ideas number twenty-nine
ideas number thirty
ideas number thirty-one
ideas number thirty-two

Four Complete Volumes of Ideas in One

Edited by Wayne Rice and Mike Yaconelli.
Previously published as four separate books.

ISBN 0-910125-32-5 (Ideas Combo 29-32)
ISBN 0-910125-00-7 (Ideas Library)
© 1981, 1982, 1983, 1987 by Youth Specialties
1224 Greenfield Drive, El Cajon, CA 92021
619/440-2333

Ideas in this book have been voluntarily submitted by individuals and groups who claim to have used them in one form or another with their youth groups. Before you use an idea, evaluate it for its suitability to your own groups, for any potential risks, for safety precautions that must be taken, and for advance preparation that may be required. Youth Specialties, Inc., is not responsible for, nor has it any control over, the use or misuse of any of the ideas published in this book.

table of contents

CHAPTER ONE: CROWD BREAKERS 7

CHAPTER TWO: GAMES 26

CHAPTER THREE: CREATIVE COMMUNICATION 72

CHAPTER FOUR: SPECIAL EVENTS **143**

CHAPTER FIVE: YOUTH GROUP LEADERSHIP **171**

CHAPTER SIX: FUND-RAISERS **176**

CHAPTER SEVEN: HOLIDAYS **182**

There are lots more ideas where these came from.

This book is only one of an entire library of **Ideas** volumes that are available from Youth Specialties. Each volume is completely different and contains tons of tried and tested programming ideas submitted by the world's most creative youth workers. Order the others by using the form below.

Combo Books

52 volumes of **Ideas** have been updated and republished in four-volume combinations. For example, our combo book **Ideas 1-4** is actually four books in one—volumes 1 through 4. These combos are a bargain at $19.95 each (that's 50% off!).

The Entire Library

The **Ideas** library includes every volume and an index to volumes 1-52. See the form below for the current price, or call the Youth Specialties Order Center at 800/776-8008.

SAVE UP TO 50%!

IDEAS ORDER FORM (or call 800/776-8008)

Your Idea May Be Worth $100

It's worth at least $25 if we publish it in a future volume of **Ideas**. And it's worth $100 if it's chosen as the outstanding idea of the book it appears in.

It's not really a contest, though—just our way of saying thanks for sharing your creativity with us. If you have a good idea that worked well with your group, send it in. We'll look it over and decide whether or not we can include it in a future **Ideas** book. If we do, we'll send you at least 25 bucks!

In addition to that, the **Ideas** editor will select one especially creative idea from each new book as the outstanding idea of that particular book—and send a check for $100 to its contributor.

So don't let your good ideas go to waste. Write them down and send them to us, accompanied by this form. Explain your ideas completely (without getting ridiculous) and include illustrations, diagrams, photos, samples, or any other materials you think are helpful.

FILL OUT BELOW

Name _____

Address_____

City _____ State ___ Zip _____

Phone (_____) _____

I hereby submit the attached idea(s) to Youth Specialties for publication in **Ideas** and guarantee that, to my knowledge, the publication of these ideas by Youth Specialties does not violate any copyright belonging to another party. I understand that, if accepted for publication in **Ideas**, the idea(s) becomes property of Youth Specialties. I understand that I will receive payment for these ideas, the exact amount to be determined by Youth Specialties, payable upon acceptance.

Signature _____

Write or type your idea(s) (one idea per sheet) and attach it to this form or to a copy of this form. Include your name and address with each idea you send. Mail to Ideas, 1224 Greenfield Drive, El Cajon, CA 92021. Ideas submitted to Youth Specialties cannot be returned.

Chapter One

Crowd Breakers

ABBREVIATED PHRASES

Here's a challenging quiz that can be printed up and passed out to your group. It can be done individually, or in teams—with kids pooling their brainpower to come up with the correct answers. Set a time limit (ten minutes should be long enough) to increase the pressure and see who can get the most right answers. Each phrase contains letters that represent a word or name that gives meaning to the phrase. In most cases, the number is the primary clue for figuring them out. Ready, set, GO!

1. 10 Y in a D _____
2. 666: The M of the B _____
3. 7 W of the W _____
4. 4 G so L the W _____
5. 54 C in a D with the J _____
6. 60 S in a M _____
7. 26 L in the A _____
8. 99 B of B on the W _____
9. 52 W in a Y _____
10. 11 M on a T _____
11. 4 Q in a D _____
12. 3 M in a T _____
13. 12 A of J _____
14. R and F of the 3rd R _____
15. 9 out of 10 D recommend C _____
16. 10 C given to M _____
17. 40 Y in the W _____
18. 66 B in the B _____
19. 31 F at BR _____
20. 5 Smooth S in a S _____
21. 12 M in a Y _____
22. 6,000,000 D M _____

Answers:

1. 10 Years in a Decade
2. 666: The Mark of the Beast
3. 7 Wonders of the World
4. For God so Loved the World
5. 54 Cards in a Deck with the Joker
6. 60 Seconds in a Minute
7. 26 Letters in the Alphabet
8. 99 Bottles of Beer on the Wall
9. 52 Weeks in a Year
10. 11 Men on a Team
11. 4 Quarters in a Dollar/or 4 Queens in a Deck
12. 3 Men in a Tub
13. 12 Apostles of Jesus
14. Rise and Fall of the 3rd Reich
15. 9 out of 10 Dentists recommend Crest
16. 10 Commandments given to Moses
17. 40 Years in the Wilderness
18. 66 Books in the Bible
19. 31 Flavors at Baskin-Robbins
20. 5 Smooth Stones in a Slingshot
21. 12 Months in a Year
22. 6,000,000 Dollar Man

(Contributed by Michael Nodland, Chicago, Illinois)

BASEBALL BAFFLER

Here's a fun quiz that might be useful sometime (around the World Series, maybe) or at a boys retreat, or whenever you choose. The object is to identify the 26 Major League baseball teams by the clues given below:

1. CIVIL WAR FACTION _____
2. "FATHER'S" TEAM _____
3. JACK'S BEANSTALK ADVERSARY _____
4. CATHOLIC OFFICIALS _____
5. TEA MAKERS _____
6. INDIAN WARRIORS _____
7. BIG CATS _____
8. ALL "STARS" _____
9. BRIGHT STOCKINGS _____
10. COMMUNISTS _____
11. APACHES, COMANCHES, ETC. _____
12. ARMY DRAFT AVOIDERS _____
13. COLORED LETTERS _____
14. BOY SCOUT GROUP _____
15. ORNITHOLOGIST'S FAVORITE _____
16. ALPHABET BEGINNERS _____
17. "ENCOUNTERED" GROUP _____
18. PARK KEEPERS _____
19. BLACKBEARD'S CREW _____
20. CLEAN HOSIERY _____
21. EXHIBITIONS OR DISPLAYS, FOR SHORT _____
22. HEAVENLY TEAM _____
23. "KINGS" OF THE GAME _____
24. YOUNG MARES _____
25. SEAFARING MEN _____
26. DOUBLE TROUBLE _____

Answers:

1. New York Yankees
2. San Diego Padres
3. San Francisco Giants
4. St. Louis Cardinals
5. Milwaukee Brewers
6. Atlanta Braves
7. Detroit Tigers
8. Houston Astros
9. Boston Red Sox
10. Cincinnati Reds
11. Cleveland Indians
12. Los Angeles Dodgers
13. Toronto Blue Jays
14. Chicago Cubs
15. Baltimore Orioles
16. Oakland A's
17. New York Mets
18. Texas Rangers
19. Pittsburgh Pirates
20. Chicago White Sox
21. Montreal Expos
22. California Angels
23. Kansas City Royals
24. Philadelphia Phillies (Fillies)
25. Seattle Mariners
28. Minnesota Twins

(Contributed by Tom Daniel, Jackson, Mississippi)

BIRTHDAY CHOO-CHOO

This is a variation of the "Happy Birthday Race" *(IDEAS Number 1)* that works best with lots of people (a big youth gathering or camp, for instance). It's a good mixer with three basic steps:

1. Announce to the entire group that you have designated 12 spots around the room according to a particular month of the year. (Let them know which spot represents which month.) On "go," they are to make a mad dash for that part of the room that represents the month in which they were born. As soon as enough people get together in each month, they lock arms and begin chanting their month over and over ("April-April-April-etc."). They stop when all the groups have gotten together. The loudest group wins.

2. After you quiet the crowd, tell each group to form a "Choo-Choo" by lining up in order of birth. For example, the April group might have someone whose birthday is April 1 on one end of the line, and April 30 on the other end. The earliest birthday (April 1) would be the "engine," and the last would be the "caboose." They hook up like a train (hands on the person's waist in front) and "ch-ch-ch-ch-ch" across to the opposite side of the room. The first team to do so is the winner.

3. Next, have the entire crowd hook up and make one huge train, January through December, and challenge them to do it in 15 seconds. The train must be able to move and everyone must be hooked up (no gaps) in order to make it legal.

The fun and excitement of such a game depends a lot on the number involved. One group did a variation of this with 850 youth and the result was wild! For added pressure, you could challenge the group to perform all three steps above in only five minutes (or less!). No one can go on to step 2 until *all* the groups have completed step one, and so on. (Contributed by Gordon Kuenemann, Houston, Texas)

BOB BOB BOB

Here's a fun way to learn everyone's first name quickly. Everyone should be seated in a circle (or casually around the room), and the leader should stand up in the middle. The leader moves around the group randomly pointing at different people. When the leader points at a particular person, the rest of the group should chant that person's name over and over again loudly and in rhythm, i.e., "BOB! BOB! BOB!. . .etc." The leader should keep it going by pointing to everyone, keeping the group chanting as loud as possible, clapping their hands in time, pointing to certain kids more than once, changing people quickly, back and forth, and so on. It's a simple idea, really wild and great for learning names. (Contributed by Glenn Davis, Winston-Salem, North Carolina)

CHRISTMAS SYNONYMS

Here's a fun "quiz" that you can use on any age group around Christmas. Print up enough copies for everyone, and have the group "translate" each of the 22 statements listed back into recognizable English. Each one is a common Christmas saying or song.

1. Move hitherward the entire assembly of those who are loyal in their belief.
2. Listen, the celestial messengers produce harmonious sounds.
3. Nocturnal timespan of unbroken quietness.
4. An emotion excited by the acquisition or expectation of good given to the terrestrial sphere.
5. Embellish the interior passageways.
6. Exalted heavenly beings to whom harkened.
7. Twelve o'clock on a clement night witnessed its arrival.
8. The Christmas preceding all others.
9. Small municipality in Judea southeast of Jerusalem.
10. Diminutive masculine master of skin-covered percussionistic cylinders.
11. Omnipotent supreme being who elicits respite to ecstatic distinguished males.
12. Tranquility upon the terrestrial sphere.
13. Obese personification fabricated of compressed mounds of minute crystals.
14. Expectation of arrival to populated area by mythical, masculine perennial gift-giver.
15. Natal Celebration devoid of color, rather albino, as a hallucinatory phenomenon for me.
16. In awe of the nocturnal time span characterized by religiosity.
17. Geographic state of fantasy during the season of mother nature's dormancy.
18. The first person nominative plural of a triumvirate of far eastern heads of state.
19. Tintinnabulation of vacillating pendulums in inverted, metallic, resonant cups.
20. In a distant location the existence of an improvised unti of newborn children's slumber furniture.
21. Proceed forth declaring upon a specific geological alpine formation.
22. Jovial yuletide desired for the second person singular or plural by us.

The Answers:

1. O Come All Ye Faithful
2. Hark, the Herald Angels Sing
3. O Silent Night
4. Joy to the World
5. Deck the Halls
6. Angels We Have Heard on High
7. It Came Upon a Midnight Clear
8. The First Noel

9. O Little Town of Bethlehem	16. O Holy Night
10. Little Drummer Boy	17. Winter Wonderland
11. God Rest Ye Merry Gentlemen	18. We Three Kings of Orient Are
12. Peace on Earth	19. Jingle Bells
13. Frosty the Snowman	20. Away in a Manger
14. Santa Claus is Coming to Town	21. Go Tell It On The Mountain
15. White Christmas	22. We Wish You a Merry Christmas

(Contributed by Bryan Schoeffler, Bath, New York)

GROUP DETECTIVES

This mixer expands on similar ideas found in other volumes of *IDEAS* like the Barnyard Mixer. It's best with a group of 25 or more. This particular way of doing it is great for group interaction, communication, cooperation, and so on. It really gets people talking and mixing up real good.

The basic idea is to have everyone gather into a specified group as quickly as possible. The groups are based upon common characteristics or descriptions. For example, you might start with "See how fast you can get into groups of people who have the same first initial." The group must then start finding out what everyone's first initials are, and getting into groups. The best way is to find someone else who would be in your group, then stick together and try to find more. At the end of a time limit, check to see how they did, and that there is noly one group for each letter. Then, move on to a new group description and try to beat the time set by the previous round, or as the game progresses: keep trying to set a "record" time.

Some other group descriptions:

1. Those who have the same number of people in their immediate family.
2. Those who have the same nationality.
3. Those who have the same favorite color.
4. Those who have the same color eyes.
5. Those with the same color shirt (or socks, hair, etc.)
6. Those who are the same age.

(Contributed by Sr. Laurice Heybl, Duluth, Minnesota)

HOW EMBARRASSING!

Give each person a piece of paper and something to write with. Have them take a couple of minutes and write down "my most embarrassing moment." They should write it in such a way as to conceal their identity. But they should also make sure that it is true.

Collect them and read them to the group one at a time. After each one, ask the kids to try to guess the identity of the writers. You can vote on each one to come up with the most likely candidate. The actual writer can then confess. It's good for a lot of laughs and it's an excellent way to "break the ice" at an informal get-together with smaller groups.

You can substitute "my most embarrassing moment" with other things like: "Few people realize that I. . .(some little known fact about yourself)" or "Ten years from now, I will be. . .(a prediction about yourself)." (Contributed by Aaron Bell, Greenwood, Indiana)

INTERROGATION

This is a good get-acquainted activity, especially when you have some new people in the group you want to get to know better. It's also great when your youth sponsors are the object of the "interrogation." Here's how it works.

Begin by dividing into teams. Each team gets a person to interrogate, like a youth sponsor. The groups are told that you (the leader) have prepared a list of twenty questions like "What is your favorite food?" or "When is your birthday?" and so on. The group, however, doesn't know what those questions are. They have ten minutes to interrogate their person and to try to get as much information out of them as possible. When the time is up, they are given the questions and must try to answer them as best they can. If they have done a good job of interrogating their person, then they will be able to answer most of the questions. The team that answers the most correctly is the winner. (Contributed by Mark Skorheim, Bullard, Texas)

KEYS TO THE KINGDOM

If you are in a big church, chances are good that there is a box or a desk drawer somewhere that has dozens of old keys in it, and nobody knows which key goes to which lock. Here's a solution to that problem. Pass out the keys to the kids in your group, and give them fifteen minutes to see how many keys they can match up with a lock in the church. Whoever matches the most keys—or any key, for that matter—can be declared the winner! (Contributed by Paul Gruhn, El Cajon, California)

THE LAND HAG

Here is an audience participation story that is particularly useful for a Halloween event, but which can be used on any occasion when a bit of silliness is needed. Names of streets, places, and events may be changed to fit your particular situation better.

To begin, divide up into five groups and assign each group a "key word" that has a corresponding action. When they hear the key word in the story, they make the sound or action as instructed.

1. "Andy Ambiguous"—shrug shoulders and say "huhhh."
2. "Count Viscosity"—with accent say, "I vant to drink your oil."
3. "Sally"—"Ahhhhhhhh" (sweetly)
4. "Land Hag"—a witch's evil cackle.
5. "Storm"—thunder, wind, rumblings

Practice with the group first so that they have their parts down, then read the following story aloud, pausing in the appropriate spaces so that the kids can add the sound effects.

THE LAND HAG

Once upon a time, long, long, ago and in the far away village of Beverly Hills, lived a beautiful and delicate maiden known simply as Sally *(ahh)*. Now Sally *(ahh)* was a tender lass, who wore gingham and calico, ate apple pie, saluted the flag, watched Mork and Mindy, and never gave anyone any trouble.

But alas, Sally *(ahh)* had a mean, cruel, ugly, nasty, horrible, crummy, witch of a step-mother known throughout the area as the Land Hag. *(cackle)*. She spent her time casting spells, running up the inflation rate, and turning innocent little children into Pac-man machines.

Now the Land Hag *(cackle)* had a regular thing going with Count Viscosity *(oil)*, a vampire who drank 10-W-40 when he couldn't get a hold of any fresh blood. Count Viscosity *(oil)* lived in a coffin underneath the music building of the local college and had been terrorizing gas stations on Hollywood Boulevard. This was one reason for the recent energy crisis.

As it happens, Count Viscosity *(oil)* had just been stringing along the Land Hag *(cackle)* in hopes of actually marrying Sally *(ahh)* and inheriting Sally's *(ahh)* fortune in a Texas oil well which the Land Hag *(cackle)* controlled.

Now also as it happens, Sally *(ahh)*, the Land Hag *(cackle)*, and Count Viscosity *(oil)* were all afraid of storms. *(boom)* The Land Hag *(cackle)* had once been struck by lightning during a storm *(boom)* while playing nine holes at a Malibu Country Club. Count Viscosity *(oil)* once slipped on an oily patch on the street during a storm *(boom)*, and Sally *(ahh)* sat through a rain drenched Rose parade. No wonder they feared storms *(boom)*.

There is one other character in our story and that is our macho hero, Andy Ambiguous *(huh)*. Andy *(huh)* never ate quiche, wore pink, or listened to Henry Mancini. Of course Andy *(huh)* was in love with Sally *(ahh)* and thought that Count Viscosity *(oil)* was a wimp. But for all his macho ways, Andy *(huh)* was also afraid of storms *(boom)*. One night while Andy *(huh)* was riding in his jeep, along came a storm *(boom)* and his cowboy hat shrank over his eyes. As Andy *(huh)* was stumbling around trying to get it off, he bungled into a theater showing "Herbie Goes to the Chocolate Factory." He

13

was humiliated.
(get dramatic)

Well, on with the story. It was Halloween night, and there was an eerie feel in the air. As the sun went down Count Viscosity *(oil)* came out from under the music building and took a bus toward Beverly Hills.

Just at that moment, Andy *(huh)* jumped in his jeep and also headed out to see his Sally *(ahh)*. The Land Hag *(cackle)* was beginning to feel strange and was turning poor trick or treaters into a complete Atari video system.

As Andy *(huh)* and Count Viscosity *(oil)* drew closer, a storm *(boom)* broke out. Count Viscosity *(oil)* decided this was the night to ditch the Land Hag *(cackle)*, marry Sally *(ahh)*, do away with Andy *(huh)* and get the oil well.

Suddenly, there was an earthquake — then the dam broke, a hurricane blew in, inflation hit 15%, and oil went up to $200 a barrel.

At that moment both Andy *(huh)* and Count Viscosity *(oil)* hit the door of the Land Hag *(cackle)*.

The Count *(oil)* shouted, "Hag *(cackle)*, we're through. I'm a-marryin' Sally *(ahh)*."

"Why you oil suckin' varmint," cried Andy *(huh)*, "I'll fix you," as he attacked the Count *(oil)*.

"Stop, stop," sobbed Sally *(ahh)*.

"Stop, stop," cackled the Hag *(cackle)*.

Meanwhile, the storm *(boom)* raged on, as all night the fight continued and the Atari machines shorted out.

By daybreak Andy *(huh)* and the Count *(oil)* were too tired to fight. Finally, the matter was settled.

The Count *(oil)* and the Hag *(cackle)* were married , moved to the oil well in Texas, and now star in their own sit-com entitled "Too Close for Comtrex."

Andy *(huh)* and Sally *(ahh)* were also married. Unfortunately, Andy *(huh)* found that Sally *(ahh)* only knew how to cook quiche.

Meanwhile, the storm *(boom)* lay in wait for the next Rose parade.

(Contributed by Dan Engle, Tallahassee, Florida)

MONEY MAKER

This is a great game for crowds of 25 or over. Before the group assembles, slip a dollar bill to about five participants (adjust the number to group size) and instruct them not to tell anyone they have it. When you get the group together tell them on the word "go" to move around and shake hands, give their name and any other pertinent information you want them to share. Explain that individuals within the group have dollar bills in their pockets and will give them to the 20th person (adjust to group size) who shakes their hand. Dollar bill holders silently keep track of the count and turn over the buck with a holler when person number 20 comes along. It's a guaranteed way to get the crowd excited and moving fast.

If this sounds too "mercenary" to you, make the prize something other than money, or simply award "points" in the same fashion. That way, whoever has the most points at the end of the game wins. Either way, it really gets people interacting with each other.
(Contributed by Phil Mininger, Macon, Mississippi)

MUSICAL SHOWDOWN

This one is great for total group involvement. Break the group down into several different teams. The number of teams is not important. Each group should have a name or a number to identify itself. Give each team pencil and paper and several minutes to think of some songs that they all know. They can write them down.

Now it's time for the showdown. The leader shouts out the name of a group. Within five seconds the group must start singing a song. Then, at any point in the song, the leader blows a whistle and shouts out the name of another group. That group must start singing a different song within five seconds. (To add excitement and a little confusion to the game, the leader can shout out the name of the group that is already singing.) This continues, calling upon all the groups until all but one are eliminated. Groups can be disqualified by (1) singing a song that has already been sung, (2) not starting a new song within five seconds, or (3) less than half their group is singing the song. Groups may add songs to their list during the showdown. To narrow things down, you might choose a particular theme for the songs, like Christmas, fun songs, hymns, etc. It's a lot of fun. (Contributed by Dan Scholten, Rhinelander, Wisconsin)

NAME THAT PERSON

Here's a good competitive game that helps kids get to know each other a lot better. Divide into two even teams. For larger groups, divide into four teams and have a play-off with the two winning teams and losing teams.

Give each person a blank 3 x 5 card (or piece of paper) and have them write down five little-known true facts about themselves and sign their name. For example:

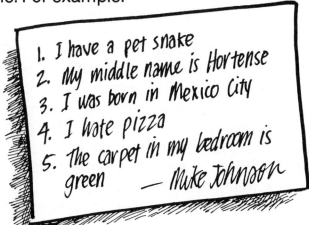

Collect all the cards and keep separate stacks for each team. The game is now ready to play.

The object is to "name that person" on the card that the leader draws (from the other team's stack of cards) in as few clues as possible. You begin by opening up the bidding between the teams: "We can name that person in five clues!", "We can name that person in four clues!", etc. The team that wins the bidding gets to guess the top card of the opposite team. They then have five seconds to guess after the reading of the appropriate number of clues. Appoint a spokesperson from each group and rotate. They can huddle together to come up with an answer. The more interaction between team members, the better. If they miss or if they don't respond in five seconds, the points go over to the other team. The scoring goes like this:

1 clue = 5 points
2 clues = 4 points
3 clues = 3 points
4 clues = 2 points
5 clues = 1 point

Proceed with the game until every card has been guessed on once. Total up the points and announce the winner. Award prizes if you wish. After each card has been played, you can read the rest of the clues that are on it (if they haven't yet been read), and if the original guess was wrong, you can let them try to guess again—just for fun. (Contributed by Bill Wertz, Los Osos, California)

ODDBALL

This is a crowdbreaker or skit that is really hilarious. It's best in a meeting format, when you have an audience and a stage or "up front" area. To begin, you select four or five contestants to compete in an exciting new game. They must leave the room (to a sound-proof area) while you set up the game.

You will need two or three tables that are the same width and about seven or eight balls of various kinds. The tables are placed end-to-end and are covered with blankets to give the appearance of one long continuous table. A hole is cut in one of the blankets, and a person kneels or sits between two of the tables so that his head sticks through the hole and above the tables. The balls are evenly spaced along the length of the table, with the head counting as one ball. All the balls (and the head) are then covered with towels so that they are completely covered. The crowd is warned not to reveal to the contestants what is going on.

Another way to do this would be to actually cut a hole in the table top for the head to stick through, but for obvious reasons, this might not go over too well with whomever owns the table. If set up properly,

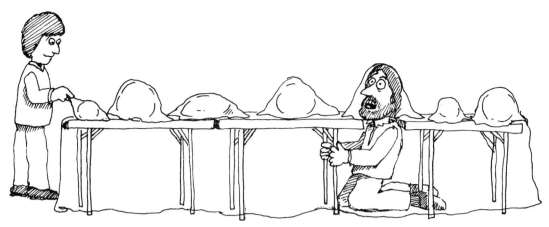

the above method will work fine. Once you are ready to go, there are several ways to play the game with your contestants:

1. *"Name that Ball:"* The announcer introduces the first volunteer and the crowd cheers wildly. The announcer explains that on the table are a number of different kinds of balls—volleyballs, footballs, soccerballs, etc. The object of the game is for the contestant to start at one end of the table, tear off the first towel and identify the kind of ball before proceeding onto the next one. A timekeeper is clocking each contestant, and the winner will be the one who has the fastest time. The crowd is encouraged to cheer them on. When they tear off the towel covering the head, the head suddenly yells "BOO!" with his eyes bugging out. Nine out of ten people will jump right out of their socks with fright. Have the contestants face the audience (rather than the head) as their reaction is what makes this so hilarious.

2. *"Guess That Ball:"* Give the head a mouthful of water before each contestant comes in. You still use the "game show" motif but this time the contestant is guessing what is under each towel. The announcer tells the contestant at the start that he or she cannot touch the ball but must guess what each ball is before taking the towel off to see if they were correct. The contestant with the most correct guesses wins. If a correct guess is made, the crowd cheers; if wrong, they boo. It is important that the head stay perfectly still. When the contestant comes to the head, he guesses, then pulls off the towel. The head spits water all over the contestant.

3. *"The Double Cross:"* For both of the games above, a good way to end is to doublecross the head. He thinks he is so funny and is really enjoying spitting and scaring people. Have your last contestant primed so that they go through the motions, but when they uncover the head, they get him with water, pie, potatoes, mud or whatever. It's really funny. (Contributed by Bob McKenzie, Calgary, Alberta, Canada)

PLAUSIBLE REASONS

Give your group three or four questions like the ones below and see who can come up with the most OUTRAGEOUS answers. It's a great way to allow kids to be creative and zany at the same time. Read them back to the entire group for some good laughs.

1. Give your reasons for the disappearance of the Mayan Civilization.
2. Other than the fact it will not come close enough, give your reason why you feel Haley's Comet will not crush you the next time it appears.
3. Give your explanation for the phases of the Moon.
4. Besides your need because of illness, explain your reasons for taking medicine.

(Contributed by Tommy Gilmore, Conway, Arkansas)

THE SALESMAN

This is a fun activity for the whole group. Pick a group member to be a "salesman"—a good sport with an art for making excuses. Explain that the salesman's job is to persuade the rest of the group to buy the product—a sample of which is in his briefcase. The trick is that the salesman doesn't know what is in the briefcase. He is sent outside to ponder his sales pitch.

The rest of the group is now shown the contents of the briefcase—a roll of toilet paper. Then the salesman is called back to sell his "product" with authority. Everyone in the room may now ask him one question about his product. The salesman must give a detailed answer. Be prepared for laughs. (Contributed by Glenn Davis, Winston-Salem, North Carolina)

SEARCH ME

For this crowdbreaker, give each person a sheet of paper, pencil, and an envelope containing a small object such as a rubber band, paper clip, bread wrapper tie, pop can tab, nail, piece of string, etc.

Next, explain that you are going to turn off the lights and they are to place the object on themselves somewhere where it is *visible* but yet inconspicuous. Turn off the lights and give them about a minute to place the object on themselves.

When the lights come back on, they are to move around the room and to search each person and discover what each person's object is. They write down that person's name and the object on their piece of paper. The winner is the one who finds the most objects and lists them (with names) within the time limit. (Contributed by Vaughn VanSkiver, Corning, New York)

SHIRT SHARING

This is a great group-building activity for a retreat or other activity that will provide a unique way for kids to learn some facts about each other.

You'll need to get enough white T-shirts for everyone. You'll also need plenty of felt tipped markers (the permanent variety work best). You'll need some open space, and some paper to put on the floor (and inside the shirts) so that it will absorb the ink that goes through the shirts.

The kids are then given instructions to write or draw a variety of things on their shirts. Here are some suggestions:

1. Write your first name somewhere on the front.
2. Your last name under the back collar.
3. Your height—written in your favorite color.
4. Draw an animal that you would like to be.
5. Draw an eye the same color as yours.
6. Identify your favorite musical instrument.
7. Write your birthdate on the sleeve.
8. Draw the logo of your favorite sports team.
9. Identify your favorite food.
10. Name a Bible verse that you can quote from memory.

Come up with about a dozen or so of these (any number you choose) and give the kids time to finish their shirts. If your markers are limited in number, have them work in groups, sharing the markers.

After they have finished, have them wear their shirts, and you can direct them in a number of other games that you can invent. For example, you can have them get into groups with the same animal drawn on their shirts. Or you can have them take pencil and paper and try to make a list of everyone's birthdate beside their name. (Whoever gets the longest list in a specified time limit is the winner.) You can probably think of other games like this to play. Or the kids can just wear their shirts and enjoy them for the remainder of the activity. (Contributed by Glenn Davis, Winston-Salem, North Carolina)

STUFFED SHIRTS

This crowd breaker is a crazy variation of the "Long John Stuff" (see *IDEAS Number One*). You can use baggy long-johns for this, but a "custom-made" shirt (see diagram) would work even better.

Make up a couple of shirts like this out of old bed sheets, and then get plenty of balloons. Next, get a couple of kids to volunteer, and

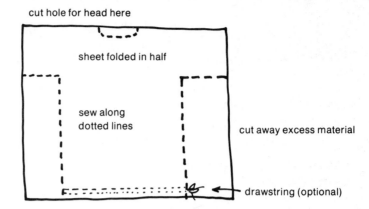

cut hole for head here

sheet folded in half

sew along dotted lines

cut away excess material

drawstring (optional)

have them put on the shirts. They leave the room with a few "helpers" who blow up the balloons and stuff them inside the shirts. They should try to stuff the same number of balloons into both shirts, and they should be about the same size. Use rope or twine to tie the waist and possibly the arms, so that the balloons won't fall out.

The two volunteers are then brought back into the meeting, looking rather "fat" with all those balloons stuffed in their shirts. You can give them names, like "Muscles McGurk" or "Fats Domino". Explain that they are going to compete to see which of them can lose the most "weight" the fastest. They will try to pop their balloons, but they can't use their hands. The only thing they can use is the floor. So they must "bounce" up and down on the floor, falling on the balloons as they try to pop them. Set a time limit of one or two minutes, or when one has successfully popped all the balloons. It's a riot to watch. (Contributed by Dan Sarian, Winchester, Virginia)

SUM FUN

Divide the group into teams and give each person a copy of the list below. Each phrase has a corresponding number which should be written in the space provided. Then, the numbers should be added up to get a "total." The team that is first to get the correct total is the winner. Teams can trade information if they want. Pocket calculators can be provided to make the addition a little easier, or outlawed to make it a little tougher.

1. Letters of the Alphabet _____
2. Wonders of the Ancient World _____
3. Signs of the Zodiac _____
4. Cards in a Deck (with Jokers) _____
5. Planets in the Solar System _____
6. Piano Keys _____
7. Baker's Dozen _____
8. Holes on a Golf Course _____
9. Degrees in a Right Angle _____
10. Sides on a Stop Sign _____

11. Quarts in a Gallon   _____
12. Hours in a Day   _____
13. Wheels on a Unicycle   _____
14. Digits in a Zip Code   _____
15. Varieties in Heinz   _____
16. Players on a Football Team   _____
17. Words that a Picture is Worth   _____
18. Days in February in a Leap Year   _____
19. Squares on a Checkerboard   _____
20. Days and Nights of the Great Flood   _____
21. Leagues Under the Sea   _____
22. Days in a Work Week   _____
23. Digits in a Social Security Number   _____
24. Jack Benny's Age   _____

Total: _____

Answers:

1. 26	7. 13	13. 1	19. 64
2. 7	8. 18	14. 5	20. 40
3. 12	9. 90	15. 57	21. 20,000
4. 54	10. 8	16. 11	22. 5
5. 9	11. 4	17. 1000	23. 9
6. 88	12. 24	18. 29	24. 39

Total: 21,613

(Contributed by William Stricklen, Clinton, Mississippi)

THAT'S THE FACT, JACK

Give your group a copy of the following story. Have them read it within the time limit (like two minutes). When time is up, have them turn the page over and answer the questions that follow. Give a prize to whomever gets the most questions right.

The Story:

> An elderly woman with young blue eyes saw an old man who was blue sitting on a light brown bench. His name was Black and he was green with illness. As the woman, who looked very young to Black, approached, he rose to his feet and asked her a question.
>
> I ate a sandwich which made me ill. Can you help me find a dock or . . .
>
> Why do you need a doctor? You don't look sick to me!
>
> But I am sick. I'm green. I can't even make it across the street.
>
> There's no street here. Only this long road and very short pathway.
>
> Just get out of my way, so I can make a long path to the shortest road into town.
>
> He rose, walked to the road, and was hit by a grey truck moving at 84.263 miles per hour.
>
> Now he really was sick!

The Questions:

1. Was the woman young or old?
2. Did the man have blue eyes?
3. Where was the man sitting?
4. What color was the thing he sat on?

21

5. What was the man's name?
6. What did the man ask the woman to help him find?
7. Besides being sick, what physical problem did the man have?
8. Was the road they were on long or short?
9. Was the pathway they were on long or short?
10. How did the man die?
11. What color was the truck?

(Contributed by Tommy Gilmore, Conway, Arkansas)

UP, UP AND AWAY

Hang some balloons from the ceiling so that the balloons are about seven feet or so off the floor. This can vary, depending on the height of the kids in your group. Select two contestants to compete in this event. They should both be the same height. Make (ahead of time) a couple of hats that have straight pins or thumb tacks sticking out the top (see diagram). If you use baseball-type hats, they are usually adjustable and will fit any size.

The object is to see which person can pop the most balloons by jumping up in the air and popping the balloons with the pin on the top of their hats. It's really funny to watch these two jumping up and down. The balloons should be almost out of reach for them. (Contributed by Dan Sarian, Winchester, Virginia)

WHAT'S MY CUE?

Here is a great new idea that is a lot of fun at a banquet or any social gathering. Each person is given a slip of paper when they arrive with a line that they are to recite each time they hear a given "cue." The "cue" is to be kept a secret. For example: Yell "Hallelujah" three times. Cue: whenever you hear the word "Please."

Then, during the course of the meal or event, whenever that person hears the word "please," they must stand up and yell "Hallelujah" three times. Everyone also has a piece of blank paper and a pencil, and they try to guess what that person's cue was. When they think they know it, they write it down. The object is to guess as many cues as possible. Whoever has guessed the most at the end of the time is the winner.

The cues can be familiar idioms or peculiar words that people say, like "thank you, um, you know, super, delicious, I don't know, Hi," and so on. Whenever a person hears their cue they must *stand up* and say their line or sing their song. Here are some sample lines you could use:

1. Act like an ape by scratching your arm pits and making an ape noise.
2. Yell "hallelujah" three times.
3. Move your head and buck back like a chicken.
4. "Polly wants a cracker, hello, good-bye" (repeat twice)
5. "The King is Coming!" (three times)
6. "Mary had a little lamb" (sing)
7. "Row, row, row your boat" (sing)
8. "Yankee Doodle went to town" (sing)
9. "Ring around the rosie" (sing)
10. "Caw, caw, caw, I'm a crow" (two times)

Obviously, the fun part of all this is watching people jump up and do their thing at the craziest times, and then trying to figure out what set them off. This works best with older youth or adults. (Contributed by Richard Baum, Jr., Lincoln, Nebraska)

ZIP ZAP

Zip Zap is a circle game designed for learning first names. The participants must know who is seated to their left and to their right. The person on your left is your "Zip." The person on your right is your "Zap." The leader stands in the center of the circle. He or she points to a person and says: "Zip, one, two, three, four, five." That person must shout out the name of the person to his or her left (or Zip) within the count of five. If the leader points to a person and says: "Zap, one, two, three, four, five," that person must shout the name of the person to his or her right (or Zap). If the person pointed to fails, he or she takes the leader's place in the center of the circle. The leader takes the person's chair. (Contributed by Glenn Davis, Winston-Salem, North Carolina)

WHAT'S THE MEANING? III

Here we go again with some "brain teasers" that are a lot of fun for kids to try and figure out. The object is to look at the arrangement of letters and to write a word or phrase that interprets each one. For more, read "What's the Meaning, Parts I and II" in *IDEAS Number 17 and Number 25.*

---

1. SLEEPING
   JOB

2. RIGHT = RIGHT

3. GOOD-BYE

4. L EL u
   L l C

5. CLOU

6. ieieceiie

7. house PRAIRIE

8. 1. D   5. U
   2. R   6. L
   3. A   7. A
   4. C

9. ping WILLOW

10. m ce
    m ce
    m ce

11. TU/LOIPES

12. SUGAR Please

13. GUN, JR.

14. SEARCH
    AND

15. SOUP

16. HOROOMTEL
    MOROOMTEL
    INN

17. T.V o

18. HOPES

19. GETTING   IT ALL

20. TEEXAMRM

Answers:

1. Sleeping on the job
2. Equal rights
3. Wave goodbye
4. Lucille Ball
5. Partly cloudy
6. "I" before "E" except after "C".
7. Little house on the prairie
8. Count Dracula
9. Weeping Willow
10. Three blind mice
11. Tip-toe through the tulips
12. Pretty please with sugar on top
13. Son of a gun
14. Search high and low
15. Split pea soup
16. No room in the inn
17. Black and white T.V.
18. Shattered hopes
19. Getting away from it all
20. Mid-term exam

(Contributed by Bruce Humbert, Richton Park, Illinois)

WHAT'S THE MEANING? SPORTS

Yes, there's more! Only these all are related to words or phrases from the sports world. Once again, the object is to decipher the arrangement of letters or numbers.

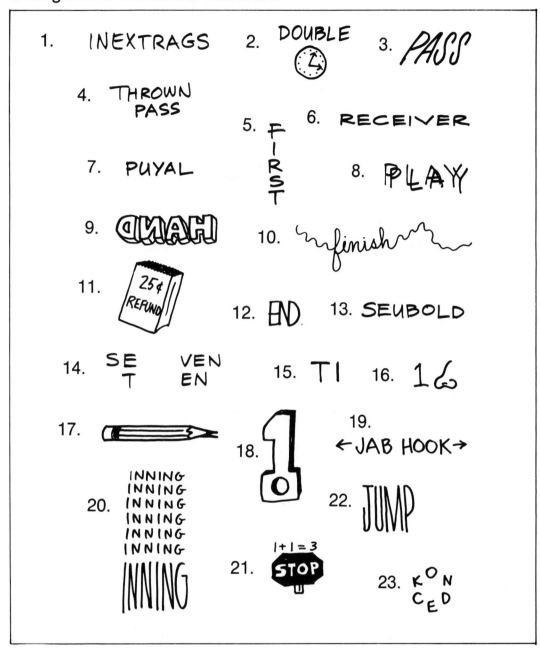

Answers:
1. Extra innings
2. Double overtime
3. Forward pass
4. Underthrown pass
5. First down
6. Wide receiver
7. Reverse layup
8. Double play
9. Backhand
10. Finish line
11. Quarterback sack
12. Tight end
13. Mixed doubles
14. Seven ten split
15. Halftime
16. Won by a nose
17. Extra point
18. Hole in one
19. Left jab followed by a right hook
20. Seventh inning stretch
21. Error on the shortstop
22. High jump
23. On-deck circle

(Contributed by Tim Spilker, Lakeside, California)

Chapter Two

Games

ALPHABET PONG

For this game, the group arranges itself into a circle. Each person holds a book with both hands. One player takes a ping pong ball and hits it with the book across the circle, calling out "A." The person on the other side then returns it to someone, calling out "B," and so forth. The whole circle works together to see how far down the alphabet they can get before they blow it. There is no particular order for hitting the ball. Anyone can hit it when it comes to them, but no one may hit the ball twice in a row. For teams, have the first team try it, and then the other, to see which one can get the farthest down the alphabet without the ball hitting the floor. It's a real challenge! (Contributed by Earnie Lidell, Tillamook, Oregon)

AMOEBA LIFT

This game is a simple variation of the game "Amoeba" (see *IDEAS Number 1-4*). This can be done as competition between teams, or as a "cooperative" game with the entire group trying to break its own record. Each group should not be much larger than about fifteen, however. If you have more kids than that, divide into more groups, all of equal size.

Each group becomes an "Amoeba." Each "amoeba" is to develop a strategy whereby they lift the entire group, and stand on as few legs as possible. The amoeba must stand in place for a minimum of ten seconds. Any legs that touch down during that time will be counted. Have several leaders available to count legs during the "lift," and to pick up the pieces when the "walls come tumblin' down." Obviously, the "amoeba" that is able to lift itself up on the fewest legs is the winner. (Contributed by Dan Scholten, Rhinelander, Wisconsin)

ANATOMY TWISTER

Here's a good game for small groups that is patterned after the old "Twister" game that has been so popular for years. To play, you'll need to make two sets of dice. You can do this by using children's blocks or something like that. Each pair of dice will have one die numbered one through six (like a normal die) and the other has six "parts of the body" either written or drawn on the die. Use any parts of the body you choose.

Teams can consist of eight people, six to comply with the instructions and two to roll the dice which give the instructions. Each roller gets one numbered die and one anatomy die. The other six members of the team number off one through six. To start the game, just roll the dice.

Here's how the game could go: The first roller tosses a number 3 on the number die and a "nose" on the anatomy die. The other roller tosses number 6 on the number die and an "armpit" on the anatomy die. So. . . team member #3 must place his or her *nose* in team member #6's *armpit*. They must hold this position until this round is over as well as comply with any further instructions given concerning their number as they come up on subsequent tosses of the dice. For example, if a succeeding roll of the dice requires #3 to place his or her nose somewhere else, then an attempt is made to position the nose in BOTH places at once. A later roll of the dice does not cancel out an earlier roll of the dice.

The winning team is the one who can successfully accomplish the most rolls of the dice before reaching the point of physical impossibility or exhaustion. Of course, with most youth groups. . .physical impossibilities don't exist. You can also play this game without team competition just for fun. (Contributed by Ken Blevens, Fresno, California)

APRIL FOOLS' GAME

At the beginning of a party or special event, give everyone in the room a card with an instruction written on it. The instruction is an April Fools trick that they must play on someone before the event is over. For example, it might say "Tell someone that their fly is open" or "Tell someone that there is a phone call for them," and so on. If the person falls for it (looks down, goes to get the phone, etc.) then that person has been officially "fooled" and is out of the game. The idea is to try and avoid being fooled and to eliminate as many others as you possibly can by faking them out. This works best when there is plenty of time (like while other things are going on as well). Check at the end of the party or event how many people were fooled, who fooled the most people, and so on. It's fun!

BLIND FOOTBALL

This is a rough but fun game that can only be played in a room without furniture. Use a ball that can be easily held onto (deflated volleyball, etc.) but which is indestructible. The object of the game is for one team to touch the ball to the wall on their opponents side of the room. Throw the ball into the middle of the room and just as the 2 teams start to fight over it—turn out the lights. From that point until a team scores—only turn the light on every 30 seconds or so. Instruct the players that when the light comes on all of them are to freeze in whatever position they are in. Leave the light on for just a few seconds so they can see who has the ball, then turn the light back off. The positions the guys get into in the dark is hilarious. It is recommended that the girls not participate in this game because it is very rough and also because clothing can become dishevelled, making for some very embarrassing moments when the lights are turned back on. (Contributed by Gary Sumner, El Centro, California)

BLIND SOCCER

This game is almost as much fun to watch as it is to play. You need a large open floor space (a carpeted floor is preferable), two teams of about five or more members per team, a couple of people to keep things going, two goals, blindfolds for each team member, and a large, heavy ball (like a medicine ball). It may also be helpful for each player to have knee pads.

The object of the game is, like soccer, to put the ball through the goal. However, instead of running and kicking the ball, the players crawl on the floor and handle the ball with their hands. They should be told not to hold the ball for more than a second or two, and this is what the two people are for (these two officials are, of course, not blindfolded). Many of the more intricate rules can be formed and reformed as you go along. For example, for the real heavyweights in the group, you *might* want to prohibit the ball from becoming airborne. (Contributed by Lew Worthington, Anderson, Indiana)

BLINDMAN CHARIOT RACES

Girls ride on guys "piggyback" style or on their shoulder to form "chariots" and "riders". Each rider must guide her chariot around an obstacle course as quickly as possible. The only catch is that the chariot is blindfolded, and the rider may not speak to the chariot at all. Directions are given by tapping or pulling on the chariot's shoulders or ears (right or left). This can be run relay-style or chariots may race for the best time. (Contributed by Gary Sumner, El Centro, California)

THE BLOB

Clearly mark off some boundaries, and put spotters on the corners. During the course of the game, anyone who steps outside the boundaries becomes part of the BLOB.

One person begins as the BLOB. The BLOB then tries to tag or chase one of the other players. If another player is tagged or is chased out of bounds, that person becomes part of the BLOB. These two join hands and go after a third person who, when tagged, joins hands and helps tag a fourth. The game continues until everyone is part of the BLOB. The BLOB's only restriction is that it cannot break hands. Thus, only people on the ends can make legal tags.

For the BLOB to be most effective, it must work as a unit. One person should act as the "BLOB Brain" and control the BLOB. No tags count if the BLOB becomes separated. Thus, the BLOB must go after one person at a time. Once the BLOB becomes large enough, it can stretch across the playing field and catch everyone. (Contributed by Glenn Davis, Winston-Salem, North Carolina)

BLOW CUP RELAY II

Here's a variation of the "Blow Cup Relay" from *IDEAS Number Twenty*. Tape two styrofoam cups together, bottom to bottom, punch a hole in the center of the two connected bottoms, and thread it onto a piece of string. The string is then connected to two stationary objects and pulled tight. Each team lines up, half on one

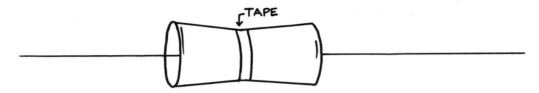

end of the string and half on the other end. The first person blows the cup along the string to the other end, and the person on that end blows it back to the other end, and so on, until everyone has gone. The first team to finish is the winner. Obviously, you will need a string and cup for each team if they compete all at once. Or, you could have the teams go one at a time, and simply time them with a stopwatch. Fastest time wins.

Another way to do this would be to have two teams line up on each end of the string. The cup is positioned in the middle. On "go," the first two players run out to the center and start blowing, trying to out-blow their opponent. A whistle is blown and they stop, run back to their team, and two new players take over wherever the other two leave the cup. The object is to blow the cup as deep as possible into the other team's "territory." The game ends when the cup reaches the end of the line, or after all the players have had their turn. The team that ends up with the cup in its territory loses the game. (Tom Bougher, Peoria, Illinois)

BOMB DRILL

This a game that can be played either in or out-of-doors. Designate one end of the room or the playing field as the "quarter deck" and the other end as the "half deck". Have the participants all line up against the wall on one end of the field. The leader then calls out the name of the opposite deck and the group must run like crazy to that place. The leader calls either "quarter" or "half" deck depending on which one he wants the group to go to. While the group is running between these two points the leader may then call out one or more of three other things. They are:

1. FREEZE!—Everyone must freeze (stop) right where they are.
2. BOMBS!—Everyone must bend over, grab their knees, and keep their heads down.
3. TORPEDO!—Everyone must dive to the floor in a push-up position.

When any of these three things are called, referees watch and eliminate the last one or two (or more) people to get into the proper position. Anyone who gets into the wrong position altogether is automatically out. The game goes on until one person is left. It's a good active game that really tires a group out. (Contributed by Brian Fullerton, Wenatchee, Washington)

THE CHOCOLATE BAR GAME

This game is best with a group of 12 to 20 players. If you have more than 20, divide into 2 or more groups and get several games going. To play, you'll need a wrapped chocolate candy bar, a hat, a scarf, a pair of gloves, a knife and fork, and one die (half a pair of dice).

Have each group form a circle and place everything except the die in the middle. The die is then passed around the circle and each person is given a turn to roll it. As soon as someone rolls a six, they rush to the middle of the circle, put on the hat, scarf and gloves, and use the knife and fork (no hands) to unwrap and eat as much of the chocolate bar as they can. In the meantime, the die is still being passed around the circle as quickly as possible, with each participant attempting to roll a six. As soon as another player rolls a six, it is his turn to go into the center, put on the hat, scarf and gloves and attack the chocolate bar with the knife and fork.

The person who was in the middle must go back to his place in the circle, even if he has not yet obtained any of the chocolate bar. It is important to remember that when a person is in the middle, he or she may not start eating the chocolate bar until the hat, scarf, and gloves have been put on. Of course, many players who get a turn in the middle will not get any of the chocolate bar, as their turn will be over before they get that far. The game is over when the chocolate bar has been completely eaten. Or, to keep the game going, just add new chocolate bars. (Contributed by Robb and Nancy Mann, Hamilton, Ontario, Canada)

CHRISTMAS FAMILY FEUD

This game is based on the T.V. game "Family Feud," but with a Christmas flavor. You also don't need all the fancy buzzers and scoreboards that are used on T.V. The game does require a little advance preparation.

First, prepare a short "survey," similar to the one below. Give the survey to one of your adult Sunday school classes, or to the entire church if you can. Have them write in anything that will correctly answer each question. After this has been done, you take all the completed surveys and tally up the results. Find out the top five answers for each question.

After you have the results, the game is ready for the youth group.

Divide into teams (like on "Family Feud"). Flip a coin to determine which team goes first. The first question is then read to the team. The team decides on an answer and tells you what it is. If they choose the #1 answer (according to the "survey" results), they get 50 points. If they choose the #2 answer, they get 40 points, and if they get the #3 answer, they get 30 points, and so on. Each team gets one guess at a time, and then the other team gets a try. In other words, the first team might guess the #2 answer on their first try, which would then allow the other team to guess the #1 answer and collect the 50 points. Any guess which isn't one of the top five answers (a "strike" on the T.V. version) can be a loss of ten points. If all the points available on one question have not been won by either team after five guesses by each team, then go on to the next question. It's a lot of fun with a lot of tension.

Here are some sample questions for your "survey":

1. Name something you hang on a Christmas tree.
2. Name a Christmas carol.
4. Name one of Santa's reindeer.
5. A role someone might play in a Christmas pageant.
6. The color of a Christmas tree light.
7. The number of days you leave your tree up after Christmas.
8. A Book of the Bible that tells about Christ's birth.
9. How old were you when you found out there was no such thing as Santa Claus?
10. Name a Christmas decoration, other than a tree.
11. Name something associated with Santa Claus.
12. Name something people usually do on Christmas day.
13. Name a food or beverage that is popular at Christmas.
14. The shape of a typical Christmas cookie.
15. How many weeks before Christmas should Christmas cards be put in the mail?

(Contributed by Tim Spilker, Lakeside, California)

COMIC STRIP MIXER

Take a Sunday paper comic strip (one that has about 8 or 9 frames to it), and cut it up into its individual frames. Take those frames and pin them on the backs of the kids in the group (one frame per person). When the game begins, the kids try to arrange themselves in the correct order, so that the comic strip makes sense. Since the frames are on their backs, it means that there will be a lot of communication required.

For larger groups, use several different comic strips (preferably ones that have the same number of frames) and pin them randomly on everyone's back. The game now has the added element of

finding others who have the same comic strip on their backs. The winning team is the first group to line up with a completed comic strip in its correct order. (Contributed by Lawrence E. Jung, Carmichael, California)

CRAZY BRIDGE

Crazy Bridge is a card game which can be played with regular cards or "Rook" cards, and in no way is it like Bridge. It is a simple game that anyone can play and anyone can win. Older youth, college age, and adults should enjoy it. It is recommended as a good way for you to get together with your sponsors and enjoy an evening together—without the kids!

You can adapt the game to almost any situation, but it is designed for mixed couples. Set up several card tables and start out with boy/girl or husband/wife combinations. Two couples (or four players) to a table, but the losers move down a table and winners move up a table and change partners each time (try to keep it male/female).

There are 16 rounds or hands, and each is played by different rules. But in all of them, you deal out the whole deck and play for tricks. High card takes the trick, or trump will take anything. You can only play trump when you do not have a particular suit in your hand. Whoever takes a trick then takes the lead and plays the next card. In this way it is similar to games like Pitch, Hearts, etc.

Each person is on his or her own, and the one with the highest total points wins. You use a lot of time for visiting because it is an easy game, plus you get to be with different people constantly. Have plenty of food on hand for between rounds. If there is an odd number of people, work them in at the last table.

The following is the Instruction and Score sheet that should be passed out to each participant:

NAME_____

CRAZY BRIDGE INSTRUCTION & SCORE SHEET

1. No bidding, no dummy, no honors counted.
2. Players on left of dealers lead.
3. Do not score as in bridge, each trick counts 10.
4. Play partners. The side taking the most tricks is the winner in each case.
5. Each hand you change tables (winners move up, losers move down) and partners.
6. Winner is the person with the highest score.

Round 1	Spades are trumps.	_____
Round 2	No-trump. Winners add 100.	_____
Round 3	Clubs are trumps. Winners & losers trade scores.	_____
Round 4	Hearts are trumps. Don't look at your hand, play from table.	_____
Round 5	Spades are trumps. Losers subtract 10 from score.	_____
Round 6	Clubs are trumps. Winners add 300 to their score.	_____
Round 7	No trumps. Winners take all.	_____
Round 8	Diamonds are trumps. Winners and losers trade scores.	_____
Round 9	Hearts are trump. Winners take all.	_____
Round 10	Cut for trump. Winners add 50.	_____
Round 11	Clubs are trumps. Don't look at your hand, play from table.	_____
Round 12	No-trumps. Loser takes all.	_____
Round 13	Spades are trumps. Winners add 50 to score.	_____
Round 14	Diamonds are trumps. Winners add 100 to score.	_____
Round 15	Spades are trumps. Winners and losers trade scores.	_____
Round 16	Hearts are trumps. Winners double score.	_____

TOTAL SCORE OF ALL ROUNDS   _____

(Contributed by Larry Jansen, Wichita, Kansas)

DESPERATION

Here's a wild game that your kids will love. Two teams get on opposite sides of the room, each staying behind a line. For each "round," one person from each team is blindfolded. A squirt gun is then placed somewhere in the middle between the two teams. On "go" the two blindfolded players try to find the squirt gun. Their teammates may help them by yelling out directions. As soon as one of the players finds the squirtgun, they may remove their blindfold and go squirt the other player who is still blindfolded. The player who didn't find the squirt gun may try to run back behind his or her team's line to avoid being squirted, but they may not remove their blindfold.

Points are scored as follows: Finding the squirtgun—50 points. Squirting the other player—50 points. Removing the blindfold illegally (before the squirtgun is found or while you are being pursued by the person with the squirtgun)—minus 100 points.

This game can also be played outdoors on a warm day using water balloons. (Contributed by Gary Sumner, El Centro, California)

DISABLED DERBY

This is a wild game that can also serve to sensitize kids to the difficulties of being physically handicapped. The game was created with that in mind. Caution should be taken to prevent the game from degenerating into a mockery of those who are handicapped. Presented and used properly, it can be great fun and a positive learning experience at the same time.

To play with two teams, you'll need a few paper bags or blindfolds, two sticks about four feet long, a pitcher of water and some paper cups, two pair of crutches, and a couple of wheelchairs. The teams line up at a starting line, and the game is run relay-style. The first person on each team puts the bag over his head (or is blindfolded), takes the stick (cane) and proceeds to a table about 20 feet away. The table has a pitcher of water and some cups. Still blindfolded, the player must pour water into the cup. He then proceeds with the cup of water (still blindfolded) to a chair several more feet away, sits down, removes the blindfold and drinks the water. The cup is deposited into a waste basket.

The player then picks up a pair of crutches lying beside the chair and walks with the crutches to the wheelchair, another 20 feet or so away. The player must keep one foot up off the ground at all times while using the crutches.

The player then gets in the wheelchair and races around a "course" that eventually ends up back at his team. Upon tagging the next person in line, the whole thing is repeated. The first team to have all its members complete the relay is the winner.

Each team will need a "runner" who runs out and replaces things for each new player. The cane will need to come back to the starting point, the wheelchair will need to be put back in its original position, etc. Create your own "obstacle course" for these events and the result will be a lot of excitement and fun. (Contributed by Lisa Larmondra, Bath, New York)

DONKEY SOCCER

Here's a game that is exciting and extremely hilarious. To play, divide your group into four teams and place each team along one of the four sides of a square playing area. Place a soccer ball in the center of the square.

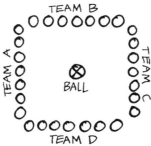

Each team then chooses a "donkey" (player on the bottom) and one rider (player sitting on top of donkey's shoulders). The donkey is blindfolded and the rider then directs the donkey to the ball and gives direction as to which foot he should use to kick the ball. The object is for the donkey to kick the ball past one of the opposing teams. No points are awarded if the ball is kicked past one's own teammates. All four donkeys are trying at the same time.

Team members on the sides of the square may block the ball with their body, legs and feet *only* (no hands). Points can only be made when the ball is kicked by a donkey. (Contributed by Ben Smith, Seattle, Washington)

DOWN THE DRAIN

For this game, you'll need to get quite a few of those plastic tubes found in most golf club bags that protect the clubs. You can probably borrow these from someone, as the game won't damage them.

Divide the group into two equal teams. Each team gets half the tubes, or one for each player. The teams line up and the players hold the tubes end to end, using their hands to secure the joints.

At the beginning of each line, the team leaders or sponsors simultaneously place a marble in the end of the first tube. The object is for the team to move the marble down all the tubes and out the other end. The team that is first to do this is the winner. If the marble slips through one of the joints and falls onto the floor, the team is disqualified. Once the kids get the hang of it, they should be able to do it rather smoothly. There is some strategy involved, however, and the kids will really enjoy the challenge.

To make the game a little longer, go for "best two out of three," or give each team ten marbles to send "down the drain." Only one marble is allowed in the drain at a time. Somebody should be assigned to catch the marbles when they come out. (Contributed by E. Parke Brown, Middleburg, Pennsylvania)

FAT BAT

Here's a version of softball that can be played out-of-doors in any kind of weather. Anybody can play. It doesn't require much skill.

You'll need to purchase a "Fat Bat" and "Fat Ball" from a toy store or department store. They are relatively easy to find and quite inexpensive. Regular softball rules apply, only there are no "foul" balls. Everything is fair. Players don't use ball gloves, either. The ball is so light that a good wind will carry it all over the place. So, the nastier the weather, the better. (Contributed by Mark S. Smith, Jacksonville, Florida)

37

FIGHTERS AND FIENDS

Here's a great "wide game" that can be played in a large area, like at a camp, where there is plenty of room to run, hide and sneak around. The game has certain affinities with the popular fantasy game "Dungeons and Dragons," but it has none of the negative elements such as false gods, demons, and the like. It looks complicated at first glance, but it's really not difficult to figure out and play with your group.

The game has two opposing teams, the Fighters and the Fiends. The object of the game is to either find or keep the most bags of treasure before the time runs out. Materials needed for the game include a deck of regular playing cards and several bags of "treasure," each worth 1000 points. You'll need to make up one bag of treasure for every four people playing. At the beginning of the game, the Fiends get to take the bags of treasure and hide it.

To begin, the "Game Master" passes out the playing cards to all the players, so that each player has one. There should be the same number of red and black cards, and there will need to be at least one "ace," "two" and "three" of each color in the cards passed out. The cards determine the players' roles in the game and how much power they have. All red cards are Fighters. All black cards are Fiends. Both Fighters and Fiends have Wizards, Assassins, and Zombies on their team. (See character descriptions below.)

Once the cards have been distributed, and all the players know their role in the game, the Fiends are turned loose with the bags of treasure. They have five minutes to hide it. There must be at least one and no more than two Fiends guarding each bag. Those guards must never stray more than twenty feet away from the hidden treasure. Hidden bags of treasure must be separated by a distance of at least forty feet. In other words, they need to spread them out all over the place.

After the five minutes are up, the Fighters head out in search of the Fiends and the treasure. To do battle, the attacking party yells "draw" and all must show their cards, with the higher cards winning. In case of a tie, the defender wins. Winners then take the losers' cards, divide them, and add them to their own, making themselves more powerful. After defeating Fiends, the Fighters may look for the treasure. Dead players may not move from the spot where they are killed. If treasure is found, Fighters carry it with them until the game is over. It may be reclaimed by the Fiends if the Fighter is attacked and killed by a Fiend, Assassin, or Zombie.

Here are the character descriptions for each of the players:

Fighters:

These are all players with red cards, 4,5,6,7,8,9,10, Jack, Queen, and King. The point value (power) for each player is the number on the card, with face cards being worth 10. Fighters may travel alone or in pairs. Fighters may kill any Fiends of less power, but they cannot kill Wizards (only one 40-point Fighter may kill a Wizard), and they cannot attack Assassins. Fighters may be killed by higher (more powerful) Fiends, equal Assassins, and any Zombie. They may, however, be restored to life (turned into Zombies) by Wizards.

Fiends:

These are the same as Fighters, only they have black cards, and they hide and guard the treasure

Wizards:

These players have cards numbered 2 or 3. The color of the card indicates which team they are on. They are worth 2 or 3 points, depending on which card they have. The mission of Wizards is to protect players of the same color, restore dead players to life, and to destroy opposing Zombies. Wizards may travel alone or in pairs. A Wizard can only be killed by one 40-point Fighter, Fiend, or Assassin. Once they are killed, they cannot be restored to life. Wizards do not attack anyone. They do not look for treasure. They move around turning their dead teammates into Zombies, and killing Zombies of the opposing team. Once a Wizard kills a Zombie, the Zombie cannot be restored a second time. Wizards may, if you choose, put some kind of mark on Zombies that they kill for identification.

Assassins:

These are players who have aces, and they are worth 15 points. Red aces are Fighter Assassins, black aces are Fiend Assassins. They travel alone at all times. They may kill at will. Because of their point advantage, they are pretty dangerous. In a tie with Fighters or Fiends, they always win. In a tie with another Assassin, the defender wins. They cannot be attacked except by another Assassin. They can only be killed by a Fighter or Fiend with more points, other Assassins with more points, or any Zombie. Once killed, there is no restoration to life for Assassins. Assassins are usually the ones who are most likely to kill a Wizard. They are able to get 40 points quicker.

Zombies:

These are dead Fighters and Fiends who are brought back to life by their Wizards. They cannot attack anyone, but when they are attacked, they may kill any Fighter, Fiend, or Assassin. They may

39

travel alone or in pairs, and they actually try to deceive Fighters, Fiends, and Assassins into attacking them. When attacked, all they have to do is raise their right hand, and the attacker is automatically dead. Zombies can then take the attackers card(s) to gain points, but they can't use those cards to attack anyone. Zombies may only be killed by an opposing Wizard. Wizards do not collect points (cards).

The game ends at the end of a time limit (like 45 minutes or an hour), or after all the players of one team have been killed, or after the fighters have found the majority of the treasure. . .whichever comes first. The treasure brought in at the end of the game is worth 1000 points to the team possessing it, plus they can add on the points captured in the game (on the playing cards) by all players, dead or alive.

This game can be adapted or changed however you see fit, but there is enough strategy and excitement in this version to make the game one that the kids will want to play again and again. If it sounds confusing, just read it through a couple of times and it will start to make sense. (Contributed by Jim Raines, Los Angeles, California)

FLOUR OF POWER

Quite a number of games can be created by using two common and easily available items: knee high stockings and regular all-purpose flour. Place about 3/4 cup of flour in the toe of the stocking (all sheer works best) and tie the end. The stocking can now be swung, thrown, or slingshotted with a resultant patch of flour being deposited on the surface of whatever it hits. Any tag game can be played with this device (regular tag, team tag, freeze tag, etc.)

One good game to try is to line everybody up on one side of a field with one person in the middle of the field armed with the stocking. At the whistle all must run to the other side without being hit by the stocking. Everyone hit is eliminated. For large groups use more than one person in the center.

These can be used in place of water balloons and they can be used over and over. One filling of flour will last for quite awhile. By using your imagination this simple device will bring hours of enjoyment for youth. (Contributed by Greg Thomas, Watsonville, California)

FOUR-CORNER VOLLEYBALL

Here's a wild version of volleyball that involves four teams at once. You can set it up with four volleyball nets, or just two, depending on the size of your teams and the number of nets you have available. You'll also need five or six poles. Arrange the nets according to one of the diagrams below. If you use two nets, then you form two right-angles with them, as in diagram A. If you use four nets, then just tie all four to the center pole as in diagram B.

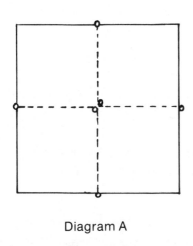

Diagram A

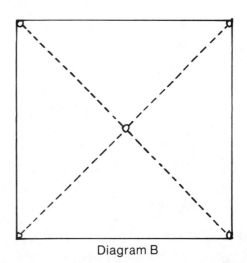

Diagram B

The four teams get in one of the four corners of the court, and the game is played like regular volleyball, except that now you can hit the ball to any of the other three teams. An interesting strategy can develop since a team is never sure exactly when the ball will be coming their way.

This game can also be played with "New Volleyball" rules *(IDEAS Number 18)* or any of the other volleyball variations found in *IDEAS*. Once you try this version of volleyball, your group may never want to play regular volleyball again! (Contributed by Ron Fay, Los Osos, California)

GOTCHA RELAY

Divide the group into two teams. Set up the room or field similar to the diagram below. Each team lines up single file behind their respective markers. On "go", the first players begin running around the track (in one direction only) just like in a regular relay race. On completing the lap, the runner tags the next player who takes off in a similar fashion.

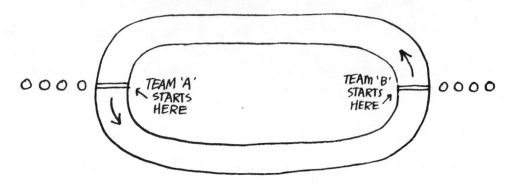

The object of the game is to try and tag the runner of the other team. The teams continue to run the laps until a person is finally caught (Gotcha!) The team that catches the other first is the winner. Be sure to divide the teams so that they are about even in speed. This can also be played piggy-back, or on tricycles, or hopping on one foot, or whatever. (Contributed by Brian Fullerton, Wenatchee, Washington)

HELP YOUR NEIGHBOR

Here's a simple card game that kids like to play. You need a minimum of four people to play and there is no maximum. If you have lots of kids, get lots of games going at once. You will need one deck of regular playing cards (or some other kind of numbered cards) for each four people who play. If you have more than four people, you'll need more cards.

Everyone gets one suit (hearts, spades, etc.) from the deck— numbers two through twelve (jack is eleven and queen is twelve). The King and the Ace is not used. The cards should be spread out in front of each person so that they can be seen (face up).

The first person in the group (it doesn't matter who starts) takes a pair of dice and rolls them. Whatever number is rolled, the player then turns over the corresponding card. For example, if the dice total comes to seven, then the player turns over his number seven card. If the dice total is eleven, then the jack is turned over, etc.

The player keeps going so long as he has cards to turn over. He can, however, also turn over the player to his left's cards in order to keep his turn alive. (That's when you "help your neighbor"). In other words, if a second "seven" is rolled, then you check your neighbor's hand to see if he has a seven still showing. If so, then you turn it over and keep going. Your turn continues until you can no longer turn over any cards from either your hand or your neighbors. The game ends when one person has turned over all of his cards. (Contributed by Malcolm McQueen, Camas, Washington)

HOW'S YOURS?

Here's a simple "living room" game that's good for a lot of laughs. Everyone gathers in a circle while one person is sent out of the room. The group then chooses a noun (such as "shoe" or "job"). When the person comes back into the room he must ask "How's yours?" Each person he asks must then answer with an adjective that describes the noun chosen by the group. "It" must guess after each response and continue around the circle until he can guess the noun chosen. The last person to give an adjective before "It" guesses the correct noun becomes the new "It." (Contributed by Glenn Tombaugh, Wichita, Kansas)

HUMAN FOOSBALL

Many churches and recreation centers have a "Foosball" table which is a table version of soccer. Using an open field the Foosball format may be reconstructed making for a wild and fast game of soccer.

Begin by dividing a playing field into ten sections. (See diagram, next page). You may divide the field by using lime on the ground or an even better method is to use string or cord strung across the field about waist high as dividers. An easy way to do this is to run the string across the field and attach it at both ends to folding chairs.

Once the field is set up then it is time to arrange the players. Each team should use an equal number of players, normally ten is about right but you may want to adjust that number depending on field size and the number of people who want to participate. Arrange the players in the sections as shown in the diagram below. The players on the outer edges of the field are called spotters.

Once set up, the game itself is simple. The object of the game is to kick the ball into the other team's goal. The ball may be advanced using any part of the body except the hands and arms. Unlike normal soccer, this rule also applies to the goalie who you will

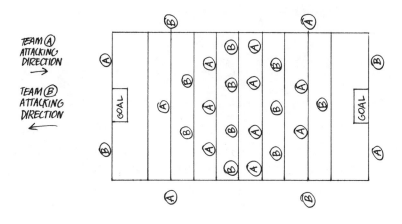

notice is not stationed directly in front of the goal but in the first section away from the goal. Every player is required to stay within the limits of their section. One may only advance the ball while it is in his section. The players may move laterally as much as they like, but they may not break the plane which serves as the boundaries for their section. To enforce this rule any player who ranges out of his section is removed from the game for two minutes along with everyone else who is in that section with him. It is the job of the spotters who stand around the field of play to roll the ball back into play once it has been kicked out of bounds. As shown in the diagram the spotters are placed around the field alternately in order to keep the game fair. Once again the number of spotters used will depend upon the number who are available to participate.

A couple of helpful hints to keep the game moving is to be sure the spotters throw the ball back in as soon as they retrieve it. Also it is best to develop a rotation system so that everyone can play the different positions. Finally any round ball will work to play with but normally a little heavier ball such as a regulation soccer ball works best. (Contributed by Billy Richter, Arlington, Texas)

HUMAN OBSTACLE COURSE

Here is a game that serves as a great community builder, as it gets people interacting and touching. The participants are instructed that they are going to build a human obstacle course. They are to use their body to somehow become an obstacle, and it is up to them what challenge they will present to the runners. They may design an obstacle with a partner if they so choose.

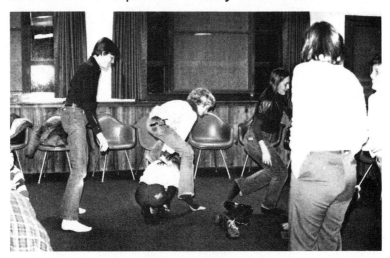

The participants are then numbered off, and a course around the room or outside is then laid out. Runner one starts and proceeds to #2, who tells what their obstacle is. . .for instance, "you have to run around me twice" or "you have to leap over me" etc. Runner one follows the instructions, and is followed by #2 to #3, where they hear instructions and carry them out. When runner one has completed the course, he/she then takes up his/her obstacle position as the other runners approach. The game ends when runner one is again the one in line to do the course. This game inspires creativity, as well as provides a fun, group experience. (Contributed by Ruth Staal, Holland, Michigan)

HUMAN PAC-MAN

Everybody is familiar with the popular video game "Pac-Man". Most kids love it. Here's one way to convert it into a game that you can play with your youth group using kids instead of computers. To play, you'll need a large playing area, like a gym floor. Then you'll need to create a "maze". This can be done with chairs, placing them end to end in such a way as to create the maze passage-ways. You could use masking tape on the floor, or if outdoors, line the field with chalk. At the four corners of the maze are the "energizers" (one group used hymnbooks), and in the middle is an open space which is home base for the ghosts.

There is one Pac-Man and up to four ghosts. You can have more if the maze is very large. The rules for the game are as follows:

1. Stay in maze.
2. Only one Pac-Man. Rotate players into game.
3. Pac-Man moves by shuffling feet along floor. Feet never should leave the ground. This is funny to watch.

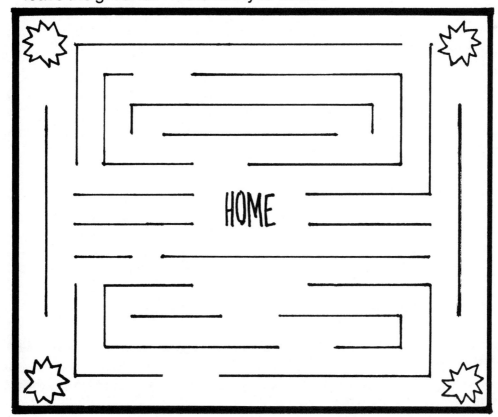

4. Ghosts walk at a moderate pace. NO RUNNING, NO RUNNING.
5. Ghosts move forward only and must follow the maze. No stopping.
6. Pac-Man can go in any direction and may stop.
7. Pac-Man's objective. . .to avoid being eaten by ghosts.
8. Ghosts objective. . .to eat the Pac-Man.
9. Pac-Man may tag ghosts only when energized (by picking up an energizer).
10. Pac-Man is energized for only 8 seconds. (timer/controller keeps time)
11. When time is up, Pac-Man must put energizer down (can not carry it around).
12. When Ghost is tagged, it must return to home-base and touch it before returning to game.
13. When Pac-Man picks up an energizer, it must say "Energize."
14. Ghosts must tag Pac-Man with both hands.
15. Pac-Man can tag Ghosts with one hand.
16. No reaching over chairs or outside maze passageway.
17. Pac-Man starts each game by saying, "go."
18. Pac-Man has three lives to a round.
19. Energizers are placed back in the corners at end of each game.
20. Game can be played as a tag game or for points.

(Contributed by Keith Curran, Huntington, Pennsylvania)

HUMAN PAC-MAN II

This game combines Pac-Man with the old game "Streets and Alleys" (from *IDEAS Numbers One through Four*). Streets and Alleys is the game that has the entire group lined up in rows (see diagram below). When "streets" is called, everyone grabs hands with their partners standing next to them in one direction (e.g. horizontally) and when "alleys" is called, they turn ninety degrees the other way, grab hands, and form rows running the other direction (e.g. vertically).

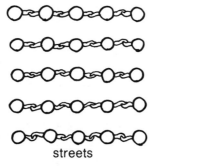

streets

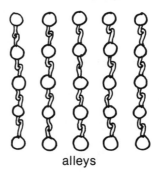

alleys

For this version of Human Pac-Man, one person is "it" (the Pac-Man), and two people are chasers ("ghosts"). You will need four tennis balls, someone to count (the "counter"), and a person to call "streets" or "alleys" (the "caller").

Place one tennis ball in each corner of the square (see diagram). Pac-Man should start each turn (he gets three turns) from the center and the ghosts should start each turn from any two diagonal corners, they should not be in the same corner.

The caller begins the game by calling "street" or "alley" and the people forming the square raise their arms, creating the correct passageway. Pac-Man then runs or walks towards any tennis ball, following the passageway. He may not reach over or under any arm to collect a ball. The object is for the Pac-Man to collect all four balls within three turns. The ghosts, also following only the passageways, chase the Pac-Man. The ghosts may not hover around any ball but must keep moving. Ghosts must move only by hopping while keeping both feet together (bunny hop). The Pac-Man may call "street" or "alley" a total of ten times in order to create a route to the balls or to get out of a jam. The "counter" counts how many times Pac-Man calls "street" or "alley." He has *only* ten calls to last all three turns, so if he uses ten calls on the first turn, he has no more calls. Each turn ends either with the Pac-Man being caught by one or both of the ghosts, failing to follow the passageway, or when all four balls are collected. Should a ghost fail to follow the passageway, all players return to start points and the turn is replayed, with the Pac-Man keeping balls collected on that turn.

The caller continuously calls "street" or "alley" (every 15 seconds or so) but waits two to three seconds after the Pac-Man uses one of his calls before changing again. The caller sets the pace by how often they make a call. The Pac-Man and the ghosts may not run from corner to corner along the outside of the square, though they may go outside to get to another row. Allow all the kids a chance to be a Pac-Man or a ghost. Feel free to change the rules or to adapt the game as you wish. (Contributed by Gary Jones, Arvada, Colorado)

HUMAN PAC-MAN III

Here's another adaptation of the Pac Man video game (see *IDEAS Number 31*) which is relatively simple to play. This one is best suited for a camp or retreat group as you will need a lot of kids—at least 50—to help build a human maze. You might be able to get by with fewer people if you also use chairs, trash cans or other objects to make up the maze.

Begin by dividing your group into four teams and removing one player from each team. Form your maze with the remaining players, making a square on the outside as large as you desire the maze to be. On the inside, form the maze by lining people up with arms outstretched to make walls and corners. Now blindfold three of the four players you have selected. These are the "ghosts." The person without the blindfold is the "Pac Man." Attach a balloon to the backs of all four. The Pac Man is to chase after the other three to try to

burst their balloons. The ghosts are to try to burst the balloon of the Pac Man. They should be required to move through the maze slowly, either by hopping or shuffling their feet. Each team member is encouraged to help direct the chasers after the Pac Man by yelling at them. You can keep score as follows: Pac Man's balloon— 1000 points, Chaser's balloons are 1 balloon—200 points, 2 balloons—500 points and 3 balloons—1000 points. The game ends after everyone has had a chance to be in the maze. (Contributed by Larry Felgenhauer. Farmersburg, Indiana)

HUMAN SCAVENGER HUNT

Divide into teams and have each team choose a leader. All team members must stay within a designated area. A "judge" stands in a position that is an equal distance from all the teams. For example, if there are four teams, then the teams can position themselves in the four corners of the room and the "judge" can stand in the middle.

The "judge" calls out a characteristic similar to the ones below and the leader on each team tries to locate someone on his or her team that fits the characteristic. As soon as someone is found, the leader grabs that person by the hand and they both run like crazy to the judge. The first team leader to slap the hand of the judge (pulling along the proper person) wins points for his or her team.

Here are some sample characteristics: someone who. . .

1. Has blue eyes and brown hair
2. Received all A's in the last marking period
3. Ate at MacDonald's today
4. Jogs daily
5. Is engaged to be married
6. Likes broccoli
7. Sent a friend a card today
8. Memorized a Bible verse this week
9. Visited a foreign country this year
10. Is wearing Nike sneakers
11. Is chewing green gum
12. Came in a blue Mustang
13. Was stopped by a cop for a traffic violation this month
14. Has a zit on their nose
15. Received a love letter today

(Contributed by Don Shenk, Lancaster, Pennsylvania)

HUMAN TIC-TAC-TOE

As suggested by its title, this game is played just like it is on paper, except that people are used. It is very active and great for smaller groups. To play, set up nine chairs in three rows of three. Team One stands on one side of the chairs and Team Two on the other. Players on each team then number off, 1-2-3-4-etc.

The leader then calls out a number, like "4." As soon as the number is called, the two "4's" on each team scramble to sit down in any two chairs as quickly as they can. When they are seated, another number is called, and the same thing happens, until three teammates from either team have successfully scored a "tic-tac-toe" by sitting in a row of three, either up, down, or diagonally. If no tic-tac-toe is made, then the players return to their team and the game is played again.

A variation of this would be to play with ten people per game (5 on a team). They all take a seat in one of the nine chairs, leaving one person without a seat. When the whistle is blown, everyone must get up and move to a different chair, while the "extra person" tries to sit down somewhere. After the mad scramble for seats, the game is scored like tic-tac-toe. Any row of three people from the same team gets points. Each round, there will always be one person left without a seat.

An even crazier way to play this game would be to play as described above, but use guys on their hands and knees as "chairs" and have girls from each team sit on the guys' backs. When the whistle is blown, they jump on a guy, and try to hang on, even though another girl may try to pull her off, or take the same guy. It's really wild. Whether you use chairs, guys, lines on the floor (like real tic-tac-toe) or whatever, it's a lot of fun to play. (Contributed by Glenn Davis, Winston-Salem, North Carolina)

I LIKE EVERYONE

This game is similar to "Fruitbasket Upset" and other games where people scramble for chairs. Everyone sits in a circle in chairs but there should be plenty of space left between the chairs. Every chair should have someone in it.

An extra person stands in the middle of the circle. That person says, "I like everyone except. . ." and names a characteristic of at least two people seated in the circle. For example, he might say, "I like everyone, except those wearing Nike shoes!" or "I like everyone except those with blond hair!" and so on.

If the people sitting in the chairs have any of these characteristics, they must immediately vacate their chairs. A scramble then takes place to find a now un-occupied chair (the original person in the middle also scrambles for a chair). Whoever is caught standing without a chair then becomes the person in the middle and repeats the "I like everyone except. . ." phrase using new characteristics.

Only those people in the chairs who have that characteristic need vacate chairs. All others can sit still. Those who vacate their chairs must find a new chair to sit in. In other words, a person cannot stand up and then sit back down in the same chair.

The person in the middle, however, may say, "I like everyone" in which case *all* must vacate their chairs and scramble to find a new one. This creates quite a traffic jam! (Contributed by Malcolm McQueen and Jeanne Norris, Camas, Washington)

INTELLECTUAL SCAVENGER HUNT

Here is a new twist to the Indoor Scavenger Hunt. Instead of simply asking for a common item, ask for it in such a way that they first need to figure out what you want. For example:

1. A cylindrical object that releases a blue medium used to communicate. (A pen that writes in blue ink.)
2. A many pronged black object used by the vain. (A black comb.)
3. A soft item which when exhaled into expands into a flimsy round ball. (A balloon.)
4. A slip of paper valued at a net worth of 20 thousand pennies. (A $20 bill.)
5. A permanent impression in color of a comrade. (A color picture of a friend.)
6. A clean soft piece of cloth used to wipe mucus from one's nostrils. (A handkerchief.)

(Contributed by Don Shenk, Lancaster, Pennsylvania)

INTERMISSION GAME

Here's a good game for a "movie night." Every movie has to have time for some Coke and popcorn, right? Well, this is a "Coke and Popcorn Relay," otherwise known as the "Intermission Game."

Teams line up relay race style. The first person in line gets a bottle of Coke (or any soda pop) and on a signal, runs to a point about thirty feet away (a chair can mark the spot) carrying the bottle as a baton. At various points the leader blows a whistle, and the players who are running must stop and drink the pop until the whistle blows again. They continue running around the marker and back to the team. The next player takes the bottle and does the same thing. If the bottle is emptied on one person's run, then a new bottle is given to the new runner. The winning team is the one which drinks the most pop within a certain time limit. The time limit should be long enough that at least everyone has had a chance to run.

Now we are ready for the second event, which involves the popcorn. Place shopping bags full of popcorn (weigh them in to make sure they are all the same to start with) a certain distance from the team. On "go" the first player runs to the popcorn, sticks his or her head in the bag and gets one big mouthful of popcorn. No hands allowed. They must swallow the popcorn sooner or later (they can't spit it out after it comes out of the bag). The teams continue until someone finishes off the whole bag, or until the time limit is up. The bags can then be weighed to determine the winner.

The two games can be combined into one with a little creativity. Just have the kids carry the Coke to one location, take a drink, then run to the bag of popcorn, take a bite, and back to the team. (Contributed by Bill Wertz, Los Osos, California)

JUNGLE FOOTBALL

This is essentially touch or flag football. However, all players are eligible to catch a pass. The "quarterback" or ball carrier can also run across the line of scrimmage and still pass the ball forward, backward, etc. to another player. Multiple passes are allowed (several passes on one play). Each team gets four downs to score. There aren't any first downs. Only touchdowns are counted (six points) and safeties (two points). The rules can be changed or modified to fit any size group, age, sex, etc. Have your own Jungle Football Super Bowl! (Contributed by Ray Kelley, Sacramento, California)

KILLER FRISBEE

This basically is a Frisbee version of "circle dodge ball," but it has a new twist to it that only a Frisbee can add. Form a circle, spacing people so there is enough room to roam in the middle,but yet not too much so no one is able to remain in the center indefinitely. With small groups (about 10) one Frisbee is enough, but use two or three Frisbees with larger groups for a real fast moving game. The object is to try to remain in the center of the circle while the others try to hit you with a Frisbee. If they hit you, then you join the others in the circle of throwers, and that person goes in the center. Use a lightweight Frisbee(s). Of course the person must be hit below the shoulders. (Contributed by Bob Stover, Minneapolis, Minnesota)

KNOCK YOUR SOCKS OFF

This is sort of like "King of the Circle"—a survival of the fittest game. It's best when not played co-ed. Both guys and girls can play. . .just not at the same time.

Draw a big circle on the floor. All the players get in the circle with no shoes, only socks. On go, the object is to take off other people's socks and keep yours on. Once your socks are gone, you are out of the game. If any part of your body goes outside the circle, you are also out. The last person to remain in the circle with their socks on is the winner. (Contributed by Glenn Davis, Winston-Salem, North Carolina)

KWIFFLE BALL

This fast-paced game combines kickball and wiffle-ball. It can, however, be played with any other kind of "baseball substitute," using a volleyball, softball, etc. A baseball diamond configuration is used (four bases) but there are two home plates (see diagram).

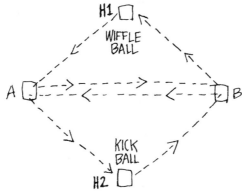

One team is in the field, the other team kicks or bats at the two home bases (H1 and H2). Kickball goes one way, wiffle-ball the other way. The team that is "up" provides its own pitcher. The base-runners only run two bases (bases A and B), then home. Runners will be running in opposite directions. Both games are played at once with half of the team that is "up" on each game rotating back and forth. The team in the field has to really be alert.

There are three outs, and the outs can be made on either of the games. Runners can be put out with either ball if they are in play at the time. Runners can occupy the same base at the same time. Otherwise, regular rules apply. It's a lot of fun. (Contributed by Jon Bollback, Silver Spring. Maryland)

LOG ROLL

There is always a great deal of value in introducing games that encourage people to work together, and at the same time gets people touching and interacting. This builds a good group feeling, and cooperative play will usually carry over into other cooperative youth group activities. The log roll is one such game to help build community.

All participants lay on the floor on their stomach, being sure that there are no empty spaces between their body and the bodies next to them. The game proceeds as the first person in the line lays across the small of the back of the participants. This enables the weight to be distributed by about 3 or 4 people. Slowly, those people start to roll together in one direction, and as they do so, the

53

person on top will begin to roll. As they make their way down the backs, the participants begin to roll when they feel the weight on them. If the participants do not continue to stay body-to-body, the log will not roll. Direction can be reversed also. When the log reaches the end, another log climbs on and the rolling again begins.

Not only is this a good cooperation game, but the "log" experiences a great deal of support from the group. It doesn't matter what the size of the participants for this game, since the weight is always distributed over several people. This is a game that you have to try to believe! (Contributed by Ruth Staal, Holland, Michigan)

MIDNIGHT FOOTBALL

This rowdy game is great for boys of all ages although it can also be played with girls. It is played indoors in a room or hallway that is relatively free of furniture, and which can be made pitch dark. Then you need two even teams.

To begin, teams line up against opposing walls. Both teams are on their hands and knees. The lights go out and one team "kicks off" by sliding the eraser over to the other team. A brief time is allowed for the receiving team to make any "hands-offs" they want, and then play is begun. The team that "kicked off" goes out to meet the other team in the dark and attempts to stop the other team from scoring (this is done by searching every person).

Scoring is accomplished by successfully crossing the room with the eraser and touching the opposite wall with it. Teams are permitted to pass the eraser, but they need to be "sneaky and careful" or they will lose it to the other team. The eraser must be carried by hand across the room. No stuffing it inside clothing. Teams must also remain on their hands and knees while the game is being played.

If there is a "fumble" or an "interception" (the kicking team somehow manages to capture the eraser), then play is stopped and the teams line up again at opposing walls. The team that recovered the eraser now becomes the receiving team. It's wild and a lot of fun. (Contributed by Michael McKnight, Oak Ridge, Tennessee)

MUSICAL BACKS

This is a lot like musical chairs and similar elimination-type games. Kids simply mill about the room and when the music stops (or when the whistle blows, etc.) everyone quickly finds another person and stands back to back. When there are an odd number of people on the floor, someone will not have a partner, and they are eliminated from the game. When there is an even number of people playing, a chair is placed on the floor, and anyone may sit in it and be safe. Naturally, every other time, the chair will need to be removed. Make a rule that everyone must keep moving and players may not pair off with the same person twice in a row. The last person to survive wins. It's a lot of fun. (Contributed by Dan Brandel, Livonia, Michigan)

MUSICAL PADDLES

This game is great indoors for large groups and requires a piano or record player and several ping pong paddles (or similar objects that can be passed easily). The group stands forming a circle passing paddles from left to right while music is played. Players caught holding a paddle when the music abruptly stops must do certain things with every subsequent paddle they receive. For example:

First time caught: all paddles from then on must be passed by the individual around his waist once before passing it on to his right.
Second time caught: all paddles must be passed around waist twice, then on.
Third time caught: all paddles around waist twice, under one leg and on.
Fourth time caught: all paddles around waist twice, under one leg and under the other, then on.
Fifth time caught: all the above, then under both legs and on.
Sixth time caught: sing a solo.

(Contributed by Glenn Davis, Winston-Salem, North Carolina)

NIT WITS

This game is a take-off on the old television show "Cross-Wits". Contestants (or teams) play against each other by trying to solve the words in a crossword puzzle, which are clues towards a "person, place or thing." Every "clue word" you guess in the puzzle is worth points (ten points for every letter in the word), but if you are first to guess the "person, place or thing," you get 100 bonus points, and you win that round.

To create the game, think of a "person, place or thing," like "George Washington." Then think of some words that could be clues, like "American," "President," "Father," "Cherry," "Potomac," "Virginia," etc. Then put those clue words into a crossword puzzle, like so:

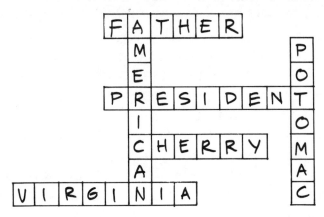

Then you'll need to write clues for the clue words, like:

1. What he is to his son. (Father)
2. A type of cheese (American)
3. The head of a company. (President)
4. Sits on top of a sundae. (Cherry)
5. Yes,_____, there is a Santa Claus. (Virginia)
6. A river. (Potomac)

You'll need to create a bunch of these, as they go pretty fast. With each one, place the empty crossword puzzle up on the board, overhead projector, etc. Give Team #1 the first clue. They get ten seconds to come up with a guess. If it's wrong, the other team can solve that word or choose another. After each correct crossword puzzle guess, the team then gets a chance to guess the "person, place or thing." You can only make guesses at the clue words or the "person, place or thing" when it is your turn. (Contributed by Andy Strachan, Keithville, Louisiana)

ORGANIC SCAVENGER HUNT

Here's a scavenger hunt list that might come in handy next time your group is near a river, by a lake, in the woods at a picnic area, or on a camp or retreat.

the words of John 15:13	a cotton ball
a piece of flint rock	a corncob
a flea	a Salem cigarette
a yellow wild flower	a dandelion
a pre-1975 penny	a magazine
a snail	a brick
a three inch twig	a cactus needle

a four leaf clover
a string of 10 pop tops
a paper clip
a pine needle
5 different soda caps
a feather
a mosquito
an acorn
a root-beer can
an old colored sock
a piece of rope
a baby diaper
a golf tee
a snuff can
a match box
a tooth pick
a little live fishie
a double pine cone
a piece of hard, used gum
a live grasshopper
a ticket stub
an apple core
3 live ants
a red shoe string
a lizzard
a cigar band

a mesquite bean pod
a live fly
a mushroom
a piece of ribbon
a button
a clean Kleenex
a red leaf
a piece of green glass
a strip of cassette tape
a red handkerchief
a pencil that isn't yellow
a new piece of charcoal
a rubber band
a walking stick
an out-of-town newspaper
a crayon
some moss
a mud-dobbers home
a plastic 6-pack holder
a straw
a popsicle stick
a roly-poly bug
a used stamp
a live frog
a bun with sesame seeds
a 1979 calendar

(Contributed by Rodney Coleman, San Marcos, Texas)

PASS THE BUCKET

Here's a good game for bus trips. Make sure you have an equal number of kids on each side of the aisle of the bus. The two sides are opposing teams. Give everyone a list like the one below and about two minutes to determine whether or not they have any of the items that are listed. Then "pass the bucket" on both sides. You will need a couple of large "fried chicken" or "ice cream" buckets (paper sacks will work) and as they are passed down the aisle, the kids toss in as many of the listed items as possible. Set a time limit for each side to collect their bucket full of stuff. Then, the leaders count the items. The side with the most stuff collected is the winner. You can make certain less-common items worth more points if you wish, and you can also have other rules—like no person may contribute more than five items total. Make sure everybody has a way of getting all their stuff back. Here's a sample list:

A comb
A pack of gum (unopened)
A hair brush
A sock
A digital watch
A coin older than 1963
A ring
Nailclippers
A Bic pen

A wallet
A pair of sunglasses
A false eyelash
A paper clip
A white T-shirt (no printing)
A pocketknife
A note from your mother
Lipstick

(Contributed by Tommy Gilmore, Conway, Arkansas)

POPPING PAIRS

This crazy relay is as much fun to watch as it is to participate in and works well with large groups. All you need is a large box of penny balloons and several *clean* inner tubes.

Divide your group into several equal teams of 20 or more. Have team members pair up in small groups of 2 each. Line the teams up behind a start/finish line. Place piles of balloons 50 feet or more from that line, one pile for each team. Make sure you have enough balloons in each pile (one for each team member).

Instruct the teams that the object is for each pair to simply run to their pile of balloons, pick up a balloon, blow it up, and pop it with his foot before returning to tag the next pair on their team. There is however a catch! Each pair must face back-to-back and place their inner tube around both of them at waist heighth. With one runner running forward and the other backward, the pair run to their pile of balloons. Each one must bend down, pick up a balloon, blow it up and break it with his foot while his partner is doing likewise. The inner tube must stay at waist heighth at all times! After both balloons are popped the pair is allowed to run back to their team to tag the next pair of runners. The one who ran forward must now run backward and vice-versa. The first team to get all its members back across the start/finish line is declared the winning team. For added variety, use two inner tubes per pair instead of just one! (Contributed by Mark W. Kaat, Sheboygan, Wisconsin)

PORKY MALLOW

This game gets more difficult but funnier as you go along. Divide your group into two or more teams. Give each player a toothpick (round ones work best) and a marshmallow. The first player puts the marshmallow on his toothpick and then holds the toothpick with his teeth. You're now ready to start the game.

Pass the marshmallow from player to player by sticking your toothpick into the marshmallow and leaving it as you pass it along. You are not allowed to use your hands. As the marshmallow is passed it accumulates one more toothpick from each player.

It's a riot to see players trying to avoid being stuck by the other toothpicks already in the marshmallow. The first team to finish is the winner. And the end product is a marshmallow that looks like a porcupine. (Contributed by Glenn Davis, Winston-Salem, North Carolina)

RANDOM SCORES

Next time your group is having competition between teams in several events, and you want to "neutralize" things so that no team is able to dominate the other teams, here's a way to hand out points which normally keeps the competition much closer.

Before the competition begins, determine the point value for each event. Make sure you have enough points so that every team will receive points following every event. For example, if you have five teams, you need at least five point entries—like 10, 8, 6, 4, and 2. After you have decided on that, make up a board for each event like the illustration below, and scramble the points so that they are in no particular order.

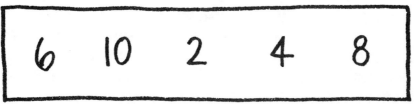

Then cover the points with construction paper squares, with a letter on each one, like so:

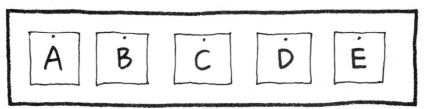

Now, following every event, the points are awarded this way: The team that comes in first gets FIRST CHOICE of the letters on the board. It's purely chance, but they do get to choose first. The second place team chooses second, and so on. Sometimes the last place team actually gets the most points because they don't know how many points lie behind each letter. Still, the first place team likes the "privilege" of being able to choose first, even though the whole thing is determined by luck. Not only does this keep the competition close, but watching teams choose their letters adds extra suspense. (Contributed by Billy Richter, Arlington, Texas)

REFRIGERATOR BALL

Here's a good game that might come in handy at your next retreat when it starts raining outside. You need an indoor playing area and a standard refrigerator (or something similar). You also need a light ball and a cardboard box.

The box is weighted and placed on top of the refrigerator. The refrigerator is moved into the center of the room. A circle is drawn on the floor around the refrigerator so that kids can't get closer than four feet or so. Then you just play regular basketball. The team that has the ball may pass it around and then take shots at the "basket", trying to get the ball to stay in the box. The excitement is increased by missed shots going over the box to the opposing team, shots being "tipped," etc. Make up your own rules as you go along. A referee can call "fouls" and try to keep things from getting out of hand. (Contributed by John Pierce, Marietta, Georgia)

ROOT BEER RELAY

Here's a good one for your next picnic or outdoor event. It always goes over great with kids. Get some cold root beer and some root beer mugs. Five contestants from one team sit on one side of a picnic table, and five from the other team take the opposite side of the table. Each begins with a full mug of root beer in front of them.

Blow the whistle and the first person on each side starts drinking down his or her root beer. When finished, they sit their empty mugs down on the table and the person next to them starts, and so on down the line. Meanwhile the ones who have finished are getting refills. When the last person is finished, it starts over again with the first person. It's that second time through that makes this game really wild. The first team to finish the second round wins. If you have a lot of teams, do it tournament style. Try to have a good mix of guys and girls on each team. (Contributed by Dan Brandel, Livonia, Michigan)

SHOCK

This is a good game for large groups. It's a lot like the game "Domino" in *IDEAS Number Nineteen.* Two teams line up single file and hold hands. There has to be the exact same number on each team. On one end of the team there is a spoon on the floor (or on a table) and at the other end there is a person from each team with a coin.

The two people with the coins begin flipping them (like a coin toss) and showing the coin to the first person in line on their team. If the coin is "tails," nothing happens. If the coin is "heads," the first person quickly squeezes the hand of the second person, who squeezes the hand of the third person, and so on down the line. As soon as the last person in line has his or her hand squeezed, they try to grab the spoon. After grabbing the spoon, the spoon is replaced and that person then runs to the front of the line and becomes the coin flipper. Everybody else moves down one. This continues until every player has been the coin flipper and the spoon grabber. The first team to get its original coin flipper or spoon grabber back into their original positions is the winner.

No one may squeeze the next person's hand until their own hand has been squeezed first. This is like an electric "shock" that works its way down the line. A referee should be stationed at both ends of the team lines to make sure everything is done legally. A false shock results in a new coin flip. You might want to have everyone practice their squeeze before starting, so that everyone knows to squeeze good and hard. Otherwise they might confuse a little twitch for a "legal" squeeze. (Contributed by Adrienne Anderson, Calgary, Alberta, Canada)

SHOE GAMES

Here are some great games that incorporate the use of shoes in some way. They can be used in conjunction with the idea "Walk A Mile in My Shoes" in the Creative Communication chapter of this book, for a retreat or series of meetings with a "shoe" theme. If you need more "shoe" games, check out former volumes of *IDEAS* for games like the "Shoe Kick," "Shoe Scramble," "Shoe Stretch," "Shoe Hockey," and others.

1. *Shoe Hunt:* Read through the following list and find someone whose shoe fits the description. Have that person sign his/her

name on your paper. Last, and most importantly, you must "borrow" that shoe until the game is over. You may only borrow one shoe from each person. Try to borrow as many shoes as possible.

A shoe with a hole on top
A shoe with a broken shoe string
A Nike
A high-top tennis shoe
A shoe with a buckle on it
A sandal
A shoe with four eyelets
A shoe belonging to an adult counselor
A shoe less than a week old
A clog

A shoe with a rawhide shoe string
A shoe that is a larger size than yours
A shoe with a hole in the sole
A 3-colored shoe
A shoe with a bow on it
A shoe belonging to someone of the opposite sex
A dirty shoe
A shoe that is a smaller size than yours
A shoe with flat shoestrings
A shoe that you would like to own

2. *Shoe Pass:* Divide into teams. Each team sits on the floor in a line. One team member takes off a shoe. On a signal, each team must pass their shoe down the line and back. That person then goes to the other end of the line (rotates), and the next person does the same thing. The first team to pass a shoe from everyone on the team is the winner.

3. *Shoe Carry:* Each team divides in half and forms two lines (facing each other). They should be about twenty feet or so apart.

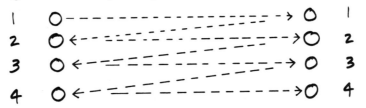

The object of this game is to transport shoes from one side of the room to the other side in a cumulative way. For example: the first person takes off his shoes and carries them across the room and gives them to person #1 on the other side. That person then takes off his shoes and carries *both* pair of shoes to person #2 on the other side. Now three pairs of shoes are carried across, and so on. The idea is to get all the shoes transported back and forth without dropping them. The first team to do so is the winner.

4. *Shoe Sculpture:* Each team puts all the shoes from the team into a big pile. The team then gets five minutes or so to create a "sculpture" from the shoes. A group of impartial judges can choose the winning masterpiece.

(Contributed by Susan Norman, Kernersville, North Carolina)

SHOE GRAB RELAY

This is a great relay game for parties or big group get-togethers (the bigger the group, the better). First, everyone needs to take off their shoes and put them in a big pile at one end of the room (shoes should be as mixed up as possible). Next divide the group into even teams for the relay. After yelling "go" the first person in each relay team must turn to the next person in line and describe his or her shoes to them. That person must then run down to the pile of shoes and hunt out the shoes described to them, bring them back, and put them on the person. If they are the wrong shoes they must go back again and get the right ones. The game continues in this manner with the last person in line describing his shoes to the first person in line. The team who has all their shoes on first is the winning team. This game is especially fun since so many kids wear similar shoes, making it almost impossible in some cases to find the right ones! (Contributed by James Hirsch, South Gate, California)

SHORT ARM BASKETBALL

This game is played relay-style and is not only fun to play, but it makes a fun spectator sport, too. Line up in any number of teams. The first player in each line runs out to a line about eight feet away with the "ball." The ball is a ball of wadded up newspaper wrapped in masking tape that is about six inches in diameter (or you could use a "nerf" ball). He tosses the ball to the second player (standing now at the front of the line) who must catch it *with his elbows* while his hands are on his chin.

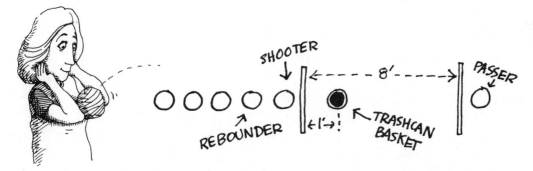

After catching the ball, that person (the "shooter") then bounces the ball off the "backboard" (his knees) and into a bucket (or trash can) that is on the floor, one foot in front of him. The ball must bounce off his knees in order for the basket to count. If he misses, the "rebounder" (the next person in line) picks up the ball and tosses it back to the first person and the whole process repeats until a legal basket is made. You might want to set a limit on unsuccessful tries (like three), but usually that is not necessary.

Once a basket is made, the shooter grabs the ball, runs out to the passer's position, and the rebounder becomes the shooter, while the passer runs to the end of the line, etc. Everybody on the team plays all three positions once. The first team to get back to the original position is the winner. (Contributed by Richard Moore, Vista, California)

SOCCER ON PAPER

Here's a new way to play soccer that is best when played indoors. It's just like regular soccer, except that you give each person, including the goalie, a piece of paper to stand on and a particular place to put the paper. They must keep one foot on the paper at all times. "Scooting" the paper is not allowed. Be sure to scatter players at both teams evenly all over the playing area. Toss in a soccer ball and watch the fun. The effect is like a giant pinball machine. (Contributed by Mitch Lindsey, Olney, Texas)

SOCK BALL

This version of softball can be played with regular softball rules or "Polish Baseball" rules (see *IDEAS Number 13*). It can be played indoors, like in a gym, because you play the game with socks. Everything is made out of socks. Stuff a large sock full of socks to make a sock "bat"; make a ball the same way. No shoes are allowed during the game, only socks. On a freshly waxed floor, this game can really be a riot. (Contributed by Louise and Jim Warnock)

SPITWAD RELAY

Divide your group into teams. Have each team line up single file facing a prepared target. (The target can be a large photo of someone or a regular target.) Each team member is given a plastic straw and told to guard it with his life, and he is given five small pieces of paper to be used as spitwads. At the sound of the whistle each person moves to the shooting position (15-20-30 paces, whatever), and waits for the whistle. At the sound of the whistle, the shooting begins. Spitwads are shot one at a time by each person in line. Spitwads are made by chewing up the small bits of paper into a little ball and then blowing them through the straw. They will usually stick to the target. After shooting one spitwad, each person goes to the end of the line and the next person then shoots, and so on until all shots have been fired. Winners will be determined by points and, of course, neatness. Any team member found shooting other targets is automatically eliminated and used for a target himself after the game is over. (Contributed by Peter A. Ernst, Salt Lake City, Utah)

SQUEAK, BUNNY, SQUEAK

Here's a fun game for smaller groups. Arrange everyone in a circle, seated in chairs. One person is chosen to be "It," and must stand in the middle of the circle. He or she is given a pillow and is blindfolded. "It" is then spun around a few times, the people in the chairs may change seats, and "It" must then find a person's lap. He places the pillow on the lap, sits on it, and says "Squeak, Bunny, Squeak." The person who is being sat on then disguises his or her voice and squeaks. "It" then tries to guess whose lap he is sitting on. If the guess is correct, the person who is identified becomes the new "It" for the next round. If the guess is incorrect, then the same "It" tries again. (Contributed by Ted Landwehr, River Forest, Illinois)

SQUIRREL

This game can be played indoors or outdoors. The group forms several small circles of four each. Then one person steps out, leaving only 3 persons with hands joined. These three people become a hollow tree and the extra person becomes a squirrel who finds a home in the hollow tree. Two extra players are needed, a squirrel and a hound. The hound chases the extra squirrel in and out between the trees. For safety the squirrel may crawl into any tree, but the squirrel already in the tree must leave and flee from the hound. If the hound tags the squirrel, the squirrel becomes the hound and the hound the squirrel, and the game continues. (Contributed by Glenn Davis, Winston-Salem, North Carolina)

TECHNICOLOR STOMP

Here's a good indoor game that is really wild. You will need lots of colored balloons. Divide into teams and assign each team a color—red, blue, orange, yellow, etc. Then give each team an equal number of balloons of their color. For example, the "red" team would be given a certain number (like 20) red balloons. They begin by blowing up all the balloons and tying them. When the actual game begins, the balloons from all the teams are released onto the floor, and the object is to stomp on (and pop) all the balloons of the OTHER teams while attempting to protect your own team's balloons. After the time limit is up (two or three minutes should do it), the popping of balloons stops and each team gathers up its remaining balloons. The team with the most balloons left is the winner. (Contributed by Christine R. Rollins, Turtle Creek, Pennsylvania)

TERRIBLE TWOS

Here is a fast competitive game that can be organized in just a few minutes using ordinary household items. Go around the house and locate about 30 or 40 pairs of things (like two shoes, two hammers, two books, two records, two bars of soap, two toothbrushes, etc.). Add several items as well which have no mate. Put all this stuff into a big box, or into a big pile. Mix it all up real good. Then divide your group into two teams. Each team should be an equal distance away from the pile or box. If this game is played indoors, it would be good to locate the pile of stuff in a separate room.

On "go," each team sends a player to the pile or box of stuff, and he or she brings one item back to the team "stockpile." Each successive team member does the same thing in turn, taking care not to bring back an item that has already been brought back by a teammate. The kids race through their lineup as many times as possible within a set time limit, bringing back as many items as they can.

If a person brings back an item that is already in the team's stockpile, it must be spotted by the team and sent back with the very next runner, and that runner may not bring back a new item on that turn. If the item is not spotted right away as a duplicate item and thrown into the team's stockpile, it will count against them when points are added up at the end of the game. When the whistle blows (this should occur before the entire stock of items is exhausted), points for each team are awarded as follows:

1. Each item is worth ten points. (Total of items times ten.)
2. Each item *with no mate* is worth 50 more points.
3. Each pair of objects stockpiled by the same team is worth a *minus* 50 points per item. (100 total minus points per pair)

For experienced players, have each team's stockpile be a large box that items are dropped into (out of sight). This means that kids must memorize each item as it goes in, and it increases the likelihood of ending up the game with more duplicate items in the box. Another way to add difficulty to the game is to make the pairs of items not identical to each other, but still creating a "pair." For example, you might have a toothbrush and toothpaste, a hammer and a nail, a cup and saucer, etc. It's a good game. (Contributed by Rob Moritz, Kansas City, Missouri)

THREE BALL

Here's a great outdoor game from New Zealand that can be used with almost any age group and any number of people. You need a baseball diamond (or a reasonable facsimile) and three balls of any kind. You can use softballs, footballs, rugby balls, soccer balls, volleyballs, or just about anything that can be thrown. You can use frisbees if you want to. The three balls you use don't have to be the same, either. You will also need a cardboard box, trash can, bucket, or something that the balls can go in.

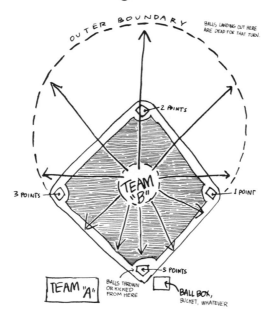

The box (for the balls) goes at home plate. One team is "up" and the other team is out in the field, just like regular baseball. There are no "positions," however. Everybody just plays everywhere. The first "batter" comes to the plate and selects three balls (if there are more than three to choose from). He then must get rid of all three of them as quickly as possible, any way he wants to—by kicking, throwing, etc. The balls must stay within the boundaries of the field.

After getting rid of the balls, he starts running the bases while the team in the field tries to return all three balls back to the box at home plate. The player who is running the bases gets a point for each base he reaches before the balls are back in the box, and five points if he gets a "home run" and makes it all the way around. If a ball is caught on the fly, then that ball does not have to be placed in the box—it is dead. If the runner is caught between bases when the last of the three balls are placed in the box, then he loses all his accumulated points. He must watch and stop so that he is safely on a base when all the balls are finally in.

There are no "outs." The best way to play is to let everyone on the team have a chance each inning and just add up the total points scored. When everybody has gone up, then the other team is "up"

67

and tries to get as many points as possible. You can play as many "innings" as you want. If you have larger groups, then get several games going at once. It doesn't matter if the fields overlap.

Since it is very easy to get to first base (at least), it means that everyone can contribute to the team score and have fun. You will need one referee for the game to blow the whistle (or whatever) when the balls come in and to help keep score. Boundaries, distance between bases, etc. can all be adjusted depending on the size and skill of the group. (Contributed by the Campus Life Staff. New Plymouth, New Zealand)

TOOTHPASTE RACES

Give each team a new tube of toothpaste and a roll of toilet paper. The toilet paper is a "track" upon which to squeeze the toothpaste, so it's easy to clean up.

Race #1: Go for the longest unbroken strand of toothpaste in a set length of time.

Race #2: Lay out an "obstacle course" where you must run your strand of toothpaste over all sorts of objects. For a really spirited group, have the members of the team lie down and the toothpaste (without TP) can run across their faces, etc.

Race #3: Go for the longest strand from one single new tube of paste per team!

(Contributed by Rob Moritz, Kansas City, Missouri)

TRIPLE THREAT BASKETBALL

Here's a new way to play basketball. It requires one basket and three teams. You can have three teams of any size, however a maximum of five players and a minimum of two would be best. The rules of the game are pretty much the same as regular basketball, but with these changes:

1. Baskets are worth one point. The game is played until one team has ten points and is leading the other two teams by at least two points each.
2. After each basket is scored, the team in last place is awarded the ball out of bounds, even if they were the team that just scored. In the event that two teams (or all three teams) are tied for last, the team that has had the low point total the longest is awarded the ball. Or, you may want to come up with some other system that seems fair.
3. In the event that play is stopped for some reason other than a basket, such as the ball going out of bounds, travelling, double

dribble, etc., the team in last place is again awarded the ball. If the last place team was guilty of the violation, the ball is given to the team which is next to last.

4. In the event of a foul, the team that was fouled takes the ball out of bounds. No foul shots.

This game can be played with two baskets on a regular basketball court, and having the teams "rotate" baskets after each goal is scored. Part of the fun then is trying to remember which basket is yours. Another variation would be to play with four teams and four bas kets on each side of a square, if you have baskets that can be moved. You could, of course, play the game with a Nerf Ball and cardboard boxes or trash cans for baskets. Use your own crea tivity and have fun! (Contributed by Merle Moser, Jr., Berne, Indiana)

VOLLEY-BALLOON WATERBALL

The crazy name is to avoid possible confusion of this game with "Water Balloon Volleyball," found in *IDEAS Number 17*. To play this unique game, you will need a regular volleyball net, lots of filled water balloons, and two king-size sheets or blankets.

There are two teams, one on each side of the net. Each team gets a sheet and the entire team surrounds the sheet, holding it by the edges. A water balloon is placed in the middle of the serving team's sheet, and the team must lob the balloon over the net using the sheet—sort of like a trampoline. The other team must catch the balloon on their sheet (without causing it to break) and then heave it back over the net to the other team. If it goes out of bounds or lands back in their side of the court, they lose the point or serve. If the receiving team fails to catch it, or if it breaks in-bounds, then they lose.

The scoring is the same as in regular volleyball. Teams can be any size, but if you get too many people around the sheets, it becomes difficult to move quickly. The game requires great teamwork, and is perfect for a hot day. (Contributed by Dan Sarian, Winchester, Virginia)

WALKY TALKY

This is a great get acquainted type of game that would be ideal next time you are on a walk or need to get your group from one place to another. You will need two lines of people with everyone having a partner. Then you start walking. The two people in the front start by going back to anyone who is in their column of people behind them (they don't have to go to the same couple) and telling them to either go forward 5 or back 10 people. They can use any numbers they want. Then after that person leaves their spot to do as they were told, the person who told them to move takes their spot. This would give them a new partner and friend to get to know. This same procedure is followed throughout the entire walk. It ends when you get to your final destination. If you have a large crowd, you might have two or three couples lead off. This will create a lot of confusion with people running back and forth, but that's the fun of it. (Contributed by Jan Schaible, Wichita, Kansas)

WRITING IN THE SAND

Here's a "mindreading" game, in which the leader and his partner try to baffle the rest of the group. The group selects a "secret word" and the partner comes in and is able to guess the word correctly following a short series of clues from the leader which the group tries to figure out.

The leader holds a stick in his or her hand, and appears to "write in the sand" some clues. However, the writing does not appear to make sense, and bears no obvious relationship to the secret word being guessed. But the partner is still able to guess the word on the first try.

Here's how it is done: The consonants in the word (let's say the secret word is "light") are L, G, H, and T. These are given to the partner through a series of verbal clues after he or she enters the room. The leader might first say, "Let's see if you can get this one." The first letter of that sentence is "L." That would clue in the partner that the word starts with an "L." Then, the leader draws on the floor with the stick, and at some point taps out either 1, 2, 3, 4, or 5 taps. These are the vowels. "A" is one tap, "U" is five taps. So, in this case, the leader would tap the stick three times for "I." Now the partner has two letters. The "G" is given next with a verbal clue, like "Got it yet?"

70

As soon as the partner has enough letters to guess the word, he amazes the group, and anyone who thinks they know how it is done may try their skill as the partner. (Contributed by Glenn Davis, Winston-Salem, North Carolina)

ZIMBAT

This game is very similar to the old game "Capture the Flag" (See *IDEAS Number 1-4*). Two teams are situated on a large playing field, with a boundary dividing the field in half. Each team is given a flag which they must place in a conspicuous position and protect. Should the other team capture their flag by taking it over to the other side, they would lose. Players tagged while in the enemy's territory are captured and sent to jail. The jail is a designated area about twenty yards from the flag zone.

So far, it's just like regular Capture the Flag. But this game differs through the addition of Frisbees. About a fourth of the players are issued Frisbees. Any player tagged by a Frisbee, whether it is thrown or held, is sent to prison, regardless of which side of the field they are on.

Additional rules include: 1) Jailed players stay in jail for 100 seconds—they just count it off themselves and return. There is no "freeing" prisoners as in regular Capture the Flag. 2) A Frisbee must be "dead" in order for someone to pick it up. Anyone may pick up a dead Frisbee regardless of who threw it. 3) Jailed players must surrender their Frisbee to the nearest person. (Contributed by Dennis James Henn, Wenatchee, Washington)

Creative Communication

AFTER THE WELL

For an interesting approach to a study of the "Woman at the Well" (John 4), have kids role-play the situation after the story ends in scripture. Someone should play the part of the woman as she confronts the man she has been living with. The scene can open up with the man asking "What took you so long? I thought you were just going up to the well for a bucket of water. . ." From there the dialogue can go in any direction. Each character should respond as they think the actual characters might have responded then, or as they (the kids) might have responded had they been in the same position. Follow up with a discussion of what happened. (Contributed by Gail Moody, Newtown, Pennsylvania)

APATHY PARTY

Here is an idea for a youth meeting which is not only a million laughs but is a good object lesson on a problem which Christ addressed in his letters to the seven churches in Revelation (Rev. 3:14-19)

Announce ahead of time that you are going to have an "Apathy Party" and that everyone is to come dressed in the most bland and boring clothing they can dig up. Have them wear what they would wear if they "just didn't care."

When they arrive have the sponsors greet them at the door and hand out a list of rules for the party (refer to the list of "Apathy Party Rules"). Each sponsor is to have several paper bags large enough to cover the heads of anyone who laughs or gets excited or shows any enthusiasm whatsoever.

The following games may be played at this party:

1. *Un-dramatic reading:* Have some books of prose and poetry and perhaps a phone book or dictionary available for finding selections and have each person read a selection from the available material as emotionless and monotonous as possible. The dryest, dullest, most boring reading will be declared the winner.

2. *Clothes judging:* Have everyone line up and have the sponsors judge everyone's costume. The winner will be the one with the most blah clothes.

APATHY PARTY RULES

Not Allowed:

Laughing (giggling, chuckling, etc.)
Crying

Smiling (grinning)
Frowning (scowling)

Loud voices (neither happy nor angry)
Fast movements

Bright eyes
Enthusiastic hand gestures
Applause

Interesting conversations
Exclamations ("wow!", "hey!" etc.)

Allowed:

Yawning
Bored looks (glazed eyes, rolling eyes, dead-pan expression)

Slow movements
Tapping fingers
Twiddling thumbs

Monotone voice
Boring conversations

Staring into space . . .

If you are caught performing any of the activities that are **not allowed—you
must put a sack over your head until you are able to control yourself and behave in
a properly bored manner.

**Anyone who cannot bring himself (herself) under control in a reasonable
amount of time will have to go into the hall until they can return apathetically.

Have a real ho-hum time . . .

3. *Dead-Pan Face Staring:* Have an elimination contest: Everyone is pared off and at the signal, they attempt to out stare their partner. The winner is the one who stares the longest without laughing or looking away or closing his eyes (blinking is permitted). Each contestant may say things to get the other one to laugh but must not get excited himself.

4. *Balancing-air-on-a-spoon Relay:* Divide everyone up into teams and tell them you were going to have them balance raw eggs on spoons for a relay but you weren't in the mood to go to the store, so they can balance air on their spoons instead. Have them (in equally divided teams) go up to a mark and back, then hand off the spoon to the next one on the team. Sponsors may decide who has dropped their air off their spoon and have them go back and start over again. The first team to come in gets disqualified for trying too hard, and the last place team gets

disqualified for trying to lose.

5. *Book balancing relay:* This is another team relay like the previous relay but they are to balance a book as they go up to the mark and back. However, they may hold the book however they want to because after all it doesn't matter anyway and besides that. . ."Who cares?"

The sponsors may then announce that all further games have been cancelled because by now everyone is thoroughly bored and utterly apathetic. Sponsors may commend those in the group who gave exceptionally fine demonstrations of apathy and boredom. Those who refused to participate in the games are to receive highest praise for their apathy and lack of cooperation. In order to really get into the feel of the luke-warmness of it all, the proper refreshments would include the following:

1. Flat, luke warm coke in small cups or better yet luke warm tap-water. (The sponsors may explain that they just didn't have time to get anything better.)
2. Small pieces of cold frozen pizza.
3. Small cups of melted ice cream.

Follow the refreshment time with a discussion on Revelation 3:14-19 about the consequences of being "luke-warm" or apathetic. Allow kids to share their reactions to the party and the refreshments. This might be a good way to creatively shock a luke-warm youth group out of its doldrums. You might wrap up with some *good* refreshments and a little enthusiasm. (Contributed by Ed Skidmore, Arcadia, Texas)

APPEARANCES

The following multiple-choice questionnaire is an excellent discussion starter on the subject of personal appearance. Most kids worry a great deal about how they look, and this can help give some direction and substance to this natural preoccupation.

This questionnaire could be combined with some other appearance-oriented exercise or crowd breaker for an entire meeting or program on this theme. Here are some suggestions:

1. Start with a fashion show. Check other volumes of *IDEAS* for some crazy ways to do this.
2. Have a "best dressed" contest. Have kids come up with a list of the ten best (or worst) dressed people in the church or the youth group. This could be a lot of fun.
3. Hang up some pictures of people with different kinds of appearances (dress, hair, etc.) and have the kids try to make some conclusions about the values or lifestyles represented. The

object is to determine whether or not there is a connection between outward appearance and the "real" person.

4. Have the youth sponsors dress in a very sloppy or bizarre manner for the meeting. Or just different from normal. Watch the kids' reactions. Or. . .

5. Encourage the kids to come to the meeting dressed in a "different or unusual" way. You might have everyone come in formal attire or as sloppy as possible, or wearing their "favorite" clothes.

6. You might have a game or drawing in which the winner gets a gift certificate to a clothing store (you might be able to get this donated).

These are only suggestions, of course. You may be able to come up with better ones yourself. The following questionnaire is the important part. Print it up so that everyone has a copy, and give the group ten or fifteen minutes to complete it. When they are finished, have them discuss the questions in small groups or with the entire group. Try to focus in on some principles which might help kids to care about their appearance without being obsessed with conformity, status-seeking, or being phony. Wrap it up however you choose.

Please answer these questions in order. Don't go back and change your answer; your initial response was probably most honest.

MY APPEARANCE

1. I think about my appearance . . .
    (a.) constantly
    (b.) regularly
    (c.) when it is called to my attention
    (d.) rarely
    (e.) never (even when looking in a mirror)

2. The money I spend on clothes and my appearance is . . .
    (a.) ridiculous
    (b.) too much
    (c.) about right
    (d.) not enough

3. I dress the way I do for chuch on Sundays *primarily* because . . .
    (a.) I feel most comfortable this way
    (b.) it is what others expect
    (c.) I don't want to be noticed, stick out
    (d.) I want others to notice me
    (e.) because I think God would be pleased
    (f.) I was taught by my parents to dress this way
    (g.) Other _____

4. I think long hair being a disgrace for men, long hair being a woman's glory and it being improper for a woman to pray with her head uncovered . . . (I Cor.-11:13-16)
    (a.) were all cultural (just applied to the time they were written)
    (b.) all apply to us today

75

         (c.) can't be put in the same category (even though they appear in the
            same paragraph in the Bible)

5. Quite honestly, I . . .
    (a.) judge people on the basis of their appearance
    (b.) don't let appearance affect the way I think of people
    (c.) let appearance affect the way I judge people some, and rightly so!
    (d.) try not to be affected by people's appearance but can't help it

6. I dress the way I do at work or school because . . .
    (a.) I feel most comfortable that way
    (b.) it is what others expect
    (c.) I don't want to be noticed, stick out
    (d.) I want others to notice me
    (e.) because I think God would be pleased
    (f.) I was taught by my parents to dress that way
    (g.) I would lose my job or be kicked out of school if I dressed otherwise
    (h.) other _____

7. Please rate the 7 reasons listed in Question 6 as to the best (#1) to worst (#7) reasons for dressing the way one does (whether that is the reason you chose or not)

8. *Most* people in our society (culture) are . . .
    (a.) hung up on appearance
    (b.) don't care enough about their appearance
    (c.) have a good perspective on the importance of appearance
    (d.) other _____

9. If I could change one thing about my appearance, it would be . . .

    _____

10. The reason I would change what I chose in the previous question is . . .
    (a.) I would impress others more favorably
    (b.) I would be able to forget about this which bothers me a lot
    (c.) I would be better in sports
    (d.) I would feel better (physically)
    (e.) I would be more attractive to the opposite sex
    (f.) other _____

11. Please rate the following three categories as to whether you think it (1) Matters very much to God, (2) Matters very little to God, (3) Matters to God if it matters to us, (4) Really doesn't matter at all to God
    (a.) how I dress _____
    (b.) whether I am overweight or underweight _____
    (c.) whether I shower, shave, keep hair combed and cut regularly ____

12. A Christian in our society . . .
    (a.) should have about the same idea as others in our society do about appearance. That is, there's little wrong with how our society thinks about appearance.
    (b.) should be distinctly different than most of society in the way he thinks about appearance.

13. When I am dressed distinctly different than others in a social situation, I feel . . .
    (a.) pleased
    (b.) embarrassed, conspicuous
    (c.) comfortable
    (d.) other _____

(Contributed by Dan Mutschler, Chicago, Illinois)

ASH WORSHIP

This idea is not really a new one, but rather a recovery of a church worship practice which can be easily used in a youth group setting. This is based on a service for Ash Wednesday, but could be used in any situation which is appropriate.

In a group setting, have the leader talk about sin and grace. After the talk, have everyone write down on a piece of paper something they wish forgiveness for. When everyone is finished, have them fold the paper so that no one else can see what was written and bring it forward to a group leader. The leader then lights the papers with a match with the whole group watching the paper become ashes (lighting the paper in a steel or carbon Wok is a good way to contain the ashes and prevent any accidental spread of fire without damaging the Wok).

After the paper has been completely turned to ash, the leader instructs each person to place his/her fingers into the ash and, with a bit of ash, make the sign of the cross on the person's forehead next to them. The leader can then explain that in our repentence, Christ has forgiven us and is with us. This can be a powerful way to understand sin, grace, and forgiveness. (Contributed by Malcolm McQueen, San Anselmo, California)

BETHANY CHURCH

This is a simulation that deals with church structure, the mission of the church, unity in the church, and a host of other issues as well. It would be most effective in a retreat setting so that plenty of time could be allowed if necessary. It will work well with any age group, junior high on up.

To set up the experience, explain to the group that they are all members of a fictional church called Bethany Church. Bethany Church is located in the city of Gitchigumi, in the heart of the downtown area. Gitchigumi has a population of 72,000. The church has a membership of 580 adult members, and membership has recently been declining. However, the church is not in any kind of serious trouble. It is served by a senior minister, an assistant minister, and a full-time secretary. The church budget is $80,000 per year and was raised last year with some difficulty. In the past, around $9,000 has been given per year to the mission of the church.

Note: You can, if you like, use the name and description of your own church here. This would make the simulation much more realistic and "close to home." You would need to adapt the entire simulation (including the "proposals" and the "interest groups") to fit your church.

Recently a wealthy resident of the community passed away and left

$250,000 in cash to the church. The church is now faced with a decision on how to use that money, since the person who left the money did not specify how it was to be used. That person did, however, insist that everyone in the church must unanimously agree on how the money would be used (within a certain time limit), otherwise the money would be turned over to another charitable organization, namely the Society for the Preservation of Begonias.

With that in mind, the group is divided into a number of "interest groups." Each interest group is provided with a role identity, an assigned number of votes, and a set of goals for itself. The effectiveness of each group will depend, to a large degree, on the ability of its members to role-play the assigned viewpoints and identity of the group.

After the groups have been assigned, a number of "proposals" are presented. Each group must decide which of these proposals, if adopted, would provide the kind of addition to the life of Bethany Church that would be desirable by its own standards. Then, they may devise a strategy for using their group's power or influence to secure other groups' assistance in getting their favorite proposal adopted. They may also try to block, by any means in line with the identity of their group, the adoption of proposals which they feel would adversely affect Bethany Church. If none of the proposals are acceptable to the group, they may suggest alternatives.

The Proposals:

Number One: In light of the large number of people still not going to church in Gitchigumi and in light of the constant tendency of others in the church to fall away, it is proposed that the money be invested in order to yield $15,000 annually in interest for a week-long evangelism crusade. This fund would allow for the obtaining of a first-rate preacher, ample advertising, funds for TV, and part-time summer help to follow up new conversions. Special music would also be included.

Number Two: In the light of severe economic and social distress of many of the aged members of the congregation, it is proposed that the $250,000 be set up as the first money in a fund to construct low-cost housing and other facilities for those elderly in need.

Number Three: The $250,000 should be used to finance a modest addition to the current Christian education building that would be helpful to the church in several ways: 1) relieve overcrowding of current Sunday School classes by constructing six new classrooms; 2) provide adequate office facilities for assistant minister; 3) provide combination gymnasium-activity room which would be used to build a more active youth program; 4) provide prayer chapel for small groups within the church and for individual meditation. Since the property is already owned, it is possible to do this for $250,000.

Number Four: Gitchigumi desperately needs more day care for children of working mothers. The church school rooms sit unused all week long, while for $100,000 they could be converted and equipped to provide one day-care facility for 15 to 30 children. The other $150,000 could be used to finance one full-time professional staff person who, with the help of church volunteers, could staff the program. This would fulfill fewer needs of our own church members, but would provide help for those outside the church membership who need that help.

Number Five: Bethany Church is understaffed. Given the current budget, it would not be possible to hire another minister in the near future. Yet there is needed a person who can go full-time calling on our shut-ins and those in the hospitals and do counseling with those having various difficulties. This would free our other ministers to do their jobs more vigorously and would lead to the eventual building up of the congregation. With the $250,000 in a savings account drawing interest of $15,000 a year; another minister could be hired.

Number Six: The organ in the sanctuary desperately needs to be replaced. The pipes are cracking and there are notes that do not even play. Since the worship service depends on the organ for music, it is imperative that the organ be replaced. This can be done for only $230,000.

The "Interest Groups":

1. *The Choir:* The choir is not the most open group in the church, since it is dominated by the members of four or five of the old families in the church. To them the worship life of the church is central, and at times, music is the center of that worship. Most of the people are over 45, and most of them are very pious, being also the active core of the pastor's adult Bible study group that meets during the Sunday School hour. (10 votes)
2. *Executive Board of Church Women:* These officers speak for the concerns of the women who compose the eight circles of the church. They are perhaps better educated than the congregation as a whole. All of them are married, most of them are homemakers, and they are quite concerned about the church's ministry to young people and children. (20 votes)
3. *The Board:* This is a group of men between the ages of 35 and 70. They are entrusted with the responsibility of raising money and supervising the activities of the church. The majority of them are businessmen. There is also a group of professionals—doctor, lawyer, engineer, and college teacher. By in large the group is rather conservative and traditional. (30 votes)

4. *Young Adult Discussion Group:* This group of post-college married couples and singles is the most lively and most progressive group within the church. They meet every Sunday night and study such things as they wish, emphasizing fellowship, study and social concern in about equal measure. The pastor speaks of them as the conscience of Bethany, because of their willingness to raise unpopular issues and their general contribution to the liveliness of the Church. (15 votes)

5. *The Church Staff:* Three people, the senior pastor (age 55), the assistant pastor (age 29), and the church secretary (who has worked here longer than both ministers, 15 years). They have particular interests and loyalties, but also feel to some extent a responsibility to look out for the general welfare of the church. (20 votes)

6. *The Youth Fellowship:* This group, made up largely of sons and daughters of church members plus a few of their non-member friends, meets weekly for fun and discussion. It has recently been developing interest in how the church can be more responsive to community needs, though a few members are pressing for a more personally oriented, evangelical emphasis. (10 votes)

7. *Neighborhood and Street People:* Though not actually members of Bethany Church, these people are interested in the use and purpose of the church. Some of them resent the church's tax exempt status and feel that it owes the community more specific community services. (5 votes)

Instructions to the Group:

1. Divide into the assigned groups.
2. Read the description of the group you are representing.
3. Decide how you will role-play that group.
4. Decide which proposals you are in favor of and which you object to.
5. Talk with members of other groups at the designated time to convince them of your argument.
6. Hand in a written ballot as to how you are voting. You may vote either for a proposal or against a proposal. For example, if you have 15 votes, you can cast 3 votes *for* the Evangelism Crusade, six votes *against* the organ, and six votes *for* the building addition.
7. The votes will be tabulated and if a certain proposal has a majority of the votes it will win. If not, another round will be played, following steps 4 through 6.
8. If at the end of four rounds no one proposal can be agreed upon, Bethany Church will lose the $250,000 gift and it will be given to the Society for the Preservation of Begonias.

Following the simulation, discuss the experience with the entire group, sharing feelings and generally de-briefing. This can be tied in with other learning strategies, Bible study, or opportunities for personal growth and commitment. (Contributed by Malcolm McQueen, San Anselmo, California)

BIBLE MATHEMATICS

Sometimes it is a good idea to use "Scripture Search" games with young people to familiarize them with their Bibles, and to give them practice at looking up verses and finding information in Scripture. It's definitely not the best way to learn Scripture, but it does get kids into their Bibles. The following five games are math problems that are solved by looking up the verses and finding the necessary

---

GAME ONE

1. Locate the number of gold pieces the burned books were calculated to be worth in Acts 19:19.

2. Divide that number by the number of measures of oil owed by the debtor in Luke 16:6.

3. Add to that number the number of years Ahaz ruled in Jerusalem (2 Chronicles 28:1).

4. Add to that number the number of generations from Abraham to David (Matthew 1:17).

5. Subtract from that number the number of years the Israelites were in possession of their land (Acts 13:20).

6. Multiply that number by number of days that Lazarus had been in the tomb (John 11:17).

7. Subtract from that number the number of years that Serug lived after the birth of Nahor (Genesis 11:23).

8. Divide that number by the number of Beatitudes in Matthew 5:3-11.

FINAL ANSWER _____

GAME TWO

1. Locate the number of years that Eber lived after the birth of Peleg (Genesis 11:17).

2. Subtract from that number the age of David when he became king (2 Sm 5:4).

3. Add to that number the number of men armed for war in Judges 18:18.

4. Add to that number the number of pigs that ran down the cliff and drowned in the lake (Mark 5:13).

5. Divide that number by the number of denarii the ointment was worth in Mark 14:5.

6. Add to that number the number of years it had taken to build the sanctuary according to John 2:20.

7. Add to that number the number of days that Paul and the crew on the boat had gone hungry (Acts 27:33).

8. Multiply that number by the number of sparrows two pennies would buy according to Luke 12:6.

FINAL ANSWER _____

GAME THREE

1. Locate the number of the total of the twelve tribes of Israel in Numbers 1:46.

2. Divide that number by the number of just men Yahweh asked Abraham to find in the city of Sodom (Genesis 18:26).

3. Subtract from that number the number of years Jared lived (Genesis 5:20).

4. Subtract from that number the number of years that Peleg lived after the birth of Reu (Genesis 11:19).

5. Subtract from that number the number of men who stayed with Gideon (Judges 7:3).

6. Divide that number by the number of plagues visited upon the Egyptians before the Pharaoh would let the Israelites go (Exodus 12:29).

7. Subtract from that number the number of years the land enjoyed peace after the battle led by Deborah and Barak (Judges 5:31).

FINAL ANSWER _____

GAME FOUR

1. Locate the number of the members of Abram's household (Genesis 14:15).

2. Add to that number the number of years that Jared lived (Genesis 5:20).

3. Add to that number the number of talents of gold that Hiram sent to Solomon (1 Kings 9:14).

4. Subtract from that number the number of years the descendants of Abraham would be oppressed (Acts 7:6).

5. Divide that number by the number of measures of oil the steward asked his master's debtor to pay back for what he owed (Luke 16:6).

6. Multiply that number by the number of times Paul was shipwrecked (2 Cor 11:25).

7. Subtract from that number the number of years the Israelites enjoyed peace in Midian (Judges 8:28).

8. Add to that number the age of Enosh when he became the father of Kenan (Genesis 5:9).

9. Subtract from that number the number of years that Judith lived (Judith 16:28).

FINAL ANSWER _____

Answers:

(The numbers needed for each step are provided, plus the final answer)

Game One	Game Two	Game Three	Game Four
1. 50,000	1. 430	1. 603,550	1. 318
2. 100	2. 30	2. 50	2. 962
3. 16	3. 600	3. 962	3. 120
4. 14	4. 2000	4. 209	4. 400
5. 450	5. 300	5. 10,000	5. 50
6. 4	6. 46	6. 90	6. 3
7. 200	7. 14	7. 40	7. 40
8. 8	8. 5	Final Answer: **50**	8. 90
Final Answer: **15**	Final Answer: **350**		9. 105
			Final Answer: **5**

numbers then doing some simple arithmetic. Print them up and give them to the kids in your group. They will, of course, need Bibles and pencils. Pocket calculators are optional. They can be solved individually or they can be worked on in teams. The object is to be first to arrive at the correct answer.

(Contributed by Mrs. Pat Andrews, Slidell, Louisiana)

THE BLACK ARMBANDS

Here's a discussion starter on the topic of authority and civil disobedience. After reading the following news item to your group (which is true, by the way), you might wish to go over the discussion questions and examine other current issues where protesters use non-violent expressions of civil disobedience. To wrap up the evening, you might tell the actual fate of the three kids in the story: while their families received hate calls, bomb threats and a bucket of red paint thrown at their house, the case of the armbands was ultimately taken to the United States Supreme Court. The court ruled that peaceful protest in a public school is legal: "School officials do not possess absolute authority over their students. Students in school as well as out of school are 'persons' under our Constitution."

In 1965, during the beginning of United States military involvement in Viet Nam, three high school students in Iowa heard of the anti-war protests taking place on college campuses. They decided that they too would wear black armbands to class as a way of saying that war is wrong.

Chris Eckhardt, John Tinker and his sister, Mary Beth, wrote an article for their school paper explaining why they were about to begin wearing black armbands. Before the article was printed, however, a copy of it reached their high school principal. He immediately instructed the three that they would not be allowed to stage their protest. The principal explained that such activity would disrupt classes and school spirit.

In spite of their principal's warning, John, Chris and Mary Beth wore their armbands anyway as they felt it was within the rights of students to express their opinions. All three were suspended from school until their armbands were removed.

Possible Questions for Discussion:

1. How do you feel about the three kids and their protest? Would you have joined them? Would you have supported their right to protest?
2. Do you think the principal did the right thing? What would you have done in his place?
3. Make a list of authorities *you* must answer to (such as the principal of your school). Under what circumstances might you have to disobey each of these authorities?
4. Look up these verses on our relationship to authorities: Rom. 13:1-7, Titus 3:1, Peter 2:13-17, Eph. 6:1-9, and Col. 3:20. Do these verses rule out civil disobedience?

5. Now look up these examples of civil disobedience: Exodus 1:15-21, Exodus 2:11, Joshua 2:1-7, I Samuel 19:9-17, Matthew 27:64, and 28:2, Acts 4:1-3, 5:17,18 and 12:6-10.
6. How does one know whether or not to obey or disobey an authority?

(Contributed by Kraig Klaudt, El Cajon, California)

THE CASE OF THE MISSING YOUTH DIRECTOR

Here's a good idea that deals with the subject of apathy and commitment, particularly as it relates to the church. It all begins when you purposely don't show up for a planned meeting. A sponsor (who has been informed ahead of time on what to do) pretends to be puzzled by your tardiness, and encourages the kids to get some of their feelings out while they wait for your arrival. The group will very likely have some negative things to say about your absence.

Let this go on for about 10 minutes (or until the group can no longer be contained) and then have the sponsor suggest that someone give you a call to find out why you aren't there. When your phone rings, tell them that, "I just decided not to come tonight. I was tired and just didn't feel like putting up with anything this evening."

While the reaction of the kids might be to leave, have the sponsor encourage them to stay and to discuss their feelings about your apathy. They could even be asked to write you a letter expressing their feelings. Questions the sponsor may wish to raise in the discussion might include:

1. How do some of the rest of you feel?
2. Is it fair to us that our youth director stayed at home?
3. What do you think we should do?
4. Has anyone else ever showed a lack of concern about the youth group, the church, or something you cared about a lot?
5. What would you say to someone who didn't care about something you really cared about?
6. What do you think is the cause of a lack of concern or apathy?
7. Have you ever been apathetic about important things?
8. What is the solution to apathy?
9. Read Revelation 3:14-21.

To wrap up the discussion, the sponsor can read a letter from you which explains why you are not at the meeting and explains how you feel about apathy. You can then either stay away the entire evening or come by later to participate in the rest of the meeting. (Contributed by Doug Tweedy, Westminster, California)

CLUES TO HAPPINESS

What are some of the clues to real happiness? Jesus spoke on the subject in his opening pronouncements in the Sermon on the Mount (Matthew 5:1-12). The word "happy" could easily substitue where the word "blessed" is found in many translations. As a way of helping the young people to think about this passage from Matthew before they study it, give each of them a sheet of paper. Ask them to list all of the things which make them happy, contented, or leave them feeling good. Then, compare their lists with the list of Beatitudes found in Matthew 5. There will probably be a great difference between the two. Yet, the sharing can prove to be fruitful as you can help the group begin to discover what it means to be poor in spirit, to be meek, merciful, pure in heart, peacemakers, etc. In short, the group can uncover some new light on the meaning of happiness. (Contributed by Vernon Edington, Decatur, Alabama)

THE COOLS AND THE NERDS

Here's an idea that will open up the topic of conformity, popularity, acceptance, and peer pressure with your kids in a fun and creative way. First, divide into two groups, the "Cools" and the "Nurds." For obvious reasons, you may want to divide up the group, then tell them which of the two groups they are. There should be at least one "artistic" type in each group, if possible. Give the two groups a drawing pad and some marking pens and have the "Cools" draw a picture of someone who is *really* cool—a stereotype of everything

that is currently "in." The "Nurds" draw a picture of a real "Nurd", someone who is totally out of it.

After the pictures are drawn. they can be posted and judged by an impartial jury (sponsors, maybe) for accuracy, humor, creativity, etc.

List on the blackboard or on poster board some characteristics of a "cool" person and a "not cool" person. For example:

COOL

Not taking school work home
Wearing a game jersey
Sports
Owning a car
Cutting class
Smoking, drinking
Dating
Swearing
Eating junk food for lunch

NOT COOL

Wearing rain boots to school
Girls carrying a purse
Guys carrying a briefcase
Going to church or S.S.
Dressing up
Being driven by parents on a date
Bringing lunch in a lunch pail
Golf

Next, discuss the following questions, or other questions of your choice:

1. Do you consider yourself "cool" or "Un-cool"?
2. What is the "coolest" thing you ever did? The "un-coolest"?
3. Why are items on the "cool" list accepted by the crowd and not the other list. What's wrong with the "not cool" list?
4. What's wrong with the "cool" list?
5. Why do we want to be "cool"? Why is it so important?
6. Is conformity good or bad? Always good or always bad?
7. What are the dangers of conformity?
8. Where do you find the most pressure to conform?
9. What does the Bible say about conformity? What does it mean?

Wrap up the discussion with some thoughts from Scripture, using passages like Romans 12:1-2, which deal with conformity. You might want to illustrate with heroes of the faith (like Noah) who had to take a lot of ridicule from the crowd, but knew that they were right. The supreme example, of course, was Jesus. John 7:5 says that even his brothers rejected him. Encourage your young people to pinpoint one problem area where they can begin to "break away" from the crowd a little bit and live for Christ's approval, not the world's. (Contributed by James Gullett, Redwood City, California)

CORINTHIANS, CANDLES, AND COOPERATION

Here's a game that will highlight the importance of spiritual gifts (I Corinthians 12) and will also encourage cooperation and teamwork in your group. You will need nine identical pieces of paper, a flashlight, a candle and a book or box of matches. Before the players arrive, you will have to: 1) place the flashlight in a prominent place, 2) hide the candle somewhere in the room, 3) hide the *empty* matchbox or match pack and 4) hide some matches in the room.

Begin by giving each person a folded piece of paper and instruct them not to read it until you give the signal. This piece of paper has each person's "role" for the game on it. Be sure to call it a "role" and not a "gift" at this point. It is also important that you *give* each person the paper rather than letting them draw one from a hat. If there are more than nine, split the group up into teams and see who can finish the game the quickest. Only one team may play at a time, the others will have to leave the room.

After distributing the papers, you can explain the rules to the kids. There are three main rules: No one may speak except the speaker, unless he is asked a direct question by the speaker. He may only respond by giving a direct answer to the question. Second, no one may move out of his chair except the Helper and those given certain restricted movements according to their role. Third, the object of the game is to get some light into the room (other than the flashlight). The game ends when the candle is lit.

Then tell everyone to read their roles silently. As soon as everyone knows what their role is, the lights go out. The following are the roles found on the nine pieces of paper:

1. You are the speaker. You have the ability to speak but you may not move.
2. Only you have the ability to hold candles. You may move but only when you are holding a candle.
3. Only you have the ability to hold a strike pad or match pack. You may move only when holding a match pack.
4. There is a match pack hidden (give location).
5. You have the ability to strike matches but you may not move out of your chair.
6. Only you have the ability to use the flashlight. You may do nothing else. You may move anywhere, but not until someone gives you a flashlight.
7. There is a candle hidden (give location).
8. There are some matches hidden (give location).
9. You are the Helper. You may move anywhere but you may not speak to anyone (not even the speaker). You may carry objects from one place to another but you may not use them.

The easiest way to begin is for the speaker to address each player and have them reveal their role. The game will flow naturally from there until the candle is lit. A discussion on the different talents in the body (see Romans 12:6-8, Eph. 4:11, 1 Peter 4:9, 10 and Matthew 25:14ff) might be an appropriate conclusion. (Contributed by Steven Clouser, Pittsburgh, Pennsylvania)

COUNTING BIBLICAL BLESSINGS

Here's a good Bible study that would be good anytime, but especially around Thanksgiving. Have the group look up the following scripture passages and discover in each what the different writers or Biblical characters were thankful for.

Psalms 30:4-5
Psalms 97:10-12
I Chronicles 29:6-13
Daniel 2:23
Acts 27:34-35
Romans 1:8
Romans 6:17-18

I Corinthians 15:55-57
II Corinthians 2:14
II Corinthians 9:15
Philippians 1:3-5
II Thessalonians 1:2-3
I Timothy 4:3-5
Revelation 11:16-17

When finished, have each person choose one or two items from the list that they also are thankful for, and then spend some time sharing these with each other and thanking God in prayer. (Contributed by Richard Starcher, Sumner, Nebraska)

CHRISTMAS CARDS FOR JESUS

Here's a good idea for a Christmas youth group meeting that will really get the kids involved. Have them create a "Christmas Card for Jesus," using construction paper, scenes from magazines and old cards, plus sayings or verses that they make up. Have the kids think in terms of what they would say on a card if it were going to be sent to Jesus on His birthday. Stress creativity and originality, and allow the group plenty of time to complete them. You might also ask the kids to present a "gift" to Jesus along with the card. After they have finished, the kids can read them and show them to each other, or simply put them on display. The results will be very exciting. (Contributed by David R. Oakes, Albuquerque, New Mexico)

CHRISTMAS COSTUME PARTY

A unique touch for a Christmas party or program would be to have everyone come dressed as a character or thing that is associated with Christmas or the Christmas story. Possibilities might include any of the Biblical characters like Mary and Joseph, the wise men, the innkeeper, the shepherds, Herod, and so forth. Or someone could dress like one of the animals, the star of Bethlehem, an angel—the list could go on and on. It could also be expanded to include non-biblical Chrsitmas characters and things like Santa, Mrs. Santa, Rudolph, Frosty the Snowman, a Christmas package, a toy soldier, a doll, or even a Christmas tree.

To add more meaning to this, have a time at the conclusion of the party for each person to share what Christmas means to them, from the perspective of the person or thing they are dressed as. (Contributed by Susan Norman, Kernersville, North Carolina)

CHRISTMAS TREE TRACTS

Secure permission to decorate a tree in a shopping mall or other public place. At least six weeks before Christmas, write to the American Bible Society to find out what Scripture leaflets (sold below cost for just a few cents) are available for the Christmas season. They usually have a good selection. Their address is: American Bible Society, Volunteer Activities, Dept. YS, 1865 Broadway, New York, NY 10023. If you live in a Spanish-speaking area, buy some Spanish selections also. Wrap the leaflets "tootsie roll" fashion in colored cellophane and dangle them from the tree. Arrange for your youth choir or other musicians (or a good tape recorder when live music is not available) to furnish background music. Also line up a person to "man the tree," inviting people to "Take One!" and to answer questions. You'll need a supply of extra ornaments to replenish your tree.

Christmas is a special time to communicate God's love. This can be one effective way to do it. (Contributed by Geri Mitsch, Aurora, Oregon)

"CROSS" WORD PUZZLE

The theme of the crossword puzzle below is the crucifixion of Christ, making it a "Cross" word puzzle in the true sense of the term. Use it around Easter or anytime you are dealing with the meaning of the Cross. Duplicate copies of the puzzle and the clues for each person, or put it up on an overhead projecter and fill it in as a group exercise. (Adapted from an idea contributed by Peter A. Ernst, Salt Lake City, Utah)

Solution:

```
S A L V A T I O N          B L O O D
  I       H       P U R P L E     W
S U F F E R       I         S I N S
O   T     E L I J A H   L     E
          E       U     C A L V A R Y
G O   D     J E S U S   T     M
O   L A M B       T     E   E L O I
L   R       I       H   C     E
G   K I N G O F T H E J E W S     R
O   L       I       L   N   S A V E
T H O R N S       C   L   T       D
H A   T O   I   C A S T   U   G R E E K
A     B     M   T   H   R       M
      R E C O N C I L I A T I O N   P
      E     N     O   E   O       T
A B B A     S O N   V   N     V E I L
      O       E     E   O
F O R G I V E N     S A T A N   W O N
      N
```

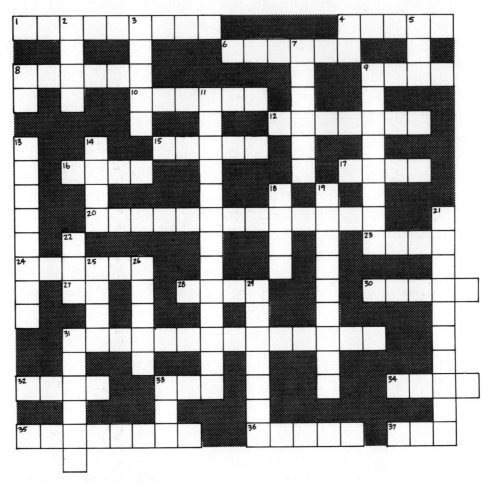

Across:
1. The result of the Crucifixion (Heb. 2:3)
4. Without it, there is no forgiveness of sin (Heb. 9:22)
6. The color of Jesus' robe (John 19:2)
8. What Jesus had to do on the cross (Luke 24:26)
9. The reason for the Crucifixion (Acts 2:38)
10. Some thought Jesus was calling him for help (Matt. 27:47)
12. The Mountain of the Crucifixion
15. The One who made Salvation possible (Rom 5:8)
16. Jesus was a _____ without blemish (I Pet. 1:19)
17. Jesus cried "_____, _____, lama sabachtani" (Matt. 27:46 NIV)
20. Pilate placed this written title over Christ's head (Luke 23:38)
23. Jesus came to seek and to _____ (Luke 19:10)
24. Jesus wore them on the Cross (Matt. 27:29)
27. Jesus came _____ die for us.
28. For His robe, the soldiers _____ lots. (John 19:24)
30. The sign above Jesus' head was written in Latin, Aramaic, and _____. (John 19:20 NIV)
31. Renewal of a once-lost relationship (II Cor. 5:18, 19)
32. A word Christ used to address God (Mark 14:36)
33. What God gave on the Cross (John 3:16)
34. It was "rent in twain" (Mark 15:38 KJV)
35. Because of the Cross, our sins are _____. (Acts 2:38)
36. He was defeated on the Cross. (Acts 5:3)

37. On the Cross, the victory was _____.

Down:
2. On the Cross, Jesus was _____ed up (John 12:34)
3. Denied _____ times; _____ crosses; raised in _____ days. (John 2:20, 13:38)
4. He said "If I _____ lifted up". (John 12:34)
7. He tried to set Jesus free. (John 19:12)
8. "For God _____ loved the World . . ." (John 3:16)
9. Characteristic of Christ's garment (John 19:23)
11. A word that means "satisfaction"; the result of faith (I John 2:2, Rom. 3:25, Heb. 9:5)
13. The place of the skull (Mark 15:22)
14. Condition of the sun when Jesus died (Luke 23:45)
18. When Jesus died, He descended into _____. (Apostles Creed)
19. This man saw and believed. (Luke 23:47)
21. To be released and gain freedom through an act of purchase, by payment. (Heb. 9:15, Eph. 1:14)
22. Similar to a "die" (John 19:24)
25. What the soldiers gambled for (John 19:24)
26. He carried Jesus' cross (Mark 15:21)
29. They were crucified with Jesus (Luke 23:32)
31. To be given new life (Titus 3:5)
33. When Jesus was buried, Mary Magdalene and Mary the Mother of Jesus went to _____ where He was laid. (Mark 15:47)

DEAR AMY LETTERS

The following letters are great for starting group discussion on a number of sensitive topics. To use them, print them on sheets of paper (one per sheet) with room at the bottom for an answer to be written. They can be used with kids, or with parents. The letters here can be used as they are, or you can adapt them, or write some of your own. They can be answered individually or in small groups. The object is to try and give the best possible solution to each problem.

Letters for Kids:

Dear Amy,

My parents are always wanting me to go places with them but I would rather be with my friends. I've had it with this "togetherness bit." How can I convince them that I don't enjoy family outings and don't want to do that scene anymore.

"Olda Nuff"

Dear Amy,

My mother insists that I go to church every Sunday, but my dad never goes, so why should I? Now that I'm older I think I should be allowed to make up my own mind about God, Church and all that stuff.

"Tired of Sunday School"

Dear Amy,

Our Bible School teacher says every family should study the Bible and pray together, but our family never seems to have the time for that. Isn't going to church together good enough?

"Busy Betsy"

Dear Amy,

My parents don't like my friends. Whenever I want to go places with my friends Mom and Dad ask me all kinds of questions. I don't think they trust me either! How can I persuade them to let me go out with whom I want to?

"Ina Cage"

Dear Amy,

I would like to talk to my parents about some of my problems but when I do I usually just get a lecture. How can I make them see that sometimes I just need to talk and do not want their advice?

"Lecture Hater"

Dear Amy,

My parents are always talking to me about being a minister or a missionary. I am very interested in mathematics and would like to study engineering. How can I talk to them about this without hurting their feelings? I think I can be a good Christian in whatever vocation I choose.

"Undecided"

Letters for Mothers:

Dear Amy,

My husband and I became Christians as adults, but we want our children to let Christ be their guide during their teen years. Our daughter says we're trying to "cram religion down her throat." How can we help her to understand that she needs Christ now?

"Worried Parents"

Dear Amy,

I try to spend time with my son and talk to him but when I ask questions about his school, friends, etc. he just clams up. How can I get him to talk over his daily activities as well as his problems?

"Clam's Mother"

Dear Amy,

My husband and I try to have open communication with our daughter. However, it seems that more and more lately she comes to me with her problems but refuses to talk with her father. He resents this and thinks I'm encouraging her in this direction. Please help.

"Caught in the Middle"

Dear Amy,

My husband and I come from very different backgrounds and our ideas on child-rearing are very different. We seem to be always at odds on rules for the children, punishments, etc. How can we change this? Our children are confused and so are we.

"Nita Solution"

Dear Amy,

I try to establish good communication with my family by listening to them, asking questions, and encouraging my children to talk about school, etc. and my husband to talk about his work. But nobody listens to me. I want to talk about my activities too but no one seems interested. Please advise me.

"Wanda Talk Too"

Letters for Fathers:

Dear Amy,

I am bewildered by the way things in the world have changed! When I was a kid life was simple and parents word was the LAW. Kids today seem to be living fast and furious. My children think my standards are old-fashioned and impossible in today's society. How can we get together on standards for our family to live by?

"Old-Fashioned Dad"

Dear Amy,

   I'd like to spend more time with my kids but I have a demanding job that requires a lot of overtime. I also try to participate in community affairs and do as much as possible for the church. There simply aren't enough hours in the day for me, yet I realize that my children are growing up fast. What do you suggest?

"Full-Schedule Dad"

Dear Amy,

   My wife and I cannot agree on how to deal with our son. I think she is too soft on him and too sympathetic. He's never going to learn to 'take it' out in the world if we're too easy on him at home. How can I convince her of this?

"Ex-Marine Dad"

Dear Amy,

   My daughter and I used to be very close. We talked a lot and did a lot of things together. But now she's in high school and she seems to have changed completely. She seldom talks to me anymore and seems to spend more and more time away from home. What can I do?

"Losing the Apple of My Eye"

(Contributed by Anne Hughes, Dickinson, Texas)

THE DEVIL MADE ME DO IT

This is an excellent simulation game which can be used to explore a number of different topics, including the role of Satan in temptation and the role of scripture in resisting temptation. Here's how it is played:

Divide into two equal groups. If there is an odd number of people, then one of your adult sponsors may have to participate. One group will be designated the "Devils" and the other group will be designated the "Pilgrims." Give each Pilgrim a game sheet (see below) containing the list of twenty instructions. Half of these instructions are good deeds and the other half are "no-no's." Unfortunately, the Pilgrims don't know which is which. The devils are given the same list, but they are informed as to which ones are "no-no's" and which ones are not. The "no-no's" on the list are No's. 1, 2, 6, 8, 9, 12, 15, 16, 18 and 19.

Now the kids pair off, with each Pilgrim getting a personal "devil" to follow them around, give them advice and to "tempt" them one way or the other. The object of the game for the Pilgrim is to score more points than his devil by doing as many good deeds as possible and by avoiding the "no-no's." The devil can score points by getting his Pilgrim to do "no-no's." Here's how the points are awarded: For the

Pilgrim—100 points are given for every good deed performed; 200 points are *subtracted* for every "no-no" committed. For the devil—200 points are awarded for every "no-no" committed by the Pilgrim. Have nice prizes available for the highest scorers to provide some real incentive.

Pilgrims can make decisions about what to do based on 1) their own judgment, 2) advice from their devil, or 3) they can get a copy of a "Good Book," which contains all the verses that are referred to on the game sheet. If a Pilgrim has a "Good Book," then he will know exactly what to do and what not to do. (Below are instructions for making the Good Books.)

But, here's the catch. The time limit for the game is only fifteen minutes. In order to obtain a "Good Book," it is necessary to memorize I Thess. 5:22, which says "Abstain from all appearance of evil." That verse must then be quoted perfectly to the "Good Book Giver" who is handing out all the "Good Books," plus a sixty-second speech must be given to the "Good Book Giver" on why that verse is important to modern-day Pilgrims. To make things even more difficult, Pilgrims must line up single file in the Good Book line and be taken one at a time. The "Good Book Giver" presents a "Good Book" to each Pilgrim after they complete the sixty-second speech, and then the next Pilgrim gets an opportunity to receive one in the same manner. Some pilgrims may consider this to be too difficult and time-consuming.

Before the game begins, the devils can meet separately and be informed that they can use any means they want (except physical force) to get their Pilgrims to do "no-no's". They can lie, act like they don't really want to win, keep a "fake" score for themselves, convince the Pilgrim that they don't have enough time to get a Good Book that common sense will do. . .etc. At the same time, the Pilgrims can be given instructions on how to obtain Good Books.

Once everyone understands the rules, blow a whistle and start the game. Let things develop in a natural sort of way. The game itself is a lot of fun with all sorts of crazy things happening. After the time limit is up, stop the game and reveal to the Pilgrims the good deeds and the "no-no's" so that everyone can tally up their scores. Award the prizes, and then discuss the following questions:

1. How many decided to get a Good Book and why? Why did some of you choose not to get a Good Book?
2. Was getting a Good Book as hard as you thought it would be?
3. For those of you who did not get a Good Book how did you determine which activities to do?
4. Was it easy or difficult to tell when your devil was lying?

5. Did your devil force you to do anything?
6. Do you think we can frustrate Satan in this same way as you with Good Book's did to your devils? How?
7. Did any of you go to other Pilgrims for counseling? What was the response you received?
8. What methods did you devils use in trying to convince your Pilgrim to "sin?"
9. Can we modern day Pilgrims (Christians) learn something from this game about the importance of scripture.

You can no doubt think of other questions besides these. In each case, help the group to make the connection between what happened in the game and what happens to them in real life. In other words, in response to question #4, you might follow that up with another question, like "How can we know when Satan is deceiving us?" You might wrap up with some thoughts on how Satan's activity is ultimately limited by God (see I Cor. 10:13, the book of Job, etc.)

Game Sheets:

The following list of twenty instructions should be printed up and handed out to the entire group.

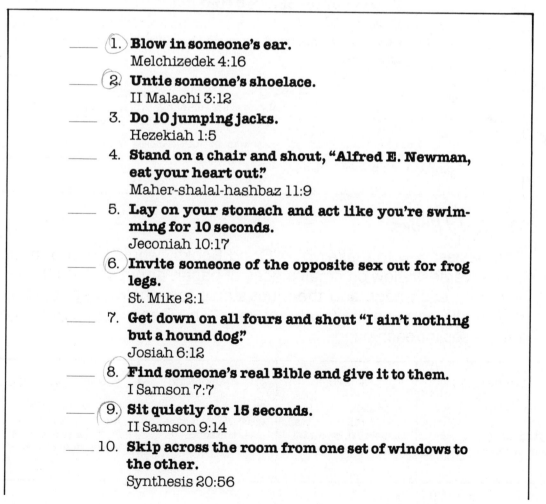

___ 1. **Blow in someone's ear.**
   Melchizedek 4:16

___ 2. **Untie someone's shoelace.**
   II Malachi 3:12

___ 3. **Do 10 jumping jacks.**
   Hezekiah 1:5

___ 4. **Stand on a chair and shout, "Alfred E. Newman, eat your heart out."**
   Maher-shalal-hashbaz 11:9

___ 5. **Lay on your stomach and act like you're swimming for 10 seconds.**
   Jeconiah 10:17

___ 6. **Invite someone of the opposite sex out for frog legs.**
   St. Mike 2:1

___ 7. **Get down on all fours and shout "I ain't nothing but a hound dog."**
   Josiah 6:12

___ 8. **Find someone's real Bible and give it to them.**
   I Samson 7:7

___ 9. **Sit quietly for 15 seconds.**
   II Samson 9:14

___ 10. **Skip across the room from one set of windows to the other.**
   Synthesis 20:56

_____ 11. **Go to the microphone and sing, "There's a sweet, sweet odor in this place."**
Exclamation 14:7

_____ 12. **Go up to someone, pound your chest, do a Tarzan yell, and say "Thanks, I needed that!"**
Bereans 16:40

_____ 13. **Find one of the devils and say, "You handsome devil, you!"**
Chaldeans 1:1

_____ 14. **Sit in the front row and shout, "Amen, preach it brother."**
Macedonians 5:8

_____ 15. **Get someone to shake hands with you.**
I Philip 8:14

_____ 16. **Find someone with a Good Book and shout "fa-natic" 5 times.**
II Philip 13:11

_____ 17. **Take one shoe off and balance it on your head for 5 seconds.**
Hilkiah 5:3

_____ 18. **Go to the microphone and whistle, "Give me oil in my lamp."**
St. Stephen 1:15

_____ 19. **Kiss one of the chairs 3 times.**
Facts 28:42

_____ 20. **Go to someone, hold your nose, and pass out from the smell.**
Naomi 19:1

You have fifteen minutes to complete as many tasks as possible. Each time you complete a task, get your devil to initial your sheet. For each good deed you receive 100 points. For each "no-no" you loose 200 points and your devil receives 200 points.

In order to get a "Good Book," you must wait in line, memorize the scripture (I Thess. 5:22) and quote it without looking. Then, give a 60-second talk on the importance of that verse for us today.

The Good Books:

The easiest way to make your "Good Books" would be to print up all the verses below on small pieces of paper, about 3" x 4". Put one verse on each page and then just staple the whole thing together with a title page on the front that says "The Good Book." Here are the verses for each page:

Synthesis 20:56	Facts 28:42	Hezekiah 1:5	Macedonians 5:8
The soul that skip-peth, it shall reach the other side.	Even a chair if it is kissed will become a slobbery mess and displease the Lord.	Bodily exercise is of great value: it exercises the body.	He that shouteth Amen is like a plat-form: he supporteth the preacher.

II Samson 9:14 Let not quietness be heard in your midst.	Exclamation 14:7 Sing unto the Lord as a sweet smelling odor in His nostrils.	Chaldeans 1:1 Even the Devils get compliments and are blessed. Where does that leave you?	II Malachi 3:12 To untie a shoelace is to loose the wrath of God.
I Samson 7:7 Hear the commandment of God, "You touch strange Bible, you die".	Melchisedek 4:16 The wind that blows through the ear is despised by the Lord.	St. Mike 2:1 One thing is an abomination to the Lord, even frog legs.	Maher-Shalal-Hashbaz 11:9 He that standeth on a chair and shouteth shall hear it and be blessed.
Jeconiah 10:7 Learn much from those who swim, for they are those who do not drown.	II Phillip 13:11 He that shouteth fanatic shall suddenly be declared lunatic and that without remedy.	I Phillip 8:14 A shaking hand is unto the Lord as a cow pie: It stinketh.	Bereans 16:40 Be ye not unequally yoked to Tarzan, for what fellowship does an ape have with a man.
Naomi 19:1 He that smells overpowering odor shall be crowned with life after the smelling salts are applied.	Josiah 6:12 Learn a lesson from the hound dog: "He that barks now, shall be heard later".	Hilkiah 5:3 A shoe on the head is like soothing ointment for sunburn: both are runny.	St. Stephen 1:15 He that whistles into microphone shall die suddenly from flying eggs and tomatoes.

(Contributed by Greg Thomas, Watsonville, California)

DOOMSDAY BUTTON

This idea, while similar to "Armageddon Bomber" (see *IDEAS 17-20*, p. 66) is a good discussion starter on the nuclear arms issue. Divide the kids into groups of 4 or 5. Have each group imagine that they are 60 feet beneath the ground as commanders of a missile silo. Each group has been entrusted with the power to launch one, one-megaton warhead at a predetermined Soviet city. It is anticipated that each warhead is the only one targeted for that city. Like all officers, they have been instructed to follow all orders, especially any command by the President to fire their warhead.

After the scenario has been set, hand each group this message:

> THE ENTIRE SOVIET PAYLOAD ... NEARLY 10,000 WARHEADS ... WAS LAUNCHED 3 MINUTES AGO AT AMERICA ... OUR DEFENSE SYSTEM WILL ONLY STOP A FRACTION OF THEM ... IT IS ANTICIPATED THAT OVER 99% OF AMERICA WILL PERISH ... INCLUDING YOURSELF. YOU ARE COMMANDED TO FIRE YOUR MISSILE IMMEDIATELY. SAYONARA.
>
> —THE PRESIDENT

The group has 10 minutes to determine a course of action before the Soviet missiles arrive and they themselves are destroyed. There are only two choices they can make: To press the button or to NOT press the button. The vote must be unanimous. Either way they vote, they will not survive nor will their country.

Questions which could be used for discussion:

1. How much was your decision influenced by your Christian convictions?
2. Was the scenario a realistic one? How did you feel about the thought of having to make such a decision?
3. Do you think that nuclear war will happen during your lifetime? What impact does the possibility have on you in terms of thoughts and feelings?
4. List the following four concepts in order of your own personal value. Give examples of when these values come into conflict in world events:
   Equality
   Freedom
   Peace
   Safety

5. What is the difference between the MEANS and the END? Give examples of where the means justifies the end; where the end justifies the means.
6. Would it be right to make peace if that peace might encourage war? Would it be right to wage war if that war would bring about peace?
7. Look up Matthew 5:9, Luke 19:41, 42, Romans 12:17-21, Hebrews 12:14, and James 3:18. List different ways peace could be kept and war could be prevented between the world's superpowers.
8. Read Joel 3:9, 10. Then read Isaiah 2:4. What do you think should be done with our country's missiles and with its tractors?

(Contributed by Kraig Klaudt, El Cajon, California)

THE ENVELOPE, PLEASE

The following idea is designed to stimulate discussion and insight into the subject of God's will. To begin, have the kids write down a question or problem that requires knowledge of the will of God. For example: "Should I go to college next year or should I join the Marines?" If the group feels comfortable doing so, have the kids share these questions with each other.

Next, give each person a sealed envelope with their name on it— labeled "ENCLOSED: THE WILL OF GOD". Instruct them to leave the envelopes sealed for now. Discuss the following questions:

1. If your envelope truly contained the will of God for your life, what do you think it would say?
2. What would you *like* for it to say?
3. Why is it important to seek God's will for questions like those we expressed? Isn't our own judgment good enough?
4. Does God always have a "will" for us in every situation?

After the discussion, tell the kids that believe it or not, the envelope does indeed contain God's will for them. They can now open them up. Inside is a piece of paper that reads (in big block letters):

PRAYER
THE WORD
CIRCUMSTANCES
ADVICE

Help the kids to see that those four words do indeed represent God's will for their particular situation. Through prayer, we make our needs known to God, and God speaks to us when we pray as well. Through the Word, we learn basic principles that we know to be the revealed will of God. Through circumstances, we see God leading us. This is the "open-door, closed-door" idea. Through the advice of parents, pastors and Christian friends, God speaks to us as well. You can elaborate on these.

You can adapt this basic idea any way you wish. You might want to save the envelopes until last—delivered by a "mailman" of some kind, direct from Heaven. The point of the envelopes is to emphasize that God's will is not just an abstract thought but something that God wants us to receive and to understand in a very real way. (Contributed by Steven Clouser, Pittsburgh, Pennsylvania)

FAITH INVENTORY

A helpful way for young people to clarify and evaluate their beliefs is to take a "faith inventory" now and then. The process is fairly simple. Create a list of faith statements or values like the ten below and print a copy for each person. Next to each statement is a continuum (1-10) with 1 representing total unbelief and 10 representing total belief. The kids are to read each statement and decide just how much or how little they believe it and circle the appropriate number.

Kids should be assured that they can be honest and not feel any less a Christian just because they express some doubts. Most everyone has doubts about certain things, and it is through those doubts that growth takes place. They need to be assured that God loves them even though they can't give every statement of faith a "10." This exercise can be useful to determine where kids need a little more help and guidance. Be sure and discuss each statement with the entire group, allowing kids to share on a volunteer basis how they rated each one and why. This can be used many times with excellent results.

1. I believe in God. (1 2 3 4 5 6 7 8 9 10)
2. God loves me. (1 2 3 4 5 6 7 8 9 10)
3. I love God. (1 2 3 4 5 6 7 8 9 10)
4. Jesus is God. (1 2 3 4 5 6 7 8 9 10)
5. God forgives me for my sins. (1 2 3 4 5 6 7 8 9 10)
6. God hears my prayer. (1 2 3 4 5 6 7 8 9 10)
7. God answers my prayers. (1 2 3 4 5 6 7 8 9 10)
8. I believe in life after death. (1 2 3 4 5 6 7 8 9 10)
9. I believe the Bible is true. (1 2 3 4 5 6 7 8 9 10)
10. I do what the Bible says. (1 2 3 4 5 6 7 8 9 10)

(Contributed by Mary McKerny, Salem, Ohio)

THE FAMILY CHAPTER

This is a study of 1 Thessalonians 2. It calls attention to the "family titles" used by Paul in this chapter:

"Brothers"—verses 1,9,14,17
"Mother"—verse 7
"Father"—verse 11

Study the chapter together, bringing in other Scripture that might be relevant. (For example, Acts 17 for info on Paul's ministry in Thessalonica; Jeremiah 31:1 and Ephesians 3:14, 15 for other references to the "Family of God.") Then give the group the following questions to work on, individually or in small groups. Close with some sharing of insights and commitments.

1. Why is the Family of God a good title for the church?
2. What are some characteristics of the love that exists in a family?
3. What are some characteristics of a brother-to-brother relationship?
4. Why would Paul call these Christians "brothers?"
5. Has anyone in the church shown you brotherly love? When? How did you feel?
6. Read verse seven again. How does a mother care for her children?
7. Has anyone in the church shown you "motherly care?" When? How did you feel?
8. Re-read verse eleven. How does a father deal with his children?
9. Has anyone in the church dealt with you in a "fatherly way?" When? How did you feel?
10. Why should the church provide all three of these relationships—brotherly love, motherly care, and fatherly correction?

11. Does your church have these relationships?
12. What can you do to improve these relationships in the church? In your youth group? With your friends? With your sponsors?

(Contributed by Doug Newhouse, Florence, Kentucky)

FEET MEETING

Here's a creative program idea that combines some fun with serious learning about servanthood and discipleship. The theme of the meeting is feet. Start the meeting with some "feet games" from past volumes of *IDEAS*. For example:

1. *Foot Signing:* Everyone takes off their shoes and socks, and receives a felt tip pen (the kind that will wash off). On a signal, the group has one minute to see how many signatures they can get on the bottom of their feet.
2. *Foot Wrestling:* Kids pair off and sit down with right feet together. They lock toes. On a signal, they try to "pin" the other person's foot, like regular arm-wrestling.
3. *Foot Beauty Contest:* Have contests and prizes for the biggest feet, the hairiest feet, the prettiest feet, the biggest big toe, longest toenails, etc.
4. *Feet by the Foot:* Teams line up with their feet in a single file line, heel to toe, to see which team has the most "footage." Longest line wins.
5. *Lemon Pass:* Teams remove shoes and try to pass a lemon down the line without using their hands, only feet. The lemon cannot drop or they have to start over.
6. *Foot Drawing:* Each team chooses some object in the room. Using only feet for patterns, they trace parts of the feet on paper to create that object. Other teams must then try to guess what the object is.

Following some of these or any other games, move to a Bible study, using whatever Bible study method your group prefers. A good passage would be John 13:1-17. Talk about the significance of feet in the passage. What was so unusual about Jesus being willing to wash the disciples' feet? What does that say about servanthood?

Following the Bible Study, gather the group around a large paper cross that has been taped to the floor. Place a pan of colored poster paint around it. Use a different color in each pan. Then talk about what it means to be a part of the cross—to be willing to walk as a servant in the same way Christ did. Invite the kids to choose a color, and (one at a time) dip in their feet and walk across the paper, leaving their footprints on the cross. This can be done as an indication of their decision to follow in the "way of the cross."

Next, you can conduct a "foot washing" ceremony, as kids wash the paint off each other's feet. Provide pans, towels, soap, etc.

This exercise can be followed up with good discussion, of course. As you view the cross together, you can talk about the significance of the different kinds of footprints upon it, how they are all unique, the blending of colors in the middle section, the plain cross that is now bright with colors, etc. You can close by having the kids cut the cross into small "posters" and taking them home to hang on their walls as a reminder of their commitment to walk with Christ. (Contributed by Ruth Staal, Holland, Michigan)

THE FOOLISH FARMER

This idea deals with materialism and more specifically the parable of the "Foolish Farmer" (or the Rich Fool) in Luke 12:13-21. Divide the group into "families" of six to eight people and give them the following instructions:

"You are a family and must make a family decision. Everyone in the family must be in agreement; any one person may veto the decision of the group.

"You have just received $100,000 from an unexpected source. You must now decide as a family how you will use that money. The only requirements are that you must say very specifically what you will do with the money and you must decide in the next ten minutes.

"Read Luke 12:13-21 before you begin your discussion."

This will obviously result in some heated discussion within each "family." It will be interesting to see how the parable is interpreted and adapted to meet the needs of the group. Some will want to take the parable very literally and radically, others will see it as hyperbole or not applicable to modern-day people.

After each "family" has had sufficient time, have them come back together and share their results, along with the reasoning that went into their decisions.

For an added dimension to this exercise, give the above instructions to all the family groups, but only give half of them the last line that asks them to read the Scripture. There should be a noticeable difference between the groups that use the Bible passage as a basis for their decisions and those who don't. This could lead to a related discussion on the importance of Scripture and how the Bible affects our day to day decision-making process. (Contributed by Richard L. Starcher, Sumner, Nebraska)

GAZING INTO THE FUTURE

The following exercise is designed to help young people think in the future tense and to explore the values of a rapidly changing world. Across the top of a blackboard, write "1963—1983—2003." Then, down the side of the blackboard, write these categories: Music, Economics, Fashion, Environment, Crime, Education, Morals, Transportation, Entertainment and Religion (of course, these can be changed or added to). Through group discussion, fill in the chart by going across the board in each category. Try to come up with a realistic prognosis for the future by looking at the past and present (it may help to have someone on hand who was around twenty years ago).

After you have filled everything in, take a look at the future column. You can draw the group's attention to the fact that most of them will be approaching middle-age then and that this is the world that they might have to live in. How does it look to them? Optimistic? Negative? Are they looking forward to it?

Here are some other possible discussion questions:

1. How do you feel about change? What causes things to change so rapidly in our world?

	1963	1983	2003
MUSIC			
ECONOMICS			
FASHION			
ENVIRONMENT			
CRIME			
EDUCATION			
MORALS			
TRANSPORTATION			
ENTERTAINMENT			
RELIGION			

2. What things do you think people will collect and reminisce about from today in the year 2003?
3. Of the predictions made for 2003, which would you want to change? How would you go about changing them?
4. What kinds of problems will your teenage children encounter in 2003? What kind of parent do you hope you'll be?
5. How accurately could a person in 1962 have predicted what the world is like now?

(Contributed by Craig Moulton, Costa Mesa, California)

GIFT GUESSING

Here's an activity that allows kids to give to each other, to share with each other, and to have fun all at the same time. To begin, make up some cards like the illustration below—so that everyone's name is on a card.

All these cards are put into a box and are randomly drawn by each person so that everyone has a name other than their own. Then they write their own name under the name they drew ("from. . .") and write in a gift that they would like to give to the person whose name they drew. It could be any gift at all. It would be best to have the group think in terms of non-material gifts, like "perfect health for the rest of your life," etc. Kids can let their imaginations run wild with this, but the gifts should be thoughtful and suitable for each recipient.

Next, have the kids tear off the top part of the card (with the two names on it) and put it in their pocket. The bottom part of the card (with the gift) is pinned or taped to the wall or bulletin board. Everyone is then allowed to examine the board and to pick out the gift that they think was given to them. They remove it from the wall and try to find the person who gave it to them. If they are wrong about the gift, then they can try to find the correct gift and trade with whoever has it. By a process of elimination, everybody eventually will come up with the right gift and giver. When they find the person who gave them the gift, they take the top part of the card from that person and sit down while others continue the search. At first there will be a lot of chaos and laughs but the results are rewarding.

You can wrap this up by discussing all that went on during the activity—how you felt about the gift that was given to you, the gifts given to others, and so on. (Contributed by Julia Thompson, Falconer, New York)

GOD IS LIKE. . .

If someone asked you to describe God to them in terms that they could relate to, what would you say? Traditionally, God has been described in terms like "the man upstairs," "a heavenly father," "a mighty judge," "a mother hen," and so on. You might begin this exercise by going over some commonly known "God is like's" with your group.

The next step is to have the group come up with some new ones that may be a little more "up to date". Each person can work individually or in a small group. After pens and paper have been given to each group, instruct the kids to think of as many "God is like's" as they can in 10 minutes. Some examples you might give them could include, "God is like Coke. . .He's the real thing," or "God is like Allstate. . .you're in good hands with Him," or even "God is like a good student. . .He spreads His work over six days instead of pulling an all-nighter." After 10 minutes are up, each group reads their comparisons while the other groups check to see if they have any of the same comparisons. If two or more groups have the same comparisons, they must be scratched off their lists. After each group has read their list, the group with the most original comparisons left is the winner. Close by discussing the various images of God presented and come to a consensus on the best four or five. (Contributed by Kathy Horton, Chesterfield, Missouri)

A GOD'S-EYE VIEW

Used in conjunction with Psalm 8, the following narrative dramatically illustrates the majesty of God's creation. It is also a good self-image booster as it reminds us of the significance we

105

have in God's eyes.

> I want you to use your imagination. Imagine that I have a long sheet of paper that stretches all the way across the front of the room, out the door, outside the building, and continues until you can't see it anymore.
>
> Now imagine that I take a pin and poke a tiny hole in the paper — that is the earth. All the cities, mountains, and oceans of our planet are represented by that speck.
>
> About 5/8ths of an inch from the pinhole, make another pinhole — that's the moon.
>
> Now imagine that 19 feet away, I draw a 2 inch circle that is the sun. Six hundred feet away, the length of two football fields, we come to Neptune.
>
> After leaving the solar system, and our pinhole planets, we would have to travel along a thousand miles of paper to come to the nearest star. That's roughly the distance between Chicago and Denver.
>
> Distances in space are so vast they are measured in light-years, the distance that light will travel in a year; light travels at over 186,000 miles per second. That's so fast that a bullet shot at that speed and circling the earth would hit you seven times before you fell to the ground, even if it took you one second to fall.
>
> At the speed of light, you could travel from Los Angeles to New York in 1/60th of a second. You could reach the moon in less than 1½ seconds, the sun in eight minutes, and cover the entire solar system in 11 hours.
>
> But even at those speeds, it would take you 4.3 years to reach the nearest star. You would need 400 years to reach the North Star, and to cross just one galaxy, our own Milky Way, would take 120,000 years. And astronomers now estimate that there are over 100 million galaxies.

After reading the narrative aloud to the group, you might want to have the kids read Psalm 8 in unison. With this as a background, you can then discuss the following questions or other questions of your choice:

1. How does this Psalm make you feel about God?
2. How does this Psalm make you feel about yourself?
3. What does this Psalm suggest a person's self-image should be? (Also see Mt. 10:29-33)
4. What do you think it means when the Psalmist says that God crowned human beings with love and honor?
5. Why do you think God needed to create such a large universe?

(Contributed by Glenn Davis, Winston-Salem, North Carolina)

GOSPEL NEWSPAPER

Here's an idea that really gets everybody involved, and allows kids to think through and express what they consider to be the important tenets of the Christian faith.

You might begin by setting up a field trip or visit to your local newspaper, just to get the feel for newspaper publishing and journalism. Then, propose to the group that they publish one issue of a newspaper containing editorials, articles, poems, song lyrics, cartoons, pictures, interviews, drawings, scriptures, etc., which communicate some of the most important aspects of Christianity to a person who knows nothing about it. The project might begin with a discussion of some of the foundational and representative truths of Christianity and how these might be expressed in printed form to an unbeliever. For example, "How can we communicate the centrality of Christ Himself in our paper so that if a person who is unfamiliar with Christianity reads this paper, he/she might come to some understanding of what it's all about.?"

The paper can be lettered, typed, or printed on an offset press—whatever the class decides. Your local paper may even publish it for you. The length of the project can vary with the elaborateness of the design of the paper and the interest of the group. The various phases of the operation can allow individuals to work on things they are interested in the most: photographer, writer, poet, artist, typist, reporter, etc. The very act of discussing the essence of the Christian faith and actually having to "put something down on paper" can be a faith-building and enlightening experience. (Contributed by Deborah Harris, Houston, Texas)

GRAB-BAG TALENTS

This is a fun activity that deals in a creative and contemporary way with The Parable of the Talents in the New Testament. That narrative, you will recall, involved a man who gave each of three others a like amount of money (talents), instructing them to trade with the talents while he was away. Upon his return, he found that each of the three had handled the talents in different ways. The first had multiplied his original amount ten times; the second man five times. The third man, however, buried his one pound talent. The full story is told in Luke 19:11-27. (Note: While it is true that the "talent" in this story is money, the emphasis is *NOT* on the money, but on what was done with the gift. Don't allow the group to get hung up on the different meanings of "talent.")

For the variation on this Parable that you are going to use with your group: Using small brown paper bags, or plastic bags (whatever is handy), fill each of the bags with a variety of good "junque:" paper clips, cotton swabs, IBM cards, popsicle sticks, rubber bands, toothpicks, straws—whatever you can find. Put a little of everything in each bag. Have them ready to hand out to your group as they arrive. Each person is simply handed a bag with the instructions: "Each person is being given one of these bags. See what you can do with what is inside." Don't say *ANYTHING* about the reason for it, don't mention the Parable—no other details at this point. Have some glue, paper, scissors, other "staple" items available if needed.

Now, see what each person will do. The options will be obvious to the leader at this point. Some will get busy creating something that will utilize much of the material, others will work at it, and some may decide they can't do anything with what they have been given; they will "bury" their talents. (Incidentally, it is okay for persons to borrow back and forth—let them work that out for themselves. The leader should not suggest it. Give the group half an hour to see what they can create. Then, have the group gather, with their "creations" and read the story, carefully. Following the reading, discuss these or other questions with the group:

1. What words or phrases do you recall from the story just read? (each person in turn—you are trying to reconstruct the story)
2. Someone briefly retell this story in your own words (group leader: allow freedom to tell it however they wish, but do be sure the "gist" of the story is understood—that is, what each decided to do with their gifts)
3. Can you share your feelings at the point where you were handed the bag with the miscellaneous items in it?
4. What did you decide to do with your talents (It is appropriate at this point for those who are willing to very specifically share what they have done with their materials.)
5. How do you feel when you know you are not using your capabilities to the full extent of your potential? How is this a problem?

(Contributed by Robin Kreider, Phoenix, Arizona)

HELP WANTED

This idea will get your group thinking about the kind of people God is looking for. Read a sampling from your newspaper's "Help Wanted" section to your group. Then pass out pens and paper and ask the kids to write a "Help Wanted" ad that could be written by God and run in the local newspaper. The ads could be titled "Help Wanted" or "Position Available," and contain a description of the kind of person God wants. Here's a sample ad:

> HELP WANTED
> NEED A CHRISTIAN WHO IS RESPONSIBLE, LOVING, UNDERSTANDING, WILLING TO SACRIFICE THEMSELF FOR OTHERS. FALSE PRETENSES ARE NOT WELCOME! PERSON MUST BE LOYAL AND NEVER LET ME DOWN. BENEFITS ARE GREAT AFTER FIRST YEAR. LIFE INSURANCE PAID FOR IN FULL. IF INTERESTED, PLEASE CALL ME AT B-I-B-L-E ANYTIME; I'M ALWAYS THERE. AN EQUAL OPPORTUNITY EMPLOYER.

After the kids in the group have had time to write their ads, have them turn their papers over and write a reply (resume) to the job offer they just wrote. Another idea would be to post all of the ads on a bulletin board and have the kids write a reply to the one that most appeals to them. Make sure they include a note to God explaining why they are qualified for the job. When everybody is finished, have the group share their "Help Wanted" ads and their replies, or else, you can collect them and read them to the group.

You could follow this with a study on God's grace and how He accepts us as His children unconditionally (Eph. 2:8-9). Or, you could follow it with a lesson on being available to God, explaining how God can use all of us regardless of our backgrounds or past failures. (Contributed by Phil Print, Denver, Colorado)

HOW GOD WORKS IN MY LIFE

Following is a good discussion starter on the topic of "Providence." A look at Psalm 121 following the discussion would be appropriate.

Have everyone divide a sheet of paper into three columns with the following headings: Primarily my Responsibility; Primarily God's Responsibility; Too Close to Call. Then read the following list (or a similar list) asking each person to classify the items by placing them in one of the columns. Afterwards share answers and discuss the reasons for placing each one as they did.

1. Making the decision whether I marry or remain single.
2. Protecting me from drunken drivers.
3. My doing well when I perform a solo.
4. My decision to become a Christian.
5. Keeping me from illness.
6. Keeping me encouraged about the Christian life.
7. Choosing my vocation.
8. My understanding Scripture.
9. My understanding geometry.
10. Keeping me from doubt.
11. My financial condition.
12. My health.

Following this exercise, it is helpful to discuss how God performs those functions which we feel He is responsible for. This discussion works very well with high school, college age, or adults. (Contributed by Dan Mutschler, Chicago, Illinois)

INTERGENERATIONAL INTERVIEWS

This idea can be used for a regular youth meeting or a special event. Divide the youth into teams of two or three kids (depending on the number of youth and senior adults in your church) and send them to the homes of some of your senior adults with the following questions (or others of your choice).

1. What are some early memories you have of attending church?
2. Would you tell us about your decision to follow Christ? (When it was, how it came about, etc.)
3. What have the Christian faith and the church meant to you and your family down through the years?
4. What is one of your favorite Bible verses or Bible stories, and why?

Have the teams return to the church and share among the whole group about the visit and the answers they received in the interview.

You will need to call the adults you want to visit in advance to arrange the visits, and let them know the questions they will be asked. You can end your meeting with refreshments, and let the adults know that you will be doing this so that they will not feel obligated to serve something. Also make sure you have enough drivers to take the teams out, and choose homes near enough for the teams to go and return within your time limit.

The adults will appreciate the visits, and it gives them an opportunity to share their faith with your youth. The youth will benefit from listening for a few moments to your older church members. (Contributed by Joy R. Jones, Canton, North Carolina)

ISAIAH'S PROPHECY

Often we fail to fully appreciate Jesus Christ's death for us. Perhaps we are too familiar with the crucifixion details. Maybe the story has become so commonplace that we forget that it was our sins that led Jesus to the cross and a horribly painful death. In this study and sharing exercise, youth group members will look at the prediction of Jesus' death by Isaiah, and recognize that it was their sins that brought the prophecy's fulfillment. Read Isaiah 53. Read the entire chapter out loud, alternating verses. Then ask these questions:

1. Who do you think Isaiah was talking about?
2. What does Isaiah say that reminds you of Jesus?

Next distribute pen and paper. Instruct students to select verses that are especially meaningful to them. They are to paraphrase these verses inserting Jesus' name in place of each singular personal pronoun. When finished, let several students read what they have written.

To complete the study, instruct students to read verses 4-6 again. They should paraphrase these verses, writing their own name in place of each plural personal pronoun. When finished, ask these questions:

1. Pretend you are the only person who has ever lived. Did Jesus

have to die? Why?

2. What has Jesus' death done for you?
3. What is your response to Him right now?

(Contributed by Doug Newhouse, Florence, Kentucky)

JUMBLED PROVERBS

You might want to try this idea as a way of getting your group into the book of Proverbs. Begin by explaining how the proverbs in chapters ten through twenty-one are written in a parallel style. Two phrases are usually separated by the conjunctions "but," "and" or "than," such as in Proverbs 11:19, "He who is steadfast in righteousness will live, *but* he who pursues evil will die." After this is explained, hand each person a sheet of paper which has a selection of 8 to 12 jumbled proverbs. The object of the game is simple: match the proper clauses together.

11:22	Like a gold ring in a swine's snout,	but the mercy of the wicked is cruel.
12:10	A righteous man has regard for the life of his beast,	that one may avoid the snares of death.
12:11	He who tills his land will have plenty of bread,	than a fatted ox and hatred with it.
12:19	Truthful lips endure for ever,	but he who is kind to the needy honors him.
13:14	The teaching of the wise is a fountain of life,	not so the minds of fools.
13:24	He who spares the rod hates his son,	but a lying tongue is but for a moment.
14:1	Wisdom builds her house,	and a word in season, how good it is.
14:31	He who oppresses a poor man insults his Maker,	but he who follows worthless pursuits has no sense.
15:7	The lips of the wise spread knowledge,	is a beautiful woman without discretion.
15:17	Better is a dinner of herbs where love is,	but folly with her own hands tears it down.
15:23	To make an apt answer is a joy to a man,	but he who loves him is diligent to discipline him.

This exercise can be done individually, in small groups or all together in a large group. There is only one rule: You cannot refer to your Bible. The winner of the game is the group or individual with the most correctly matched proverbs.

Wrap things up with a discussion on the proverbs themselves. You will find that most of the proverbs in the Book of Proverbs and in other Old Testament books like Ecclesiastes contain "definitions by implication." For example: "He who trusts in his own mind is a fool, but he who walks in wisdom will be delivered" (Proverbs 28:26). The definition: walking in wisdom is not trusting in one's own mind.

This sort of thing can be done with all the proverbs. Find the truths that are there and then look for ways that they can be applied to our lives today. (Contributed by Jerry Daniel, Westfield, New Jersey)

LEGAL BALL

The following is a game that was created to illustrate how we cannot expect to please God by living strictly by a set of rules of "do's and don'ts." The game is a form of softball which is best played with a "whiffle" ball or "Nerf" ball and a light bat. It can be played indoors or outdoors. Layout the ball diamond (bases, etc.) and divide into two teams of any number.

Before the game begins, read the following rules to the game. Read them with authority and let the group know that they must adhere to them strictly. Anyone who is caught breaking a rule will be called "out" and their team penalized one run. These rules could be printed up and passed out so that everyone knows what they are at all times.

The Rules:

1. Thou shalt play the game with one hand and one eye. Example: A right-handed person must cover his right eye with his right hand and use his left hand and eye. A left-handed person vice versa.
2. Thou shalt not run! You may only walk at all times.
3. Thou shalt not throw the ball. You may only hand it to another person.
4. Thou shalt receive one (1) pitch. If you do not hit the ball you are out.
5. Thou shalt ask permission to walk the bases. If you hit the ball you must turn to the umpire and ask permission to walk to first base. If the umpire says "no," you are out.
6. Thou must apologize to thy teammates each time you make an out.
7. A foul ball is an out.
8. Thou shalt not disagree with the umpire or question any of his calls.
9. Thy team must score 4 runs each inning.
10. Thy team must score 15 runs to win.
11. Thy team must win.

Following the game (play it as long as the group can take it) have a discussion of what it means to live in the Spirit according to Galatians, Chapter 5. You might also use Romans 7 and 8, or other Scripture for further Bible study.

The game can be both fun and frustrating. The experience will open up good discussion on the futility of the law to provide "abundant living." Good luck, and may the most "religious" team win! (Contributed by Don Thomas, Garden Grove, California)

MADISON AVENUE

For a youth meeting where you want to have fun but also learn something, get yourself a video camera or a super-8 camera with sound that can photograph indoors. Divide your group into as many teams as is practical for your size group and have them develop a 60-second commercial to sell Christianity to the world. The most fun is for them to do a "take-off" of a well-known commercial on TV, adapting it to Christianity. Make sure that everyone is involved in the commercial and then show them within a week or two. They all love to see themselves on film. Follow up with a discussion of the experience that focuses on whether or not it is possible to present an accurate picture of Christianity in 60 seconds. (Contributed by Ken S. Williams, Woodland, California)

MALE AND FEMALE

This is an exercise designed to help the members of your group come to a better understanding about what it means to be a man, what it means to be a woman, and what God has to say about the whole issue of men's and women's roles. Begin by giving each person a questionnaire with the following questions:

1. What does it mean to be female? (Or what does it bring to your mind?)
2. What does it mean to be male? (Or what does it bring to your mind?)
3. Girls: I feel most feminine when. . .(tell when)
   Guys: I feel most masculine when. . .(tell when)
4. I think a man/woman feels most masculine/feminine when. . .(describe how you think the opposite sex feels)
5. List a few "personality" differences between men and women. Do you think there are many generalizations that can be made?

After the group has had a few minutes to fill out the questionnaire, have them share their answers to these questions. Have someone then read Genesis 1:27 and 28, 2:18-25, Galatians 3:25-29 and Philippians 2:1-8. Summarize what you as the leader heard the group saying: the main points and any similarities or differences between the way the girls answered the questionnaire and the way the guys did. In light of the scripture, discuss the following questions:

1. Why do you think God made different sexes?
2. What do you think God's attitude towards men and women was then (and is now)?
3. What are some of the benefits (good things) about the differences between the sexes?
4. Having read the passage in Galatians and Philippians, how should we as Christians view the sexes? Is one superior to the

other? How do they compliment each other? How should we treat each other as a result?

Conclude by having the group think of some specific things they could do to help understand the opposite sex better, like learning more about the types of things the opposite sex is interested in, stopping to think the next time they are about to make a disrespectful or prejudicial comment, or becoming aware of how they may have locked themselves and others into certain roles which don't allow for the unity we have in Christ. (Contributed by Anna Hobbs, El Cajon, California)

MASQUERADE MIXER

This idea can be used as a "get acquainted" excercise for groups that don't know each other, or as an effective community-building experience for more established groups.

To begin, give each person a paper bag, several marking pens or crayons, some magazines, glue, scissors and the like. They are instructed to make a mask for themselves, and depending on the purpose of the exercise, these masks can be humorous, realistic, or symbolic. You might have them make a mask of themselves "ten years from now," or "as they wish they were," or whatever you decide. They can draw the mask, or cut out images and glue them onto the bag to create the proper impression. Give the group ten or fifteen minutes to do this.

Next, have everyone wear their masks and sit in a circle. Go around the group and have each person talk about themselves for one minute, and then relate this to the mask that they are wearing. When each person finishes, they may remove their masks (and give their name if the group doesn't already know it). Gradually the entire group will become "unmasked" and they will learn a great deal about each other in the process.

Use your own creativity as to how you choose to use this basic idea. It can be a simple mixer, or it can be used as a serious learning strategy that can be tied in with a discussion on phoniness, the wearing of masks, discovering who we really are, and so on. However you use it, it has the potential of being a great success with any group of young people. (Contributed by Hal Herwick, St. Charles, Missouri)

MATTHEW ONE

It's not easy to make the genealogy of Jesus in the first chapter of Matthew seem exciting to a group of young people, but this idea does exactly that. The following reading is an "annotated" version of

Matthew 1:1-16 (that is, it has some material added that explains who a few of the people were). The annotations reveal to the group what otherwise might be evident only to those who are well educated in the Old Testament. The reading also allows for the group's response to many of the people in Jesus' family tree.

Here's how it works. As the genealogy is read, someone holds up cue cards to the group, who respond as each card indicates. One cue card says "Applause," another says "Boo," another says "Cheer," another says "Hiss," another says "Moan," and another says "Huh?" (The last cue card is used after names of persons in the genealogy who are unknown even to Biblical scholars or who did little or nothing of consequence.) Before the actual reading, it would be a good idea to rehearse the group with the cue cards, just to get everybody "in the spirit." When they are ready, then proceed with the reading, pausing as indicated by the parentheses for the appropriate response.

Matthew One

The Book of the genealogy of Jesus Christ (*APPLAUSE and CHEER*), the son of David (*APPLAUSE*), the son of Abraham (*CHEERS*). Abraham was the father of Isaac (*APPLAUSE*), the father of Jacob who stole his brother's birthright (*BOO*), and Jacob was the father of Judah and his brothers who sold Joseph into slavery (*HISS*). And Judah was the father of Perez and Zerah (*HUH?*) by Tamar (*HUH?*), and Perez was the father of Hezron, and Hezron the father of Ram, and Ram the father of Amminidab (*HUH?*), and Amminidab the father of Nahshon the father of Salmon who was the father of Boaz by Rahab, the prostitute (*BOO*), and Boaz was the father of Obed by Ruth (*CHEERS and APPLAUSE*); and Obed was the father of Jesse the Father of David the king (*CHEERS*). And David was the father of Solomon by the wife of Uriah whom he had murdered (*HISS*); and Solomon was the father of Rehoboam who was a good king but abandoned God's way for several years (*BOO*), and Rehoboam was the father of Abijah who had fourteen wives (*CHEERS and BOOS*), and Abijah was the father of Asa, a good king but who did not walk in the way of the Lord at the end of his life and so died of gangreen of the feet (*MOAN*), and Asa was the father of Jehoshaphat who was a fine king ruling wisely most of the time (*APPLAUSE*). Jehoshaphat was the father of Joram who was the father of Uzziah whose pride brought his fall (*BOO*); but Uzziah was the father of Jotham, a very good king in every way (*CHEER*), who was the father of Ahaz, a very bad king in every way (*HISS*). And Ahaz was the father of Hezekiah who cleansed the temple and the kingdom (*CHEERS and APPLAUSE*). Hezekiah was the father of Manasseh who ruled for fifty-five years (*APPLAUSE*), but who was evil for most of that time (*BOOS*). He was the father of Josiah who did right in the eyes of the Lord (*CHEER*); and Josiah was the father of Jechoniah and his brothers at the time of the deportation to Babylon (*HUH?*). And after the deportation to Babylon, Jechoniah was the father of Shealtiel who was the father of Zerubbabel, a governor of the people and chosen by God (*APPLAUSE*). And Jerubbabel was the father of Abiud (*HUH?*), and Abiud was the father of Eliakim (*HUH?*), who was the father of Azor (*HUH?*), who was the father of Zadok (*HUH?*) who was the father of Achim (*HUH?*), who was the father of Eliud (*HUH?*), the father of Eleazar (*HUH?*), the father of Matthan (*HUH?*), the father of Jacob (*HUH?*), the father of Joseph (*APPLAUSE*), who was husband of Mary (*CHEERS*), of whom was born Jesus whom we call Christ (*APPLAUSE and CHEERS*).

A good way to use this (for more than just laughs) would be to have the group pay attention to who in fact Jesus' ancestors were. One would think that all of Jesus' ancestors would be good people, but that was hardly the case. Instead, we find prostitutes, murderers, bigamists, and all sorts of evil people in Jesus' family tree. Yet Jesus turned out great. So, maybe this means there is hope for us, and for our children. We may not be able to blame the way we are on our parents or anyone else. We are all responsible before God for who we are. A discussion of this concept might be a good way to tie this to reality. It would also be appropriate to use this reading at Advent, or in a Bible study as a way of beginning the book of Matthew. (By Doug Adams, reprinted by permission from *Modern Liturgy* magazine, Saratoga, California)

MISSION IMPROBABLE

Here is a great learning game that can be used with groups of young people, or with youth and their parents. It is a lot of fun to play, and it opens up good discussion on the topics of motivation and communication. The game board is provided on the next page and the basic directions and rules for the game are printed on it. To play, remove the game board,duplicate it with a copy machine, or make your own "reasonable facsimile." Then, you will need to make the "Task Cards," the "Energizer Cards," and the "Squelch Cards." These are printed on the next few pages also, and may be removed and cut up into little cards if you like. Or, you might want to make your own cards, using construction paper and writing the sayings on them by hand. Use a different color for the three different kinds of cards.

The object of the game is to complete various "Tasks" by accumulating enough "motils," which you get on the "Energizer Cards." The "Squelch Cards" take motils away. If you get too many negative motils, you may fail to complete the task. Incidentally, all the sayings on the "Squelch Cards" (put downs, for the most part) were suggested by a group of high school students. Perhaps your group can think of others. Make up a few cards of your own.

One great way to use this game is to print it up so that each young person in your group has one to take home. Then encourage them to play it at home with their parents. The game is great for family interaction. It can also be used effectively at a family retreat. (Contributed by Mike Jarrett, Tampa, Florida)

MISSION IMPROBABLE

Energize

Tasks

Squelch

Start

How to Play

WHEN THE GAME WITH PRAYER (YOU'LL NEED IT). SHUFFLE AND DEAL EVERY PLAYER A TASK. EACH TASK REQUIRES 200 UNITS OF MOTIVATED ENERGY, OR MOTUS, AS WE LIKE TO SAY IN THE TRADE, TO COMPLETE. A TASK HAS ALSO FAILED IF YOU GET 200 NEGATIVE MOTUS.

TO ACCUMULATE MOTUS AND COMPLETE TASKS, TAKE TURNS ROLLING DICE AND MOVING YOUR PLAYERS AROUND THE BOARD. IF YOU DO WHAT THE SQUARES SAY YOU'LL SOON REALIZE YOU'RE EITHER GAINING OR LOSING MOTUS.

WHEN YOU EARN ENOUGH MOTUS TO COMPLETE A TASK OR WHEN YOU FAIL YOUR TASK, DRAW ANOTHER AND WORK ON IT. THE GAME IS OVER WHEN ALL TASKS HAVE BEEN USED. THE WINNER IS THE ONE COMPLETING THE GREATEST NUMBER OF TASKS.

Board Spaces

DRAW TWO ENERGIZERS AND ROLL AGAIN.

IN A REVENGEFUL ACT OF SENSELESS VIOLENCE, YOUR YOUNGEST DAUGH-TER BAKED THE FAMILY'S PET HERMIT CRAB IN AN EASY BAKE OVEN. DRAW ONE SQUELCHER.

REMEMBER MURPHY'S LAW? YOU'VE JUST BEEN GIVEN THE UNIQUE OPPOR-TUNITY OF PROVING IT. GIVE SOMEONE ONE OF YOUR TASKS, THEY CAN CONSIDER IT ACCOMPLISHED.

YOU MIGHT AS WELL GO TO THE KIT-CHEN AND GET SOMETHING TO SCARF DOWN, BE-CAUSE YOU MUST SKIP YOUR NEXT TURN.

YOUR NEW BOOK, MILKING RATTLE-SNAKES FOR FUN AND PROFIT, JUST REACHED THE BEST SELLER'S LIST. DRAW AN ENERGIZER.

NOW'S YOUR CHANCE TO BE A SQUEL-CHER. TAKE A TASK CARD FROM ONE OTHER PER-SON AND CONSI-DER THAT TASK COMPLETE.

CAN YOU QUOTE ONE BIBLE VERSE MEMORIZED THIS WEEK? IF SO, DRAW TWO ENERGIZERS.

HAVE YOU READ AT LEAST SEVEN BOOKS IN THE LAST SIX MONTHS? IF SO, DRAW AN ENERGIZER. IF NOT, DRAW TWO SQUELCHERS.

"BORED WALK" MAY BE THE BEST PROPERTY IN MONOPOLY, BUT ITS DEATH TO MOTIVATION. DRAW A SQUELCHER.

HAVE YOU GONE ALL DAY WITHOUT QUARRELING WITH ANYBODY? DRAW AN ENERGIZER.

DIVIDE YOUR WEIGHT BY YOUR AGE. IF THE QUOTIENT IS LESS THAN SIX, DRAW AN ENERGIZER. IF NOT, DRAW A SQUELCHER.

GO TO START. TELL YOUR PARENTS THEY NOW OWE YOU TWO HUNDRED DOLLARS, AMERICAN MONEY.

IF YOU THINK SAN DIEGO IS THE CAPITOL OF MONGOLIA, MISS TEN TURNS. IF NOT, DRAW AN ENERGIZER.

IF YOU ARE WEARING SIX PAIRS OF UNDER-WEAR, DRAW TEN SQUELCHERS. IF NOT, DRAW AN ENERGIZER.

IF YOU HAVE VISIBLE HAIR IN YOUR NOSTRILS, DRAW TWO SQUELCHERS.

YOUR BELIEF IN EARWAX AS THE MOST PROMISING OF ALL ALTERNATE ENERGY SOURCES JUST LOST YOU ONE TURN!

THIS MAY BE THE HAPPIEST DAY OF YOUR LIFE. NOT ONLY DID YOUR GINSU KNIFE AND SIX IN ONE KITCHEN TOOL COME IN THE MAIL, BUT YOU MAY DRAW FOUR, COUNT 'EM, FOUR ENERGIZERS.

DOES THE NAME OF THE MONTH YOU WERE BORN IN HAVE A VOWEL IN IT? IF SO, DRAW THREE ENERGIZERS. IF NOT, YOU'RE IN BIG TROUBLE.

HAVE YOU EVER BEEN IN A CAR THAT WAS STOPPED BY THE POLICE? DRAW TO SQUEL-CHER CARD. IF NOT, DRAW TWO ENERGIZERS.

GET SOMEONE TO OPEN A DICTIONARY AT RANDOM. IF YOU KNOW THE MEANING OF THE WORD AT THE TOP OF THE PAGE, DRAW TWO ENERGIZERS; IF NOT, LEARN THE WORD.

DID YOU BRUSH YOUR DOG'S TEETH TODAY? IF NOT DRAW A SQUELCHER. IF SO, YOU'RE WEIRD.

YOU BELIEVE THIS GAME IS A WORK OF ART AND A BEAUTIFUL EXPRES-SION OF ONE'S SPIRITUAL GIFT. DRAW AN ENERGIZER.

YOU ARE AFRAID TO OPEN CANS WITH THE LABELS FACING DOWNWARDS. DRAW A SQUELCHER.

STAND UP, STRETCH, TURN AROUND IN CIRCLES TEN TIMES AND DRAW AN ENER-GIZER.

CAN YOU SPELL THE FIFTH BOOK OF THE OLD TESTAMENT BACKWARDS? IF SO, DRAW TWO ENERGIZERS.

YOUR YOUNGEST SON JUST RAN AWAY FROM HOME TO FORM A ROCK GROUP WHERE THEY ALL DRESS UP LIKE PET ROCKS. THEY ARE CALLED THE PUNK PETS. DRAW A SQUELCHER.

WHAT?

ENERGIZER CARDS

OF WHAT USE IS MONEY IN THE HAND OF A FOOL, SINCE HE HAS NO DESIRE TO GET WISDOM? PROVERBS 17:16
35 MOTILS

THINK THROUGH TASKS FIRST
25 MOTILS

A SIMPLE MAN BELIEVES ANYTHING, BUT A PRUDENT MAN GIVES THOUGHT TO HIS STEPS. PROVERBS 14:15
35 MOTILS

HOPE DEFERRED MAKES THE HEART SICK, BUT A LONGING FULFILLED IS A TREE OF LIFE. PROVERBS 13:12
45 MOTILS

NEED RELATED TASKS = MUCHO MOTILS

A PATIENT MAN HAS GREAT UNDERSTANDING, BUT A QUICK-TEMPERED MAN DISPLAYS FOLLY. PROVERBS 14:29
25 MOTILS

EVERY ACTION HAS ETERNAL CONSEQUENCES.
75 MOTILS

DO NOT WITHHOLD GOOD FROM THOSE WHO DESERVE IT, WHEN IT IS IN YOUR POWER TO ACT. PROVERBS 3:27
25 MOTILS

GOD KEEPS THE BOOKS
50 MOTILS

THE EYES OF THE LORD ARE EVERYWHERE KEEPING WATCH ON THE WICKED AND THE GOOD. PROVERBS 15:3
35 MOTILS

ACQUITTING THE GUILTY AND CONDEMNING THE INNOCENT— THE LORD DETESTS THEM BOTH. PROVERBS 17:15
25 MOTILS

ONE HUNDRED DOLLAR REWARD
25 MOTILS

LONG TERM GOALS CAN MOTIVATE
50 MOTILS

HAVE A GOAL
50 MOTILS

LET YOUR EYES LOOK STRAIGHT AHEAD, FIX YOUR GAZE DIRECTLY BEFORE YOU. PROVERBS 4:25
50 MOTILS

PURPOSE TO ENJOY MEANS AND NOT ENDS ONLY.
50 MOTILS

AN HONEST ANSWER IS LIKE A KISS ON THE LIPS. PROVERBS 24:26
40 MOTILS

GOOD MOTIVATES THE RIGHTEOUS PERSON.
25 MOTILS

WHO ARE YOU DOING IT FOR?
25 MOTILS

COMMIT TO THE LORD WHATEVER YOU DO, AND YOUR PLANS WILL SUCCEED. PROVERBS 16:3
75 MOTILS

GET YOUR TIMING RIGHT
A MAN FINDS JOY IN GIVING AN APT REPLY— AND HOW GOOD IS A TIMELY WORD. PROVERBS 15:23
35 MOTILS

ATTITUDES MAKE A DIFFERENCE
A HAPPY HEART MAKES THE FACE CHEERFUL, BUT HEARTACHE CRUSHES THE SPIRIT. ALL THE DAYS OF THE OPPRESSED ARE WRETCHED, BUT THE CHEERFUL HEART HAS A CONTINUAL FEAST. PROVERBS 15:13,15
25 MOTILS

REWARDS WORK
THE LABORER'S APPETITE WORKS FOR HIM; HIS HUNGER DRIVES HIM ON. PROVERBS 16:26
50 MOTILS

FOLLOW THROUGH
50 MOTILS

THE REASON YOU DO SOMETHING IS ALL IMPORTANT.
ALL A MAN'S WAYS SEEM INNOCENT TO HIM, BUT MOTIVES ARE WEIGHED BY THE LORD. PROVERBS 16:2
50 MOTILS

WHEN YOU GIVE SOMEONE A JOB, LET THEM DO IT.
LIKE ONE WHO SEIZES A DOG BY THE EARS IS A PASSER-BY WHO MEDDLES IN A QUARREL NOT HIS OWN. PROVERBS 26:17
40 MOTILS

MAKE TASKS A CHALLENGE WITHOUT BEING UNREASONABLE.
25 MOTILS

IT IS NOT A SIN TO OVERLOOK AN ERROR. IT IS A SIN TO KEEP BRINGING UP THE PAST.
HE WHO COVERS OVER AN OFFENSE PROMOTES LOVE, BUT WHO EVER REPEATS THE MATTER SEPERATES CLOSE FRIENDS. PROVERBS 17:9
25 MOTILS

UNCONDITIONAL LOVE MOTIVATES
100 MOTILS

WORDS HAVE POWER
THROUGH PATIENCE A RULER CAN BE PERSUADED, AND A GENTLE TONGUE CAN BREAK A BONE. PROVERBS 25:15
35 MOTILS

GIVE REASONS FOR TASKS EVEN IF THOSE REASONS ARE APPARENT
40 MOTILS

Variety does it!
25 MOTILS

TASKS ARE A GREAT WAY OF SHOWING SOMEONE HOW MUCH THEY'RE NEEDED. TRY TO CONVEY THIS FEELING TO THEM.
25 MOTILS

MAKE TASKS A GAME.
25 MOTILS

TRUST and FAITH
50 MOTILS

UNCONDITIONAL LOVE MOTIVATES
100 MOTILS

ALWAYS BE OPEN TO CREATIVITY.
25 MOTILS

EDIFY!
AN ANXIOUS HEART WEIGHS A MAN DOWN, BUT A KIND WORD CHEERS HIM UP. PROVERBS 12:15
50 MOTILS

ASK DON'T TELL.
50 MOTILS

MIX GENTLY/DON'T STIR
A GENTLE ANSWER TURNS AWAY WRATH, BUT A HARSH ANSWER STIRS UP ANGER. PROVERBS 15:1
25 MOTILS

SQUELCH CARDS

"BUT MOM, WHY DO YOU WANT ME TO WASH THE DISHES? WE HAVE A DISHWASHER."
— 50 MOTILS

"IS THIS THE BEST YOU CAN DO?"
— 30 MOTILS

DAD SAYS, "MAKE SURE YOU GET THE YARD DONE," THEN HE GOES INSIDE, SITS IN HIS FAVORITE CHAIR AND READS THE PAPER.
— 25 MOTILS

"REMEMBER, JOHNNY, FEEDING THE DOG IS YOUR JOB, WASHING THE DISHES IS NANCY'S JOB."
— 25 MOTILS

"I REALLY THINK YOU'RE BLIND. YOU JUST MOWED OVER MY FAVORITE PLANT."
— 25 MOTILS

"I KNOW WE HAVE A DISHWASHER, DARLING, BUT IT WILL BUILD CHARACTER AND DISCIPLINE IN YOU TO WASH THEM LIKE I USED TO WHEN I WAS A CHILD."

"DATE THAT CUTE LITTLE GIRL. YOUR MOM AND I LIKE SO MUCH INSTEAD OF THAT CREEP YOU HANG OUT WITH."
— 40 MOTILS

SAYING "CHEER UP, CHEER UP," DOESN'T GET TO THE BOTTOM OF A PROBLEM. IN FACT, IT CREATES A PROBLEM. LIKE ONE WHO TAKES AWAY A GARMENT ON A COLD DAY, OR LIKE VINEGAR POURED ON SODA, IS ONE WHO SINGS SONGS TO A HEAVY HEART.
PROVERBS 25:20
— 25 MOTILS

"THAT'S A GOOD JOB, SON, BUT..."
— 75 MOTILS

"I DON'T CARE IF YOU DID FINISH THE JOB, WITH AN ATTITUDE LIKE YOURS, I JUST DON'T THINK I CAN REWARD YOU."
— 25 MOTILS

"I CAN'T BELIEVE A GIRL YOUR AGE..."
— 45 MOTILS

NOBODY'S SANG ANY PRAISES TO YOU SINCE YOUR LAST BIRTHDAY.
— 25 MOTILS

"DON'T FORGET, CHRISTMAS IS COMING."
— 50 MOTILS

PUNISHMENT STRIKES!!
— 25 MOTILS

NAG CARD
— 25 MOTILS

"YES, FRANKLIN SAYS YOU NEVER ACT LIKE THIS AROUND HER."
— 25 MOTILS

"YOU KNOW AS WELL AS I DO, YOU DIDN'T FORGET WHAT DAY THE GARBAGE MAN COMES."
— 25 MOTILS

"AIN'T IT FUN WHEN YOU'RE THE GUINEA PIG FOR AMATEUR PSYCHOLOGISTS."
— 40 MOTILS

AFTER THE JOB IS DONE:

"YOU KNOW THERE WAS AN EASIER WAY TO DO THAT."
— 75 MOTILS

"YOU DID THAT ALL WRONG!" (SAID WHILE DESTROYING THE PROJECT)
— 100 MOTILS

RECESSION
MAKES MONEY SCARCE
— 25 MOTILS

"SORRY, YOU'VE JUST BEEN YELLED AT."
— 75 MOTILS

"WELL, I GUESS I'LL JUST HAVE TO DO IT MYSELF."
— 50 MOTILS

"I REMEMBER LAST TIME..."
— 40 MOTILS

HAVE YOU FINISHED THAT JOB I ASKED YOU TO DO?
THAT TURKEY, HE KNOWS I HAVEN'T EVEN STARTED IT YET
— 25 MOTILS

"YOU NEVER DO IT RIGHT. I END UP HAVING TO DO IT OVER ANYWAY."
— 30 MOTILS

"YOU NEVER DO ANYTHING AROUND HERE." "GO CLEAN YOUR ROOM."
LATER
— 25 MOTILS

"WHY CAN'T YOU BE LIKE..."
— 50 MOTILS

"I'M SORRY I DIDN'T TELL YOU WHAT A GOOD JOB YOU DID. YOU KNOW HOW BUSY I'VE BEEN."
— 25 MOTILS

"A TWO YEAR OLD COULD DO THIS JOB."
— 30 MOTILS

"DON'T JUST SIT THERE WHEN THERE'S SO MUCH TO DO." THIS IS GENERALLY SAID WITHOUT TELLING ANYONE WHAT NEEDS TO BE DONE.
— 30 MOTILS

BUSY WORK BLUES
— 25 MOTILS

"WELL, I'M GLAD TO SEE YOU HAVEN'T BEEN SITTING AROUND LIKE USUAL."
— 30 MOTILS

I COULD ASK THAT LITTLE BRAT, BUT HE WON'T DO IT. UNLESS HE'S TOLD, THE WAY I WANT. BESIDES HE NEEDS TO LEARN RESPECT FOR AUTHORITY. THEY WON'T TREAT HIM WITH KID GLOVES WHEN HE GETS OUT INTO THE REAL WORLD.
— 100 MOTILS

"I DON'T WANT TO HEAR YOUR IDEAS, DO IT THE WAY I ORIGINALLY SAID."
— 25 MOTILS

"WHAT HAVE YOU EVER DONE FOR US?"
— 75 MOTILS

MOTIVATION OUT OF GUILT:
"WE ONLY ASK YOU TO DO A FEW THINGS AROUND HERE."
— 50 MOTILS

TASK CARDS

- SMILE FOR FIFTEEN NON-STOP MINUTES
- TAKE OUT THE GARBAGE.
- TAKE YOUR GERBIL'S BLOOD PRESSURE.
- CLEAN YOUR ROOM. TAKE OUT EXTRA LIFE INSURANCE IF NECESSARY.
- COOK A MEAL.

- GO TO A REAL NURD'S BIRTHDAY PARTY.
- MOW THE LAWN.
- TURN DOWN YOUR STEREO.
- OPEN A DOOR FOR SOMEONE.
- HUG YOUR SISTER.
- TELL MOM "I LOVE YOU."

- LOSE TEN POUNDS.
- WRITE A LETTER TO YOUR GRANDPARENTS.
- LISTEN TO AN OPERA.
- MAKE UP YOUR BED.
- GET WISDOM AND UNDERSTANDING.

BECOME SKILLFUL

DO YOU SEE A MAN SKILLED IN HIS WORK? HE WILL SERVE BEFORE KINGS; HE WILL NOT SERVE BEFORE OBSCURE MEN. PROVERBS 22:29

- THROW THOSE TENNIS SHOES OF YOURS AWAY THAT HAVE THE AROMA PECULIAR ONLY TO THE CITY DUMP.
- TRY A FOOD YOU HAVE NEVER EATEN BEFORE.
- BE NICE WHEN THAT MOUNTAIN OF FLESH, AUNT BERTHA, HUGS YOU.
- HAVE A DOG WASH INSTEAD OF A CAR WASH.
- MAKE STRAIGHT A's ON YOUR REPORT CARD.
- MAKE PLANS BY SEEKING ADVICE; IF YOU WAGE WAR OBTAIN GUIDANCE. PROVERBS 20:18

SEEK COUNSEL

- WEAR A TIE.
- CALL AN OLD FRIEND ON THE TELEPHONE.
- BUY SOMEONE A FLOWER.
- WASH BEHIND YOUR EARS.
- PACKAGE THE LEFTOVERS FROM TONIGHT'S SUPPER AND MAIL THEM TO INDIA.
- FINISH YOUR OUTDOOR WORK AND GET YOUR FIELDS READY; AFTER THAT BUILD YOUR HOUSE. PROVERBS 24:27

- WASH THE DISHES
- PAINT A PICTURE.
- WASH AND WAX THE FAMILY CAR.
- GET YOUR HAIR CUT.
- PICK YOUR NOSE CONTINUOUSLY FOR THREE DAYS.
- MAKE A POINT OF STUDYING MOTIVES: THE PURPOSES OF A MAN'S HEART ARE DEEP WATERS, BUT A MAN OF UNDERSTANDING DRAWS THEM OUT. PROVERBS 20:5

MONOPOLY MORALITY

An ordinary "Monopoly" game (available in department stores, toy stores, etc.) can be used very effectively as a way of understanding the significance of unjust distribution of goods in the world.

The rules of the game have to be altered in the following way. There should be four teams. Two of the teams (Team #1 and #2) should only have two or three players at the most. The other two teams (Teams #3 and #4) should be much larger, with the rest of the group divided between those two teams. All decisions regarding strategy, etc., must be made by the entire team as a unit.

The money should be distributed as indicated below, but it's value should be multiplied by 1000. In other words, a $1 bill is now worth $1000, and a $5 bill is actually worth $5000. But all of the prices for property, etc. are also multiplied by 1000, thus "Virginia Avenue" now costs $160,000. This makes the game a bit closer to reality.

Team #1 and Team #2 receive the following:

        6   $500 bills
       10   $100 bills
        5   $50 bills
       10   $10 bills
       10   $5 bills
       10   $1 bills

This amounts to a total of $5,530,000 (with the 1000x inflation).

Team #3 and Team #4 each receive the following:

     zero $500 bills
        1   $100 bills
        2   $50 bills
        2   $20 bills
        2   $10 bills
        2   $5 bills
        2   $1 bills

This amounts to a total of $272,000 (with the 1000x inflation.)

Some "role-playing" will be required as follows: Team #1 is a Christian team. They should play the game making all their decisions from a "Christian" point of view. Team #2 is a non-Christian team. They can do anything they like. Team #3 is also a Christian team. Team #4 is a non-Christian team.

As play proceeds, each team should play out its role according to their resources and assigned religious/moral persuasion. Team #3 and #4 will probably get bored pretty fast. The non-Christians may lie and cheat and steal. The bored players may drift away and refuse to play. These developments are all part of the game.

Play for as long as the group wants to. It can end when one or more groups are out of money or they are at each others' throats. Each team should have a leader/spokesperson who handles the team's money, rolls the dice and so on. If the leadership is good, the game will be lively and lots of fun as kids try to outwit or take advantage of each other. Following the game, you will need to "de-brief" the group and talk about what happened. This is the most important part. Discuss the decisions that were made and how close to reality they really were. Compare the game to the current world situation. The discussion possibilities are great. (Contributed by Steve Yamaguchi, Santa Barbara, California)

MORE THAN JUST A PRETTY NAME

There are a number of books on the market that list thousands of common names and their original meanings. Get one or more copies of a book like this (from a local bookstore, or from your local library) and try the following exercise with your group. Break into small groups and have the kids look up each other's names in the reference book and find out what it means and the character quality that it represents. Then have them (as soberly as possible) use that meaning as a way of affirming and encouraging each other.

A second phase might be to have the kids choose a new name for themselves or for the others in their group, based upon the meaning of a particular name found in the book. When you first present this, you can point out from many different places in scripture how the meaning of a person's name was important and had great significance (Jacob's children, Hosea's children, Jesus, Peter, etc.). An exercise like this can be very enlightening. (Contributed by John Collins, Springfield, Missouri)

A NEW HUMANITY

The "declaration" printed below can be used as an effective discussion starter. Give everyone a copy of it, discuss each paragraph one at a time, and try to arrive at a consensus on the three principles which are called for. The process should get everyone thinking, and should be an interesting exercise in communication and group problem-solving as well.

THE DECLARATION OF A NEW HUMANITY

WE gathered here together in the presence of each other do hereby and forthwith solemnly covenant and agree wholeheartedly to the formation, preservation and perpetuation of **A NEW HUMANITY**—the ordering and governance of which is entirely up to us.

ON this momentous and historic occasion, therefore, let us duly establish and confirm, once for all, the manner and means by which our **NEW HUMANITY** will forge a history of its own from within the womb of the prevailing social milieu.

IT is not ours to condemn that humanity which is old and passing away, but rather to affirm and commend that **HUMANITY** which is **NEW** and ours—and thereby promulgate a vital and viable alternative to the status quo.

THIS being the case; and we, being of one heart and one mind, do here and now lay down and enscribe, for posterity's sake, the following fundamental principles upon which our **NEW HUMANITY** is now and ever hereafter eternally founded.

PRINCIPLE ONE: _____
_____
_____

PRINCIPLE TWO: _____
_____
_____

PRINCIPLE THREE: _____
_____
_____

** Agreed to and witnessed by:

Conclude the exercise by looking at 2 Corinthians 5:17-20. Help the group to realize that as Christians we are *in fact* members of a "new humanity"—a community called out by Christ with a specific mission. This session can be followed up with a definite plan for implementing the principles and putting them into action in some concrete way. (Contributed by Brad Davis, Newport, Rhode Island)

PARABLES FOR TODAY

Here is a study on the parables of Christ that allows kids to create a parable of their own. To begin, have the kids read a parable from Scripture, like the parable of the Sower in Mark 4:3-9. Then discuss the following questions. They can be presented and discussed orally with the entire group, or you might want to print the questions up and have the kids write out their answers and discuss in small groups.

1. What is a parable?
2. What does the parable of the Sower try to teach?
3. Why do you think Jesus chose to teach in parables instead of some other way?
4. What advantage does a parable have over other ways of teaching?
5. What other parables do you know. . .from the Bible?. . .from elsewhere?

The next step is to challenge the kids to come up with a parable of their own—now that they understand something about the nature of parables. Give them the following six steps (put them up on a blackboard or have them printed up so that they can be passed out) and let them work on their parable for ten minutes or so. Let kids know that their parables don't have to be very long or complicated or "heavy." In fact, the simpler, the better.

1. Pick an object or idea for your parable (Hint: like *seed*)
2. Think of how this "thing" relates to some truth God gives us. Use as many ways of showing that truth with your "thing" as possible.
3. Now write out your "parable" and title it.
4. Have your "thing" with you (if possible) when it is your turn to read your parable, to use as a visual aid to your listeners.
5. Think of some questions you can ask the listeners to see if they understood your parable.
6. Gather back with the group, and wait for your turn to read. Listen to the others.

After the parables have been written, allow the kids to share them with each other and to discuss each one briefly. You'll find this to be a great way to encourage creativity and to provide some excellent learning, too. (Contributed by Jeff Pool, Owatonna, Minnesota)

PATHWAY OF PRAYER

Here's a good way to help your kids learn a lot about prayer while playing a game. It can be played by individuals or by teams. You'll need to create a "game board" similar to the diagram below. It can be small if you play the game in small groups, or it can be large—if you play the game with the entire group divided up into teams. If you have a big blackboard, you could just draw a "reasonable facsimile" up on the board, and each player could keep track of his or her position with different colored chalk. An overhead projector could be used the same way. You can make the "pathway" as long or as short as you want, depending on the size of the group and how much time you have.

If you choose, you can get a little more "creative" with the game board and have a few obstacles along the way ("You fell asleep during prayer—go back two spaces."), or you could make some "chutes and ladders" similar to other board games. It's all up to you. Players start out on one end of the path and end up at the "Throne of Grace" (see Heb. 4:16) or whatever you prefer as a goal.

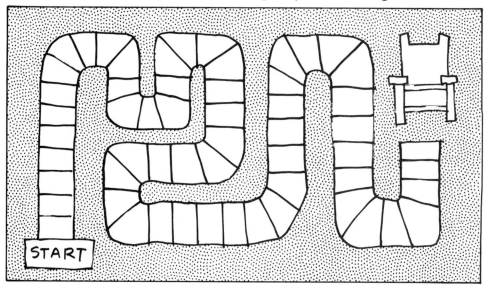

Also needed for this game are "Scripture Cards." These cards can be made by simply using small slips of paper. One side of the card should have a verse printed on it (either the whole verse of just the reference). These verses all have something to do with prayer. The other side of the card should have one or more "prayer categories" listed that the verse specifically deals with. There are seven different "categories" that a verse might touch on. They are:

1. Prayer Promises (results of prayer)
2. Prayer Petitions (what to pray for)
3. Prerequisites to Prayer (conditions)
4. Places to pray
5. Prayer Periods (when to pray)
6. Pathetic Prayer (not pleasing to God)
7. Prayer Positions (bodily positions for prayer)

As the game progresses, each player or team will select a card on their turn. They should read out loud the verse on the card, and then note which categories the verse deals with. These categories determine the number of "spaces" on the game board that the player gets to move:

1. Promises—Move ahead 1
2. Petitions—Move ahead 1
3. Prerequisites—Move ahead 1
4. Places—Move ahead 3
5. Periods—Move ahead 2
6. Pathetic—Move back 1
7. Positions—Move ahead 3

So, if the selected verse deals with Places, Petitions, and Promises, the player gets to move ahead a total of 5 spaces on the game board.

Listed below are 75 verses that you can use for your "scripture cards." Also listed are the categories that go with each verse.

II Chron 7:14 Prerequisites (*humble, turn, seek, pray*)
    Promises (*hear and heal land*)
Nem 8:6 Positions (*hands lifted, head bowed, face to ground*)
Psalm 5:3 Periods (*in the morning*)
Psalm 32:6 Periods (*while there's still time*)
Psalm 50:15 Prerequisites (*call*)
    Periods (*day of trouble*)
    Promises (*deliverance*)
Psalm 55:17 Periods (*evening and morning, noon*)
    Promises (*He shall hear*)
Psalm 66:18 Pathetic Prayer (*cherish sin in hearts*)
Psalm 88:13 Periods (*morning*)
Psalm 122:6 Petitions (*peace in Jerusalem*)
    Promises (*love Jerusalem shall prosper*)
Psalm 145:18 Prerequisites (*call in truth*)
    Promises (*Lord is near*)
Prov 15:29 Prerequisites (*righteous*)
    Promises (*He hears*)
Prov 28:9 Pathetic Prayer (*refuses to obey the law*)
Isaiah 26:16 Pathetic (*only in distress*)
Isaiah 56:7 Prerequisites (*keep sabbath*)
    Promises (*make joyful*)
Jer 33:3 Prerequisites (*call*)
    Promises (*will answer*)
Jer 42:3 Petitions (*where to go*)
Lam 3:25 Prerequisites (*wait & seek Him*)
    Promises (*Lord is good*)
Matt 5:44 Petitions (*those who use you*)
Matt 6:5 Pathetic Prayer (*seen by men*)
Matt 6:6 Prerequisites (*in secret*)
    Promises (*rewards*)
Matt 6:7 Pathetic (*repeating over and over*)
Matt 6:10 Petitions (*His kingdom come*)
Matt 6:11 Petitions (*daily bread*)
Matt 6:12 Petitions (*forgive our sins*)
    Prerequisites (*as we forgive others*)
Matt 7:7,8 Prerequisites (*ask, seek, knock*)
    Promises (*receives*)
Matt 9:38 Petitions (*Lord will send laborers*)
Matt 18:19-20 Prerequisites (*two agree*)
    Promises (*done for them*)
Matt 21:22 Prerequisites (*believe*)
    Promises (*receive*)

Matt 26:41 Petitions (*enter not into temptation*)
Mark 1:35a Periods (*before day*)
Mark 1:35b Places (*solitary place*)
Mark 11:24 Prerequisites (*believe*)
    Promises (*it will be yours*)
Mark 11:25 Positions (*stand*)
    Prerequisites (*forgive*)
    Promises (*be forgiven*)
Luke 2:37 Periods (*day and night*)
Luke 6:12 Periods (*all night*)
    Places (*to a mountain*)
Luke 11:13 Prerequisites (*ask*)
    Petitions (*for Holy Spirit*)
    Promises (*give Holy Spirit*)
Luke 18:1 Periods (*always*)
Luke 20:47 Pathetic (*long showy prayers*)
Luke 21:36 Petitions (*counted worthy*)
    Periods (*always*)
Luke 22:41 Places (*away*)
    Positions (*knelt down*)
John 9:31 Prerequisites (*does His will*)
    Promises (*He will hear*)
John 14:14 Prerequisites (*in Jesus name*)
    Promises (*God will do it*)
John 15:7 Prerequisites (*abide in me*)
    Petition (*ask what you will*)
    Promises (*it shall be done*)
Acts 8:15 Petitions (*receive Holy Spirit*)
Acts 8:22 Petitions (*forgiveness*)
    Prerequisites (*repent*)
Acts 16:25 Periods (*midnight*)
Acts 21:5 Positions (*knelt down*)
    Places (*seashore*)
Romans 8:26 Promises (*Spirit intercedes*)
Romans 10:1 Petition (*others saved*)
Romans 10:13 Prerequisites (*call*)
    Promises (*be saved*)
I Cor 14:13 Petition (*interpretation*)
Eph 6:18 Periods (*always*)
    Petitions (*for all saints*)
Phil 1:9-11 Petitions (*have fruit of righteousness*)
Phil 4:6,7 Petitions (*in everything*)
    Promises (*peace*)
Col 1:3 Periods (*always*)
Col 1:9 Periods (*don't cease*)
    Petitions (*filled with knowledge, etc.*)
I Thess 5:17 Periods (*without ceasing*)

II Thess 1:11 Petition (*counted worthy and fulfill purposes*)
II Thess 1:12 Petition (*Jesus be glorified and you in Him*)
II Thess 3:1 Petition (*God be glorified*)
I Tim 2:1,2 Petitions (*for all men*)
      Promise (*live peacefully*)
I Tim 2:8 Positions (*lifting up hands*)
      Prerequisites (*without anger*)
James 1:5 Prerequisites (*ask*)
      Promises (*gives*)
      Petitions (*for wisdom*)
James 1:6a Prerequisites (*ask in faith nothing doubting*)
James 1:6b,7 Pathetic (*doubter*)
James 4:2,3 Pathetic (*wrong motives*)
James 5:15 Prerequisites (*faith*)
      Promises (*save the sick*)
James 5:16a Prerequisites (*confess faults*)
      Petitions (*for each other*)
      Promise (*be healed*)

James 5:16b Prerequisites (*earnest, righteous*)
      Promise (*effective*)
I Peter 3:7 Prerequisites (*honor wife*)
      Promises (*prayers not hindered*)
I Peter 3:12 Prerequisites (*righteous*)
      Promise (*He hears*)
I John 1:9 Prerequisites (*confess*)
      Promises (*forgive and cleanse*)
      Petition (*forgiveness*)
I John 3:22 Prerequisites (*keep His commands*)
      Promises (*receive*)
I John 5:14 Prerequisites (*ask according to His will*)
      Promises (*He hears us*)
I John 5:16 Pathetic (*sin that leads to death*)

To maximize learning along with the game, be sure that the kids understand the verses as they are being read. Have them locate in each verse the details of the category that is being discussed. Exactly what is the "promise" in that verse? What are the "prerequisites to prayer" in this verse? And so on. This game should be used as a springboard to further thinking and learning about the role of prayer in their lives. It can be a very effective tool. (Contributed by Sheila Dudney, Bethlehem, Pennsylvania)

PHOBIA MONTH

Here's an idea you need not be afraid to use. Plan a "phobia month" in which you have lessons in areas your kids are finding difficult. To build interest, keep the subject matter of each session a secret except for the name of the related phobia. For example, advertise a discussion on Christmas season depression as "Santa Claustrophobia Night." Here are some other possibilities:

FEAR OF	CONDITION (Name)
aloneness	monophobia
crowds	ochlophobia
darkness	nyctophobia
death	thanataphobia
devil	demonophobia
failure	kakorrhaphiophobia
God	theophobia
hell	hadephobia
jealousy	zelophobia
being looked at	scopophobia
marriage	gamophobia
pain	algophobia
poverty	peniaphobia
responsibility	hypengyophobia
ridicule	categelophobia
school	schoolphobia
sin	hamartophobia
work	ponophobia

Most likely your kids won't have any of these phobias, but they are topics that sometimes can cause fear and concern. Hopefully this will give you a different approach to some important topics for your youth. (Contributed by Aaron Bell, Greenwood, Indiana)

PHONY MATRIMONY

This idea works well as a culmination to a Bible study or seminar done on dating, courtship and marriage. Have the kids take part in a mock wedding ceremony so they can think through the meaning and importance of the tradition.

Planning should begin well in advance of the wedding as many different items will be needed. You may wish to make or purchase wedding announcements, programs, wedding attire (which might be found at the Salvation Army), two dime store rings, rice and an inexpensive cake for the reception that will follow. Announcements should be sent out to each member of the youth group the week of the wedding. You may even want to include your church congregation on the guest list.

> *Pastor Bob and Mary Gail*
> *request the honour of your presence*
> *at the marriage of their students*
> *? ? to ? ?*
> *on Sunday, the eighth of June*
> *nineteen hundred and eighty*
> *at nine, forty-five a. m.*
> *Beverly Park Community Church*
> *Everett, Washington*
>
> *Reception following*

The participants for the wedding can be elected or drawn out of a hat. To add to the excitement, you may wish to wait until right before the wedding ceremony begins before picking the bride and groom at random.

On the day of the wedding you might find it appropriate to lead a discussion on the importance of the marriage ceremony and how it can be used as a worship service. While the ceremony itself should be done with some resemblance of seriousness, a few theatrical mother's tears are to be expected. And whatever happens, make certain that the pretend bride and groom are NOT officially pronounced "man and wife!" (Contributed by Mary Gail Hadley, Everett, Washington)

PROGRESSIVE WORSHIP SERVICE

Here's an interesting way to involve young people in worship. It can be done in a church, in homes, or on a weekend retreat. There really is no limit to its possibilities. It works just like a progressive dinner.

A worship service has a variety of elements, just like a dinner does. By taking each element of worship separately and in a different location, it provides a good opportunity to teach young people about these elements of worship. Acts 2:42 and Colossians 3:16 provide a good scriptural base. Here's one way to do it:

1. *Fellowship:* Begin with some kind of group interaction or sharing that provides a chance for the kids to get to know one another better. Something that would put the kids in a celebrative, but not rowdy mood would be appropriate.
2. *Spiritual Songs:* At the next location, have someone lead the group in a variety of well-known hymns and favorite songs of worship.
3. *Prayer:* Move to another location that provides a good atmosphere for prayer. If outside, a garden would be nice, as Jesus often chose a garden for prayer. Have the kids offer prayer requests, thanksgivings, etc. and have several kids lead in prayer.
4. *Scripture Reading:* At the next location, have several kids read a lesson from the Old Testament, the New Testament, and perhaps the Psalms. Use a modern English translation.
5. *Teaching:* The next stop can be where the sermon is preached. If you prefer, you could accomplish the same thing without being "preachy" by substituting a dialogue sermon, a film, or something of that nature.
6. *Breaking of Bread (Communion):* The last stop can be around the Lord's table, with a communion service. Conduct this however you choose, but it should be a time of celebration and joy.

There are other ingredients that go into worship (like the offering), which you can incorporate into the others or take separately. Design your own progressive worship service, and you can be sure that your group will never forget it. (Contributed by Al Michael, Russiaville, Indiana)

PSALM OF THANKSGIVING

Here's a good creative worship idea that would be most effective at Thanksgiving. Of course, it could be used any other time of the year as well. Have your group meet in small groups and study Psalms 136. They will readily see the repetitious pattern that exists. Point out that in the first nine verses, the psalmist thanks God for the great things He has done for all mankind, and the remainder of the psalm gives thanks for particular actions of God that the Israelites and David would be especially thankful for.

Now challenge each youth to write a statement of thankfulness for one thing *he* is glad God has done. Combine all the statements and a short psalm will have been created. Later on, in the worship service, have a representative (a good loud reader) from each small group be ready with his group's psalm in hand. Begin with someone leading the congregation in a responsive reading of the first nine verses of Psalm 136. The leader will read the first half of each verse, and the congregation will respond, "for His steadfast love endures forever." (RSV) At the conclusion of the first nine verses go right into the psalms you've recently composed. Have each group reader read one line from his group's psalm with the congregation continuing to respond in the same way. Rotate among the readers until all the psalms are completed. If the readers stand in various parts of the room it creates an effective antiphonal reading. (Contributed by Chuck Orwiler, Denver, Colorado)

PUTTING MYSELF IN A BOX

Here's a great way to allow kids to share some deep feelings about themselves with each other. It's a good community-builder and it's fun to do.

First, you'll need to get some boxes, not too big, so that everyone has one. You might try getting those small (about shoe-box size) boxes that department stores have by the thousands in their gift-wrapping department. It's not important that everyone have the same size box, but it is important that they not be too large. You'll also need some magazines, newspapers, scissors, glue, marking pens, and so on.

After everyone has their box, explain that they are to make a collage on the *inside* of the box that represents how they see themselves, or how they feel about themselves. These feelings should be expressed through pictures, words, symbols, or whatever. On the *outside* of the box, they should make a collage that represents how they think others see them—how they are seen through the eyes of people who

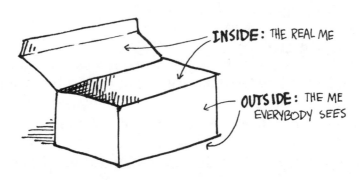

come in contact with them. If they want, they can let each side of the box represent how different people or groups of people see them (they will often be different).

After the boxes have been made (allow enough time), let the kids get into small groups and share their boxes (themselves) with each other. It will help kids to open up with each other in a relatively non-threatening way, and provide a chance for kids to be supportive of one another. Discussion can center on why there is a difference between the inside and the outside of the box, and how we can improve both. (Contributed by Eric Finsand, Azusa, California)

THE RECIPROCAL COMMANDS

If community-building is a priority for your youth group, then this study of the "Reciprocal (i.e. mutual or back and forth) Commands" would be an excellent idea. It helps kids to see that community is not just "good feelings" in a group, but that it requires commitment and responsibility. Here are the "Reciprocal Commands:"

A. COMMANDS BEARING UPON INTER-RELATIONSHIPS:
1. Love one another (Jn. 13:34; 15:12, 17; Rom. 12:9-10; 13:8; Gal. 5:14; I Th. 3:11-12; 4:9-10; Jas. 2:8; I Pet. 1:22; 4:8; I Jn. 3:11, 23; 4:7, 11, 12, 21; 2 Jn. 5; Eph. 5:1; Heb. 13:1).
2. Receive one another (Rom. 15:7).
3. Greet one another (Rom. 16:16; I Cor. 16:20; 2 Cor. 13:12; I Pet. 5:14; Rom. 16:3-6).
4. Have the same care for one another (I Cor. 12:24-25).
5. Submit to one another (Eph. 5:18-21; I Pet. 5:5; Heb. 13:17).
6. Forbear one another (Eph. 5:18-21).
7. Confess your sins to one another (Jas. 5:16).
8. Forgive one another (Eph. 4:31-32; Col. 3:12-13: Matt. 18:21-22; Matt. 5:22).
9. Members of one another (Rom. 12:5).
10. Be of the same mind with one another (Rom. 15:5; Phil. 2:1, 2).
11. Accept one another (Rom. 15:7; 14:1).

B. THE NEGATIVE COMMANDS:
1. Do not judge one another (Rom. 14:13).
2. Do not speak evil of one another (Jas. 4:11).
3. Do not murmur against one another (Jas. 4:11).
4. Do not bite and devour one another (Gal. 5:14-15).
5. Do not provoke one another (Gal. 5:25-26).
6. Do not envy one another (Gal. 5:25-26).
7. Do not lie to one another (Col. 3:9-10).

C. COMMANDS BEARING UPON MUTUAL EDIFICATION:
1. Build up one another (Rom. 14:19; I Th. 5:11).
2. Teach one another (Col. 3:16).
3. Exhort one another (I Th. 5:11; Heb. 3:12-13: Heb. 10:24-25).
4. Admonish one another (Rom. 15:14; Col. 3:16).
5. Speak to one another in psalms, hymns and spiritual songs (Eph. 5:18-20; Col. 3:16).

6. Worship together (Ps. 133:1).
7. Take material care of each other (Deut. 15:7; Rom. 12:13).
8. Honor one another (Rom. 12:10).

D. COMMANDS BEARING UPON MUTUAL SERVICE:
1. Be servants of one another (Gal. 5:13-14: Eph. 5:21: I Pet. 4:9).
2. Bear one another's burdens (Gal. 6:2; Rom. 15:1).
3. Use hospitality to one another (I Pet. 4:7-10).
4. Be kind to one another (Eph. 4:21-22).
5. Pray for one another (Jn. 5:16; Eph. 6:18-19).
6. Be patient with one another (Eph. 4:2).
7. Discipline each other (Gal. 6:1-2; Matt. 18:15; II Thess. 3:14-15).
8. Bearing with one another (Eph. 4:2).

You might begin by having the kids study these commands individually or in pairs. With their Bibles, paper and pencil, they can work on the following instructions:

1. Study the Scripture verses that deal with each of the commands.
2. Write out your own definition of each command.
3. Find a Scriptural example, or non-example, for each command.
4. List the implications, or applications of each command for your personal and relational life.

For group discussion, here are some questions that can be discussed by the group after the individual study on the commands:

1. How many of these responsibilities are getting met in our group?
2. Are there any that surprise you or which you find unreasonable?
3. Are there any which you find impossible to do? Why?
4. Are these responsibilities optional or are they to be expected of all Christians?
5. Is there one you would like to especially see our group work on?
6. How can we apply these commands to our group and make them work?

The above questions and procedures are only suggestions. Add or subtract any that you choose. You might want to take several weeks to study these commands—perhaps by taking only one of the four command groups (A,B,C,D) each week. It would certainly be worth the time. Try to find some practical ways for your group to *apply* the commands, to put them into action, and to see what the results can be. (Contributed by James Taylor, Bellevue, Nebraska)

RECYCLED FILM STRIPS

If your church is "typical", then you probably have some old youth film strips laying around somewhere. Though they are usually outdated or old-fashioned, they can still be used. Find one that is particularly outdated, and show it to the group. The older the better. It is usually a good laugh for the kids, especially if it deals with a topic like "dating" or "good grooming." Afterwards, discuss the film strip. Here are some general discussion questions:

1. Why was the film strip old-fashioned?
2. What was the most outdated thing about it and why?
3. Which principles are still valid and why?
4. How could you update some of the principles of the film strip to apply today?

You may be able to think of more pointed questions depending on the film strip and the topic. You can also do the same with old Sunday School curriculum, youth pamphlets, and the like. (Contributed by Steve Ziemke, Kalispell, Montana)

ROCK MUSIC COUNCIL

This idea deals with rock music and its effect upon young people. Very often the trend in churches is to either forbid rock music (burn the records, etc.) or to just ignore the whole issue. Probably the more sane approach is to allow kids the chance to evaluate the music and make a decision for themselves.

Get a few volunteers in your youth group to form a "rock music council," who will once a month listen to the current "top 20" records and evaluate them carefully. The records can be taped off the radio, purchased, borrowed, or whatever. Sometimes it is possible to get the records free from a local radio station. They usually have lots of extras that they use for promotion. The council should listen to the records, get the lyrics (if possible), and rate the songs in areas like: musical appeal, word content, values of the song (compared to Christian values), hidden meanings (if any), and so on. The results can be shared with the total group, and the kids can decide how to respond. You can get a lot of mileage out of something like this in terms of discussion and interest. (Contributed by Mike Murray, Dallas, Texas)

THE SCIENCE TEST

The topic of cheating is always relevant for young people, since cheating on exams and homework is almost accepted behavior on many campuses. The following situation requires kids to face a tough decision and to respond as they think they might if the situation were real. A few discussion questions are provided to stimulate thought. As you wrap-up the discussion, try to give kids some positive help and guidance rather than condemnation and/or moralizing. Here is th situation (to be read to the group):

You are walking into your science class on a particular day, everyone in the class being rather nervous about a very difficult test coming up the next day. As you sit down at your desk you notice a sheet of paper on the radiator next to you and you inadvertently glance at it. It doesn't take you long to realize that what you are looking at is the master copy for the test being given tomorrow. Before you realize all of what you are doing, you find your eyes carefully reading down the whole page. Your friend behind you, out of curiosity, looks over where he sees you are staring and also realizes what it is. Before long a small crowd has gathered around the test, and around your desk, all rapidly soaking in the questions, some even writing them down. Upon hearing the teacher approaching, they scatter to their seats, leaving the paper exactly where it was, next to you. As soon as the teacher enters he asks if anyone has seen a ditto master, and both automatically as well as prudently, you respond that there is one here next to you. As the teacher comes to pick it up, he looks at you and says, "This is tomorrow's test. Do you know if anyone looked at it?" You feel as if the eyes of the world are upon you. How will you respond?

Discussion:

1. How will you respond? What are the various options that you have?
2. What will be the outcome of each of the options?
3. What would be the motivation behind each of the options?
4. Why would it be so hard to do the right thing?
5. What is at stake in each of the options?
6. What does it reveal about values?

(Contributed by Jim Walton, Fitchburg, Massachusetts)

SENSE SCRIPTURES

Here's a good way to add a new dimension to your next Bible study or lesson that involves a Bible passage. To begin, read the passage to the group and then explain that you are going to read it again while they (the group) close their eyes and tell you what they "sense" from the story or situation. In other words, you want them to put themselves into the actual scene of the incident being described as you read. Then they are to tell you what they see, hear, smell, taste, and feel. With the active imaginations that most kids have, the results should be exciting.

For example. when Jesus calmed the storm in Matthew 8, responses might sound like this:

SEE—dark clouds, lightning, big waves, seagulls
HEAR—thunder, splashing, men hollering, boat creaking
TASTE—water, salt, cottonmouth (fear), lunch coming up
FEEL—seasick, the boat rocking, the humidity, the cold

SMELL—rain, salt, wet people who smell bad anyway, fish

On the "feel" part, you might want to consider *emotional* feelings as well—fear, anger (because Jesus was sleeping), confusion, frustrations. etc. This approach can really help young people to relate to the Bible in a fresh and intimate way. (Contributed by John Collins, Houston, Texas)

SYMBOL WALK

The New Testament Gospels use many different symbols and metaphors to explain spiritual realities. The following Symbol Walk is designed to help your kids come into a personal understanding of the meaning of these different symbols.

Before you begin, you will need seven separate rooms (Sunday School rooms would be ideal) and the following items: a candle, a book of matches, paper plates, a few ounces of salt, a bowl filled with water, paper cups, mustard seeds or other small seeds, a sewing needle, a loaf of bread, and a couple of apples sliced into sections.

To begin, divide the kids into smaller groups of 4-6 people. It is important that each group have a sponsor with them, so be sure to have enough lay helpers present. Explain to the kids that they are going to be visiting seven rooms with seven different common-place objects in them. Their task is simple: they are to exhaustively describe the objects in each room. The accompanying sponsor should make sure that they only describe the objects, *not* explain their uses or any meaning they might hold. They can use all of their senses (taste, smell, etc.) in describing the object. "The pile of salt is white; each particle is very small; all of the particles appear to be the same size; the individual particles are not pure white but are almost transparent; there is a shiny quality to the particles; the particles feel hard; the shape of the salt particles is square; their taste is not sweet; there is no smell to the pile of salt until your nose is an inch away from it; etc."

After the description is complete, the sponsor should read the Gospel verse which uses the object as a metaphor. The small group can then spend a few minutes reflecting on why that particular object was used in the verse. When finished, they can then move on to the next room and begin the description-reflection process again. Here are some of the symbols you might wish to use:

SYMBOL	VERSE
Light (candle)	John 1:1-9
Salt	Matt. 5:13
Water	Matt. 3:13-17
Mustard Seeds	Matt. 17:20

Bread	John 6:50, 51
Needle	Matt. 19:23, 24
Apple	Matt. 7:16, 17

After all of the rooms have been visited by each group, bring the kids together and discuss the Symbol Walk. You may want to go over the verses again and discuss the meaning of the objects used in the verses. Here are some possible questions you might want to use along with your own:

1. Which stop made the biggest impression on you?
2. What new things did you learn about the objects which you carefully described?
3. Why do you think symbols are used in the Bible?
4. Think of some other symbols and metaphors that could be used in place of the ones in the verses.

(Adapted from an idea contributed by Vicky Roark and Sam Deputy, Plant City, Florida)

TEN-MINUTE ALL-NIGHT PRAYER MEETING

All night prayer meetings are not very common with most youth groups these days. In fact, they aren't all that common, period. But, they can be very meaningful and effective, especially for the participants. The problem with long prayer meetings (for most people) is endurance, or lack of it, and the fact that it is difficult to pray for more than two or three minutes at a time, let alone two or three hours. But this idea—*Ten Minute All Night Prayer Meeting*—just might be the answer to problems like these, particularly for youth groups.

Here's how it is done. The prayer meeting starts at midnight. This could be a gathering of the committed kids in your group following a youth group activity, a concert, or something similar. They should be adequately prepared—that is, aware of the need for "continuous" prayer and the power of prayer. A Friday night would be ideal.

Each hour is then broken down into six ten-minute sections. The first hour would go something like this:

12:00—12:10 *Concern for Each Other:* A map of the world is on the wall showing all the major continents. Someone takes a dart or a suction-cup gun and shoots it at the map until one of the countries or continents is hit. The leader then gives some information on the needs in that area of the world, and the group joins in prayer for those needs.

12:10—12:20 *Concern for Each Other:* Break into small groups.

Give them a subject, like family, school, friends, God's Will, etc. The kids then share in their small groups their needs in that area and pray for each other. Next hour, kids will form new groups.

12:20—12:30 *Random Needs:* Prepare ahead of time on small slips of paper a number of prayer requests that you know of—for people in the church, things in the news, whatever. Roll them up and put them in balloons and hang them on a bulletin board. One person tosses a dart to try and pop a balloon. The paper inside the popped balloon is read to the group and the kids spend some time praying for that special need. If you have a lot of these, then take two or three of them each hour to pray for.

12:30—12:40 *Teaching Time:* Have someone prepare a ten minute talk or some kind of learning strategy for each hour at this time dealing with the subject of prayer. One good way to do this would be to break the Lord's Prayer down into five or six sections, and cover one part of the prayer each hour.

12:40—12:50 *Youth Group Needs:* The emphasis this time is on special needs within the youth group itself. A different need can be taken each hour, selected in similar fashion to the "Random Needs" section. Be creative here. You can devise any number of novel ways to choose a need each hour. You can draw them out of a hat, put them in milk bottles and try knocking them over from a distance with a tennis ball, etc. Once the need has been selected, however, spend some serious time in prayer for that particular need.

12:50—1:00 *Break:* This is the time for some refreshments and fun. Play a game, serve some refreshments, give kids a chance for a potty break, etc. Don't leave this part out.

The whole cycle starts over again at 1:00 and continues until morning. The whole experience can be wrapped up with breakfast, perhaps prepared by some mom's who get up early and do the honors.

Obviously, the key to this is the variety and the mixing of fun activities with serious prayer. Use your own judgment on how to plan something like this. It has been found that kids will really respond well to this, and for some it can be a genuine life-changing experience. (Contributed by Spencer Nordyke, Dallas, Texas)

THEOLOGICAL FICTIONARY

If your young people sometimes get stumped trying to figure out the meanings of those big "theological" words, here's a game that will whittle those words down to size. It's played like the game "Dictionary" found in an earlier volume of *IDEAS*.

Simply make a list of those words, like "justification," "atonement," "sanctification," "vicarious," etc., and read them to the group. Taking the words one at a time, have each person come up with a definition for that word. The correct definition is not given by the leader until after everyone has given their definition. If a person is not sure, then they should just make up a definition that sounds good.

Scoring is as follows:

1. For getting the correct definition—five points.
2. For each time someone agrees with your "phony" definition—five points.

As the game progresses, it would be wise to "rotate," so that each person has a chance to be the first guesser (hence improving their chances that someone will go along with their definition). Also, you might want to allow kids to change their answer after all the definitions have been given (but before the "official" correct definition has been given). The person with the most points is the winner of the game. You'll be surprised at the ingenuity of your kids to come up with wild new theological definitions. You can use this game with ordinary words, too. (Contributed by Rick Harris. Minneapolis, Minnesota)

WALK A MILE IN MY SHOES

Here's a clever idea for a retreat or series of meetings. The theme is "shoes," and it can be tied in nicely with the basic ideas of "walking with Christ," or " putting yourself in the shoes of others," and so on. The shoe theme can be incorporated throughout the event, using "shoe-shaped" posters for publicity, "shoe games" (see the Games Chapter of this book), name tags shaped like shoes, and the like. The title "Walk a Mile in My Shoes" is the name of an old popular song by Joe South, and you might want to use it for some group singing. The following are some suggestions for learning and group interaction:

1. *Shoelace Sharing:* Give each person a shoelace. Have them, one at a time, wrap the shoelace around their finger, telling one thing about themselves with each time they wrap the shoelace. Shoelaces should be of various lengths.

2. *Shoe Search:* Have all persons put their feet inward (so that the group forms a figure similar to the spokes of a wagon wheel). Have each person pick a shoe (in the circle) that they feel they are like and tell why.

3. *Important Steps:* Give each person a sheet of paper and a pencil. Have them write down 15-20 important "steps" in their lives. These could be events, people, decisions, etc. Allow time for

some small group sharing, but don't force them to share things they don't want to.

4. *When the Shoe Fits:* Print up the following list of incomplete statements so that each person has one. Allow them time to complete the sentences, and then have them pair off and share their answers.

> I often feel *worn-out* because. . .
> One thing I am really *tight-laced* about is. . .
> One thing (from my *"sole"*) that I would really like to share with others is. . .
> One thing in my life that may really be *wearing a hole* in me (putting a lot of strain on me) is. . .
> One thing I really like to "wag my *tongue*" about (talk a lot about) is. . .
> A time that I feel that I was really *stepped on* was when. . .
> A memorable *step* (time) in my life was. . .
> One thing I've been a real *heel* about lately is. . .
> A person's shoes that I would really like to fill is. . .

5. *Wear My Shoe:* Have each member of the group write down a problem that they have and place it in a shoebox. Then have the kids draw out a problem (not theirs) and offer a solution to the problem. The leader may want to "fatten the box" with other situations. Spend about five minutes (or less) on each problem.

6. *Walking With God:* Have the group write answers to the following questions:

God first felt close to me when:
The time I felt closest to God was when:
The time I felt farthest away from God was when:
I would like my relationship with God to be:

7. *Coat of Feet:* This is like a "Coat of Arms," only you use a shoe diagram, with a number of compartments, like the one pictured. Give everyone a copy of the diagram and have them draw or write something different in each section, like: Something they have learned about themselves, something they have learned about others, something they have learned about God, a phrase to summarize the week, and a dream or goal they have for themselves.

There are also other ideas from past volumes of *IDEAS* which can be used (with a shoe or "foot" theme). You can also use "foot terminology" throughout such as:

"Shoebox" (small group—for sharing, discussion)
"Shoelaces" (time for "tightening things up"—summarizing)
"A Really Big Shoe" (Talent Show)
"Happy Feet" (Dance)

With a little creativity, something like this can go over great with either junior high or high school youth. (Contributed by Susan Norman, Kernersville, North Carolina)

WHO'S WHO—THEN AND NOW

Here's something that is not only a good discussion starter, but a good crowd breaker as well. You will need to compose and print up two "quizzes," putting one on each side of the same piece of paper. One quiz is titled "Who's Who—NOW" and it consists of twenty or so questions concerning people in your church. Here are some sample questions:

1. Who works at Winchell's Donuts?
2. Who is the chairman of our church board?
3. Who teaches our sixth grade class?
4. Who puts the sermon titles up on the church sign each week?
5. Who is in charge of getting the church bus ready for Sunday?

On the other side of the sheet is a second quiz: "Who's Who—THEN." There should be the same number of questions as the other quiz, but this one is about people in the Bible. Here are some sample questions:

1. Who built the first temple in Jerusalem?
2. Who led the "exodus" out of Egypt?
3. Who did Jesus raise from the dead in the Gospel of John?
4. Who was the first murderer?
5. Who took a ride inside a fish?

Everybody takes both quizzes and their score is based on the number of correct answers on each quiz. Each person will have a score which is a fraction, with the answer to the first quiz on top and the answer to the second quiz on the bottom. For instance, a score of 16/19 means 16 correct on the quiz about people in the church, and 19 correct on the Bible quiz. Scores are then compared, and it will be surprising to see just how much they vary. Discussion can then center on the relative importance of how much we know about people in the Bible and how much we know about people in the church. Is it good to learn all about people in the Bible and not know each other very well? Or vice-versa? Is one more important than the other or are they equally important? These questions are both thought provoking and significant. (Contributed by Wilber Griffith, South Gate, California)

YOUR MAJESTY

Here's a good discussion starter that deals with popularity, fame, and related topics. The activity begins with a few games. Any games will do, but the first one should produce an individual "winner." A game like "People Bingo" in *IDEAS Numbers One through Four* would be a good one.

The winner of the first game is then pronounced to be the "King" or the "Queen" for the rest of the night. For the rest of the meeting, or during the games that follow (this is up to you), everyone is to treat that person just like they were royalty. If the King (or Queen) asks you to do something, you must do it (go get him a drink of water, kiss his ring, act like a pillow for sitting upon, etc.). At the same time, everyone is to bow down to or salute the King or Queen whenever the occasion arises, and they must address him or her by using a variety of favorable titles. No one may use the same title they already used, but they may use one that someone else has used. Here are some sample permissable titles:

1. Your Loveliness
2. Your Majesty
3. Your Highness
4. Your Intelligence
5. Your Talentedship
6. Your Grace
7. Your Sweetness
8. Your Muscle-boundness
9. Your Handsomeness

Kids can be creative with this part of it. As the next game progresses, the King or Queen may or may not play (whatever he/she wants) and if he feels slighted in the least by someone ("Your Ugliness!"), or if a command is not obeyed, then that person may be thrown out of the game (banishment from the kingdom, put in stocks, etc.), or some other punishment administered. Make sure that you as the leader are exempt from the peasantry—so that you can keep some semblance of law and order in the midst of the chaos that might develop.

You can play as many games as you want during the "reign" of the royal one. Following the game time, the ruler may be "dethroned" and the following questions can then be discussed.

First, to the ex-Ruler:

1. Did you feel special?
2. How did it feel being the center of attention?

3. Do you wish this could be an everyday experience?
4. How do you think everyone else felt?
5. Is this how movie stars and politicians feel?

Then, to the whole group:

1. Did you feel like a nobody?
2. Did you envy the attention he or she was getting?
3. Do some people deserve to be treated better than others?
4. Do you have family or friends who seem better treated than you? How do you feel towards them?
5. Is there someone you know who is a "class pet?" What do you think of them?
6. Was Jesus a popular person? How did these groups treat Him: Family? Friends? Apostles? The People? Pharisees and Sadducees? The Romans? Satan? God the Father?
7. Where do you think you stand in God's sight? What about famous people?

These questions are just starters of course; perhaps you could add to them. Depending on the answers given or your own personal choice of themes, this activity could lead to a discussion on being "popular" or in "the in group," or on the subject of fame. Or it could lead to the concept of one's self-image and the desire to be special versus feelings of inferiority, or feeling just average. There are numerous passages and personalities in the Scriptures that could be used as well. There are plenty of passages indicating how special or famous we are to the Lord, such as 1 Peter 1:9-10, 1 John 3:1-3, and Ephesians 2:4-7. (Contributed by Mark Prestridge, Deerfield Beach, Florida)

Chapter Four

Special Events

AGING SCAVENGER HUNT

Divide into teams and give each one a list of years (1982, 1981, etc.) from the present year working backwards for about thirty years. Now the kids have to go out and see how many items they can bring back that have those years marked on them (indelibly). They can bring back license plates, coins, drivers licenses, books with copyright dates printed on them, deeds, certificates, and so on. You can specify that only one item per date is allowed or that only one kind of item per team is allowed. In other words, if the team brings back a book with the date 1964 printed on it, then they cannot use a book for any other date. This forces them to be a little more creative than bringing back a whole pile of books. Set a time limit, and the team with the most years matched up with items wins. (Contributed by Dan Brandell, Livonia, Michigan)

ALL-CHURCH OLYMPICS

Here's a way for your church to have its own Summer Olympic Games. Divide the entire congregation up into "nations," or just make the youth group one country and the rest of the church the other country. You will need an "Olympic committee" to organize and schedule the events over a period of a month, with different events slated for each week. An "opening ceremony" can kick things off, and a "closing ceremony" can wrap things up. You will need to obtain awards (gold, silver, and bronze medals) for the winners in each event.

Events can include both individual and team competition. Volleyball, racquetball, tennis, pool, bowling, tug-o-wars, frisbee throwing, cow chip tossing, anything that you can think up. You will need events that the older folk can participate in (like horseshoes or darts) and events for the children (relays, bike riding, etc.). Something like this can really perk up a dull summer and draw your entire congregation closer together. (Contributed by John Herbert Jaffry, Alton, Illinois)

ATARI OLYMPICS

Now that just about everybody has one of those video-game attachments for their television sets, why not have an evening of competition and fun with them? Get several portable T.V. sets and a video-game unit for each one, with as many game cartridges as you can get. You can have either team or individual competition. Print up in advance some score sheets with the name of each game (Pac-Man, Laser-Blast, Combat, Asteroids, etc.) and a place for scores to be recorded. Set up a rotation system so that everyone has a chance to play equally on each game.

This can also be done at a "Video-Arcade" if you can arrange to take over one of those places for a night, or if you can get a special deal on the tokens that are used in them. Promote it well, serve refreshments, provide prizes for the best scores, worst scores, etc. You might also pick some "secret" scores in advance (put them in sealed envelopes) and whoever comes closest to hitting them wins a prize. Use your own creativity and this event can be a real winner. (Contributed by Tom Hopewell, Springfield, Ohio)

BLIZZARD BLAST

Here's a special event or party idea that would be great for a hot day. The theme is "snow" or "ice" and you play games that incorporate that theme. Teams can have names like "The Icicles," "The Snowdrifts," "The Snowflakes," and so on. Here are some sample games that you can play:

1. *Snowball Fight:* Teams wad up stacks of newspaper into "snowballs" and throw them into the other team's "territory." The team with the least amount of snow in their territory at the end of the game is the winner.
2. *Ice Melting Contest:* Each team gets a block of ice and must try to melt it using only their hands (rubbing it). The ice is weighed at the beginning of the game and again after the game is over. The ice block that has lost the most weight wins. The game can go for about ten to fifteen minutes.
3. *Mining for Marbles:* Team members try to find marbles hidden in a large pan of crushed ice. . .using only their toes.
4. *Ski Relay:* Make skis (old shoes nailed to strips of wood) and have the kids put them on and race in them. You can also do this with snowshoes.
6. *Snowman Feed:* Hold a pie-eating contest, using lots of whipped cream. No hands are allowed.

If done during the winter, or if you live somewhere where you can go to the snow (like up in the mountains), then you can add some "authentic" snow games. Refreshments can include varieties of ice cream, snow cones, iced tea, and so on. Use your own creativity and this event can be a lot of fun. (Contributed by Robert McDonald, Des Moines, Iowa)

BLOW-OUT II

This is a sequel to the Blow Out in *IDEAS Number 1-4*. In fact, by combining this idea with that one (and the Blow Out III that follows), you will have the ultimate "tire" event of all time. Invite all the "big wheels" in your group to come in their grubby clothes and play the following games:

1. *Tire Scavenger Hunt:* Divide into teams and have the kids go out and find one tire (no rim or wheel) for each person in the group. The first team to return is the winner. Set a time limit. They are not allowed to go to tire stores or service stations, nor are they allowed to swipe tires without asking permission. If a team is unable to find enough tires for their whole team in the time limit, have some extras on hand so that everybody has one.

2. *Obstacle Course:* Arrange the tires into an obstacle course that the kids must run through. One tire can be set on its end (standing) with someone holding it up (or it could be hung from a rope). Another set of tires could be set up in a slalom course, and another set laid flat on the ground, side by side (like those that a football team uses for exercises and to teach coordination).

3. *Pit Crew Contest:* One kid stands at the starting line. Eight tires are placed over his head and stacked, with him in the center. When all eight tires are stacked, he then moves to the finish line, ten feet away. There the tires are unstacked, one at a time. Do this with several different people being in the middle, but leave the pit crew the same. They may help him move with the tires.

4. *Indy 500:* Each team lines up, in single file, with one tire to be their race car. Your race track needs to be an oval shape with something sturdy to mark the corners. Each team member must make at least one lap of the track, rolling the tire.

To add to the flavor, you should have someone on hand in a striped shirt, with a checkered flag. A good refreshment would be donuts (tire shaped) and cider (looks like gasoline). There are also plenty of other races that can be run if time allows, like a "three man, two tire race" (where one person lies inside the two tires while the others

push), a "tire toss" (for distance), tire painting and lots more. Be creative and your group will never "tire" of this one. (Contributed by Hal Herwick, St. Charles, Missouri)

BLOW-OUT III

Here are a few more games to incorporate into your big "Blow Out":

1. *Tire Transfer:* This event is timed. You stack a bunch of tires at one spot and the team must transfer and stack the tires at another spot about thirty feet away as quickly as possible.
2. *Tire Toss:* Kids compete to see who can throw a tire the farthest distance.
3. *Tire Stack:* See which team can stack, one on top of the other, the highest stack of tires.
4. *Tire Ball Toss:* Place tires at different distances from a line behind which players toss softballs or bean bags. The tires farther away are given higher point values. Each person gets the same number of tosses to try and get as many points as possible.

(Contributed by Dan Scholten, Rhinelander, Wisconsin)

BLUE JEAN BANQUET

This is an informal banquet in which the only acceptable dress code is to wear blue jeans. The best setting is an old barn or some other rural setting, with wooden tables and bales of hay for seats, etc. Then give awards for the oldest blue jeans, dirtiest blue jeans, clean jeans, best fitting jeans, best decorated jeans, and so on. You can give away blue jeans for door prizes, and you just might even get a local pants store to donate them. This could be combined with "The Pants Game" in *IDEAS Number 26*. (Contributed by Doug Crabb, Piedmont, Oklahoma)

BACK TO SCHOOL NIGHT

Here's a good idea for a high-school end-of-the-summer event. Decorate the location (wherever you hold this event) in a "school" motif, and have the kids arrive early enough that they won't be "tardy." Each kid can bring a lunch-pail or a sack lunch to make it really seem like school. Before the event begins, the kids can gather in the "school yard" and play hopscotch, foursquare, and other "playground" games. Get a buzzer or school bell to start the action.

The first step is "Orientation," in which the "principal" explains what is going to happen. Then divide into "classes" (teams) for all the games. Each class will get a grade (A,B,C,D or F) for how they do in the games. At the end, the "grade point average" is figured out to determine the winning class. Here are some ideas for the games (you can play any games you want under the headings below).

1. *Home Room:* The "Barnyard" game from *IDEAS 1-4* would be a good one.
2. *English Class:* Kids could act out "What I did during the summer." Each class presents a skit or charade while other classes try to guess the activity. The leaders ("teachers") judge for the best job and assign grades.
3. *Speech Class:* Any game that involves speaking, like the old "Gossip" game.
4. *Science Class:* Perhaps a scavenger hunt of some kind.
5. *Study Hall:* Maybe a word game of some kind, like "Hangman." Each group can be given a word to guess.
6. *Gym Class:* Any game that involves physical activity.
7. *Lunch:* Any game that involves food, like an egg toss.
8. *Pep Rally:* Some singing, any rowdy activity that gets everybody yelling, cheering, etc.

(Contributed by Fred Coates, Mooresville, North Carolina)

BUBBLE BUST

Here's a crazy event that your kids will enjoy. Get some dishwashing soap and make blowing hoops out of any old wire, or go out and buy the commercial stuff, but have enough for everyone. Besides having a free-for-all blowing bubbles try these ideas.

1. Form groups of three, one blowhard, one counter and one stopper. See who can get the most bubbles in the air before the first bubble hits the floor. It's the job of the stopper to say "stop blowing" when the first bubble hits the floor. This is a team effort and the counter has to be quick and honest. If they pop before he can count them they don't count. Do this inside or the wind will give you trouble. Rotate the blowhard, counter and stopper and continue. Add up the individuals' score and the overall team score.

2. Bounce the bubbles. How many times can you bounce one

bubble off another bubble that is resting on the hoop. If the bounced bubble is swallowed up by the bubble on the hoop, count that as a bounce and continue on. If your hoop bubble breaks, catch another one and continue on until time is called. Set a one minute time limit and rotate the team as above. One person needs to be blowing bubbles for another member of the team to bounce, the third member is the counter.

3. Bubble burst. How many bubbles can you burst with a toothpick in a given time period. Variation: hold toothpick in your mouth.

4. Nose blow. Blow bubbles with your nose. Make sure nobody has a runny nose who tries this or you may have more bubbles than you desire.

You may want to make this a part of a Bubbles theme for the night by adding bubble gum blowing contests, or balloon bubbles, etc. (Contributed by Richard Moore, Vista, California)

BUS BANQUET

Here's a unique idea for a banquet. Decorate the inside of your church bus to fit the occasion (Christmas, Valentines, etc.). Then save the back two seats for the food. Have your sponsors act as stewardesses and stewards. Serve one dish at a time while driving around town or wherever. This can be a really fun experience and a change of pace from the normal banquet. (Contributed by Rick Wheeler, Springfield, Missouri)

BUS WASH

Fill some water balloons with soap and water. Fill others just with water. Throw them at the bus while washing it. Use mops to scrub the top and sides. You can even have a water balloon fight inside the bus with teams at each end (no soap, though, it gets in the eyes). This helps make a big job fun! (Contributed by Mark Reed, Creve Coeur, Missouri)

CAROLING TREASURE HUNT

Here's a great way to go Christmas caroling this year. Divide into "Caroling Groups" of between six and ten people each and make a treasure hunt out of it. Each group is given a first "clue" which (when figured out) gives the location of the first place where they are to sing Christmas carols. It could be at someone's home, at a rest home, at a shopping center, or anywhere you choose. The group must go there and sing at least four Christmas carols (chosen ahead of time) all the way through, ending with "We Wish You a Merry Christmas." They pick up the next clue at that location (or they might have the next clue already with them in a sealed envelope), and then head for the next location, and so on. It could be worked out so that none of the caroling groups duplicate locations, or some locations could get lots of carolers in one night. The last destination can be the location of a Christmas party with refreshments and games.

CHURCH CHALLENGE

If you've ever wondered why churches in your area don't do more things together, it's probably because no one ever bothered to set anything up. So why don't you? Invite three to five other youth groups in town to come and participate in a volleyball, softball, or basketball tournament. You could substitute other crazier games for any of those, of course, so long as they are fun and involve everyone. Award a trophy to the church that accumulates the most number of wins. This could turn out to be an annual event. Close with some refreshments, some singing, and give the kids a chance to get to know each other better. The rewards will be great. (Contributed by Daniel Turner, Duncanville, Texas)

COLLEGE SURVIVAL KIT

Here's something you can give to your graduating seniors who are heading off for college this year. Purchase a nice gift box (about the size of a cigar box), and fill it with the items below, or similar items. Label it "Your College Survival Kit," include "instructions for use" and wrap it up. These kits can then be presented at your graduation banquet, social event, or church service. It will go over great.

Here's what the survival kit can include:

1. A small tin of aspirin—for the headaches of registration.
2. Some kleenex tissue—for tears of loneliness while you're away.
3. Pepto Bismol tablets—for your first meal in the college cafeteria.
4. A Granola bar—for added nutrition while studying late at night.
5. A small toy—for something to do between classes.
6. A ball—because we want you to really have a ball!
7. Hershey's kisses—because we love you!

Your own creativity can add or change items on this list, but make it a lighthearted way of letting your graduates know that you care about them. You might even have the freshmen, sophomores, and juniors contribute the money and put the survival kit together for a little added meaning. (Contributed by Marilyn Dear, Jackson, Louisiana)

CRAZY CAROLING CONTEST

Here's another creative way to go Christmas caroling this year, if your group likes a little more excitement than the usual way. Divide into caroling "teams" and print up the following sheet so that each group has one. Everybody starts from the same place, and returns at the end of a specified time, or when they have completed all ten items. Have a party afterwards.

CRAZY CAROLING CONTEST

INSTRUCTIONS:

(1) Go to houses in the neighborhood and at each house sing a carol while following one of the directions below.

(2) After you have completed the carol, get the signature of a resident of the house in the space provided.

(3) Do a different number at each house, only one per house.

(4) 30 minute time limit. Do all you can in that time.

(5). Have fun and spread some Christmas cheer!

CAROLING DIRECTIONS:

1. Sing all verses of a carol (in the book) backwards_____

2. Sing a carol over the phone to Charlie (889-0781)
    _____

3. Sing a carol sitting crosslegged (Indian Style) on the porch_____

4. Sing a carol opera style_____

5. Form a human pyramid and sing a carol
    _____

6. Sing a carol to someone under 5 years old.
    _____

7. Sing a carol in a kitchen
    _____

8. Sing a carol around a Christmas tree
    _____

9. Sing a carol to someone over 60 years old.
    _____

10. Sing all 3 verses of "Deck the Hall" (pg. 14) and act out all the lines (everyone participates - and ham it up.
    _____

(Contributed by Charlie Cornett, Scottsdale, Arizona)

CRAZY ROCK CONCERT

Everyone would like to be on TV, but few really make it. Here is a chance for your whole group to become stars.

Have your kids come dressed as one of their favorite recording stars and bring one of their records. Then have them imitate the star to the music.

No real instruments can be used. They will need to make these ahead of time (i.e. a guitar would be a tennis racket, a set of drums may be made from trash cans). The only noise you will hear is the record.

Record the show on a video system that can be played back that night. There is nothing better than seeing yourself on TV. (Contributed by Rodney L. Puryear, Birmingham, Alabama)

DRIVE-IN MOVIE NIGHT

If your church has a big parking lot, or if you have another large area that's useable, here's a great event that can be used as a fundraiser, or just for fun. Get a large movie screen and set it up on one end of the parking lot. If you have a building adjacent to the parking lot, you might be able to just hang the screen over the side of the building. You will also need a 16 mm projector, and a few large speakers. And of course, you will need a movie to show.

You can then have a drive-in movie in your church parking lot and invite all of your church and neighborhood to come. If you are in a heavily populated neighborhood, you may need to check with local ordinances, or with the neighbors, about the potential noise that might be generated. If that is a problem, then you might want to try and find a parking area that is far enough away from houses as to not be a problem.

You can charge admission per car or per person. You can also set up a refreshment stand and sell soft drinks, popcorn, and candy. Make sure you do it on a warm night, and encourage people to bring chairs, chaise lounges, and so on. Be sure and book a good film that everyone would want to see, as well as a couple of shorts (like cartoons) and advertise it well. You might even put an ad in the theater section of your local newspaper. With plenty of advance planning and enthusiasm, an event like this can be a real success. (Contributed by Ray Peterson, St. Paul, Minnesota)

EGGSTRAVAGANZA

How about an event based totally on eggs? Here are some things you could do:

1. Play a few games from previous *IDEAS* books that incorporate the use of eggs, like "The Egg and Armpit Relay" (*IDEAS* #1), "The Great Chicken Race" (*IDEAS* #7), "The Egg Toss" (*IDEAS* #1), "The Egg Drop" (*IDEAS* #13), "The Egg and Spoon Relay" (*IDEAS* #3), "Water Eggs" (*IDEAS* #1), and so on. There are lots of these to choose from.

2. Use one of the crazy "quizzes" from previous *IDEAS* books. Whoever gets the best score wins the "Egghead Award."

3. For background music, see if you can get a copy of the record "In the Mood," by the "Henhouse Five." If you can't, how about getting some good "cluckers" together and make your own "chicken" music?

4. For refreshments, serve egg salad sandwiches, omelettes, quiche pie, "Egg McMuffins", and the like.

(Contributed by Dave Hodgson, El Paso, Texas)

FAST FOOD FOLLIES

Here's an event that is fun and delicious, too. Each kid brings a specified amount of money (not too much, but enough to handle a normal meal at a fast food place). Divide into teams which travel by car to various fast food locations around town. Each team is given a list like the one below. You'll have to adapt the list for the fast foods that are available in your area.

_____A double hamburger from Wendys
_____One scoop of chocolate ice cream from Baskin Robbins
_____One hush-puppie from Long John Silvers
_____One apple turnover from Burger Chef
_____One bag of fries from Burger King
_____One hamburger from White Castle
_____One cheese coney from Gold Star Chili
_____One taco from Taco Bell
_____One chicken leg from Kentucky Fried
_____One peanut butter shake from Dairy Queen
_____One liver or gizzard from Famous Recipe
_____One root beer float from A&W
_____One roast beef sandwich from Arbys
_____One burrito from Zantigo's
_____One ICEE from 7-11
_____One TAB from Frisch's

The team can pool their money and decide which team member eats which item at each location. When that person eats the specified item, they sign the list next to that item. Set a time limit and the team that completes the list first, or that has the most items checked off, is the winner. Use adult drivers and make sure there's no speeding, rudeness at the various locations, etc. (Contributed by Doug Newhouse, Florence, Kentucky)

GOOFY GOLF

For a junior high or high school party, build your own miniature golf course. Go to a sporting goods store or a golf pro shop and buy nine tin putting cups (about $1.50 apiece). They're not hard to find. Either have kids bring a putter and a golf ball or find some putters to use and buy some inexpensive balls. Your local golf course probably has some old putters they would let you use. Then, set up a 9-hole miniature golf course. Do it in your church basement, youth room, or gymnasium. It can go up ramps, through water traps, down stairs, and all over. Use tape on the floor for tee-off boxes Use old 2 x 4's for banking the balls (save the woodwork). Make a night of it and have tournament prizes and score cards. Kids love the fun and competition! (Contributed by Steve Ziemke, Kalispell, Montana)

GROTESQUE SCAVENGER HUNT

This crazy scavenger hunt idea can be done at any time during the year, but would probably go over the best during the ghoulish season of Halloween. Like most scavenger hunts, kids are divided into teams and sent out with a list of items to bring back. Here is the list:

1. 1/4 cup or more of ketchup
2. 1 raw egg
3. 1 bone (any kind)
4. 1/4 cup or more of mustard (or horseradish)
5. 1/2 cup of leftover vegetables (any kind)
6. 1/2 cup flour
7. Any portion of jello or pudding
8. Two inches of toothpaste
9. Any portion of leftover meat (any kind)
10. 1/2 cup of leftover coffee or tea

Each team should be sent out with 10 small "zip-lock" plastic sandwich bags that will hold each of the items listed. Each team should also appoint a captain, who must be courageous and daring. The captain can organize the scavenger hunt.

After the teams return with the items on the list, the next stage of the event may begin. The captain should be seated in a chair, in front of a table where there is a bowl. The rest of the team should be about 20 feet away. Each team member must bring one of the bags collected on the scavenger hunt and (one at a time) deposit the contents into the bowl. (The egg must be cracked and the shell thrown away.) After all the contents of all ten bags are in the bowl, the last person must stir the whole mess around ten times, take one big spoonful and feed it to the team captain. After the captain swallows it, he must stand up and shout, "My compliments to the chef!" The first team to complete this wins.

A slightly simpler version of this would be to skip the scavenger hunt and to provide all the ingredients for the teams. That way you would have a little more control over the cleanliness of the food items. Of course if you choose to go with the scavenger hunt, lay down some rules like: only one food item per house may be collected; no item can come from the garbage, and so on. (Contributed by Gary Harris, Sepulveda, California)

GROUNDHOG BANQUET

Do something really different next year and put on a "Groundhog Banquet" on Groundhog Day (February 2). If you make a big deal out of it, it will generate a lot of interest and excitement. By writing the Chamber of Commerce in Punxsutawney, Pennsylvania (where Groundhog Day originated), you can have them send you some colorful brochures that tell all about the history of Groundhog Day. You can also get souvenir groundhog statues, glasses, notepaper, decals, pennants, and all kinds of good groundhog things from them. The address is 123 S. Gilpin, Punxsutawney, PA 15767.

For the banquet, you can call the various dishes things like "Groundhog Stew," "Groundhog Pie," and so on. You could have a "shadow casting" contest by having contestants try to create the most interesting shadow against the wall (you could use a slide projector for light). You could play some games with groundhog names, "Groundhog Relay," "Catch the Groundhog," and so on. And you could sing some Groundhog carols like those below. With a little creativity, this could be the highlight of the year!

I'M DREAMING OF THE GREAT GROUNDHOG

I'm dreaming of the Great Groundhog
Just like I do this time each year.
When he brings nice weather
And brings us together
To wait for him to appear.

I'm dreaming of the Great Groundhog
With every Groundhog card I write.
May your Groundhog's Day be bright
When the Great Groundhog visits you tonight.

GROUNDHOG WONDERLAND

Groundhogs hoot, are you listening?
'Neath the sun, all is glist'ning
A real warm sight, we're happy tonight
Waitin' in a Groundhog wonderland.

In the field, we're watching for the Groundhog
We've been waitin for this day all year.
Do you think that he will see his shadow?
And will we know if springtime's almost here?

Later on while we're eating
What we got on Groundhog's Day
We'll share all our sacks
Of good Groundhog snacks
Waitin' in a Groundhog wonderland.

DECK THE FIELD

Deck the field with brown and black
Fa la la la la la la la la.
Take along your good sack
Fa la la la la la la la la.
Don we now our groundhog apparel
Fa la la la la la la la la
Toll the ancient groundhog carol
Fa la la la la la la la la.

See the groundhog rise before us
Fa la la la la la la la la.
As we sing the groundhog chorus
Fa la la la la la la la la
Follow him as he ascends
Fa la la la la la la la
Join with true great groundhog friends
Fa la la la la la la la la.

(Contributed by Steve Couch, Mt. Pleasant, Pennsylvania)

HE-MAN OLYMPICS

The purpose of this event is to build relationships between fathers and sons, or with men and teens in your group whose Dad may not be around for one reason or another. It would be appropriate to conduct this event around Father's Day (maybe the Saturday before). It's an all-day event that includes lots of games and activities that involve fathers and sons working and playing together. Eligible are fathers with sons at least in the fourth grade, or men of the church who would like to sponsor or "adopt" a son for the day. In the case of fathers with more than one son, the father should flip a coin to determine which one he will team up with, and the others can be "adopted" for the day. Here are some sample events:

1. *The Scripture Search:* The object of this is for each pair to find as many Scriptures as possible that refer to fathers, sons, or "men." They must be written out with the Scripture references. Set a time limit and don't allow anyone to use a concordance.
2. *Two on Two Volleyball:* Set up a round robin volleyball tournament with each pair playing volleyball against another pair for three minutes each. The pair scoring the most points in three minutes wins.
3. *The Great Hunting Trip:* Each pair gets two slingshots and ten ping pong balls. Set up some cardboard "animals" that will fall over if hit with a ping pong ball. You could set this up so that the animals are in different rooms and the pair is led around by a guide, with safari hats, etc. The larger the animal, the fewer points it is worth. The object is to score as many points as possible with your ten ping pong balls.

4. *Stock Car Race:* Set up a track around the church parking lot. The son drives (steers) a VW "bug" and the father must push it around the "racetrack." Each pair is timed.
5. *Handyman Game:* This event is designed to bring out the craftiness of each father and son. Give each pair a long (like eight feet long) piece of wood, a saw, and a few other tools

(hammers, nails, etc.) and give them a certain amount of time to make something useful. These can be judged by an impartial panel for points.

6. *Optional Events:* You can invent a lot of other games and events which the father and son teams can enter like a fishing contest, a tire changing contest, a home-run hitting contest, or whatever. Use your own creativity and don't forget to plan some activities for the "non-athletic" types.

Wrap up the day with a banquet (invite mothers and sisters) and award trophies or prizes for different categories. You might want to have a speaker who can talk about fatherhood, or the family, or men from the Bible, etc. This same kind of activity could be adapted to mothers and daughters by simply changing the games. (Contributed by Bill Wertz, Los Osos, California)

HOT OR COLD CAR RALLY

Here's a great car rally idea, especially for small groups or junior high groups. For this one, the adult youth leaders drive the cars and the kids in the car give the drivers their directions. To avoid confusion, it is best to have the riders elect one spokesperson. This person is the only one the driver will take directions from, although all the riders may have a part in the decision.

The driver knows the destination in advance, but the kids don't. Every five-tenths of a mile (0.5) the driver tells the passengers if they are getting "hot or cold" in relationship to the destination. When the car is getting closer to the destination, it may become necessary to reduce the clue times to two or even one-tenth of a mile in order to let the kids find the location.

To avoid cars just following each other, do it car rally style with each car leaving at intervals, one after the other, separated by about five minutes. The time is recorded when they leave, and someone else records their time of arrival at the final destination. Best time wins. (Contributed by James L. Hamilton, Oceanside, California)

INSTANT REPLAY

Here's a great way to attract a lot of kids to an "After the Football Game" social on a Friday night. Pick the "big game" of the season, and videotape it. See if you can put one camera in the press box at the stadium, and another on the sidelines for some close up shots. You can also tape the halftime activities (marching band, cheerleaders, etc.). If this is advertised well, you will attract a lot of kids and automatically gain an audience with the football teams, the bands, the drill team, the cheerleaders, and others. This kind of event is an excellent way to expose your youth program to a lot of new kids and to make some good contacts. Serve refreshments and just provide a fun time after the game for everyone. (Contributed by Chris Liebrum, Dallas, Texas)

MONDAY MORNING PRAYER BREAKFAST

If your church is located near a local high school, then this idea would be ideal for you. Sponsor a free "prayer breakfast" every Monday morning at the church for anyone who wants to attend. Schedule it at least one hour before school starts and get a few adult volunteers to show up early enough to prepare the food. As kids arrive, sing some songs, have some music playing, or play a few games until breakfast is served. While the kids are eating, present a short devotion, and perhaps have several of the kids lead in prayer (ask them in advance). Get some sponsors to help cover the cost of the food (business people, church members, etc.) and make sure the food is good (no cold cereal or donuts). As the breakfast becomes better known, you will find that more and more kids will come, making it a tremendous outreach program for your youth group. (Contributed by Rick Wheeler, Lubbock, Texas)

MYSTERY SWEETHEART BANQUET

Do you have a youth group that is relatively free of any "heavy" love affairs? If so, this will go over without much preparation or grumbling. If not, you may need to convince a few of those great lovers that this event will help develop some trust between them and their sweetheart, plus it will give them a rare opportunity to have a good time with "another" teen.

The basic idea is to put on a banquet (or some other event if you hate banquets) in which all the kids draw names to get their dates. Couples are selected randomly, with the boys in one hat and the girls in another. As they are pulled out, they become instant dates. If there are slightly more girls than guys, or vice versa, then even things out somehow by borrowing some people from another group, or you could just put the appropriate number of girls' names in the boys hat, or vice versa. If someone winds up with a date of the same sex, then it will really be a surprise.

The date should be "dutch treat," and the program should be good. During the early stages of the evening, give everyone a ballot so that they can vote for the "oddest couple," the "cutest couple," the "couple least likely to get married," the "shortest couple," etc. Tabulate the votes and then give out awards to the winners. This can be an unusual and funny night. Don't forget to take pictures so that the kids will never forget "that" date. (Contributed by Bruce Humbert, Richton Park, Illinois)

158

PORTA-PARTY

This is a great way to please and surprise even your longtime youth group members and have a great time doing it. The idea is to show up at an unexpected time during your regularly scheduled meeting or at a kid's house with a suitcase filled with a "party!" For any outrageous reason or no reason at all, you stage an instant party by bounding into the room with your party hat and your suitcase filled with a cake, ice cream, bowls, spoons, napkins, streamers, everything. You can do it for random birthdays or in celebration of some obscure event. (National Pickle Week, maybe?) You might even try taking a "Porta-Party" to some kid's house at 6:00 a.m. on his birthday. Use your own imagination for the reason and time and your surprise party will be talked about for a long time by some quite thrilled kids. (Contributed by Jan Augustine, Washington, D.C.)

PRISON PARTY

Here's a special event with a "prison" theme that can be a lot of fun by itself, or it can be combined with a field trip to a local police headquarters or county jail. Decorate a gym or large room in a prison "decor." Put "bars" on the windows, have the youth sponsors dress up like guards. Have a siren handy for crowd control. Everything can look pretty drab—like a prison would be.

When the kids arrive, they have to be arrested, of course. One way to do this (you could think of other ways) would be to have them meet in a separate room that has play money hanging from the ceiling from pieces of string. Each person is called out of the room, one at a time, and they are instructed to bring with them a piece of string. When they leave the room, they can then be arrested for having stolen money in their possession. If they say the money was just attached to the string, too bad. They are under arrest. Being framed is no excuse. You can use handcuffs, take them to an interrogation room, question them under a bright light, confiscate their personal belongings, fingerprint them, etc. The "prisoners" can then be given prison clothing, or prison hats, or an identification number or whatever.

Now you're all set for some "prison games" like these:

1. *BALL AND CHAIN STOMP:* This is the old "balloon stomp" with a new name. Tie balloons around each person's ankles and the object is to stomp (and pop) other prisoners' balloons while keeping yours from getting stomped. Whoever lasts the longest wins.

2. *THE TUNNEL ESCAPE:* This is similar to the old "Car Stuff." Set up a tunnel (made of cardboard boxes, tables, or just about anything) and divide into teams (cell-blocks). The idea is to see

how many can "escape to freedom" through the tunnel within a set time limit (like two minutes). Each prisoner crawls through the tunnel, with the next one right behind him. As soon as each person leaves the tunnel, they run around, get back in line and go through again. A "warden" or "guard" can count the prisoners as they come out and keep the official time. Each team can go one at a time. That way you only have to make one tunnel.

3. *MURDER IN CELL BLOCK FIVE:* This is a great game that can be played in the dark. The details for this game ("Murder") are in *IDEAS* #5, but briefly, here's how it is played. One person is secretly chosen to be the murderer. When the lights are out, that person walks up to others in the room, who are milling about, and

whispers in their ears, "you're dead." The victim counts to five, screams and falls to the floor. This continues, and as soon as someone thinks they know who the murderer is, they take an "official" guess. But if they are wrong, then they are dead too. The idea is for the murderer to see how many people he can knock off before his identity is discovered.

4. *BREAK OUT:* This one can be played outside in the parking lot if it is good and dark. Set up a "guard tower" of some kind that can hold a couple of people. Two kids are chosen to be guards and they are given powerful flashlights. A bell is placed underneath the guard tower. On a signal, the rest of the kids try to sneak up to the guard tower and ring the bell without getting "shot" with the flashlight. As soon as someone successfully rings the bell without getting hit with light, they may trade places with one of the guards. When you get "shot", you must go back to the starting place (back inside the prison, or 100 feet or so away from the tower) and try again. Some sponsors can referee this to make determinations as to whether or not someone got through

successfully. This can also be played with teams. One team can provide the guards while the other team tries to get to the bell.

5. *FIND THE LOOT:* This game is a lot like "Hunters and Hounds," found in *IDEAS #4.* Divide into teams with each team choosing a team captain, or leader. The object is for each team to find as much loot as possible. The loot can be play money which has been hidden all over the place ahead of time by the sponsors. If you are using a church, then the loot can be hidden in classrooms, trees, desks, trash cans, or anywhere else. On a signal, the teams take off looking for the loot, but the team captains must stay in a central "waiting area." As soon as a team member finds some loot, they must run back and tell their team captain where it is. The team captain may then go get the loot himself. No one else may touch it. The team captain must return to the waiting area before being allowed to go after more loot. The rules can be adapted or changed as you see fit. It's a lot of fun.

6. *EXERCISE YARD:* Under this general heading, you can play all kinds of relays and games from the *IDEAS* series. Take your pick.

Don't forget to serve refreshments ("Mess Hall"), and/or combine this event with any number of other activities with the same theme. You could put on a mock trial or have a discussion of issues like justice, freedom, the prison system, or whatever. Use a little creativity and something like this can be a real winner. (Contributed by Dan Craig, San Diego, California)

PROGRESSIVE DESSERT PARTY

The idea is in the title. For a tasty variation of a progressive dinner, just have different kinds of desserts at each stop. The portions should be small at each location—kind of a "sampler" of each dessert. Serve ice cream, cake, pie, cookies, mousse, cheesecake, cobbler, and the like. Guaranteed to go over great with any group of kids! (Contributed by Jerry Pattengale, Marion, Indiana)

PROGRESSIVE PICNIC

This is done exactly like a regular progressive dinner, only adapted for nice warm summer weather (or any time of the year, depending on where you live). Everybody should bring three or four paper plates, plastic forks, napkins, etc., and each "course" is served outside on the ground (blankets) or on picnic tables. You can go to several public picnic areas or just use the backyards of the folks who prepare the food. You might play a different outdoor game at each location as well. It's a nice change of pace. (Contributed by Bruce Humbert, Richton Park, Illinois)

PROGRESSIVE SPRINKLER PARTY

Here's a good idea for this summer. It works just like a progressive dinner, with several homes hosting the group. Everyone should wear bathing suits and bring towels. The first house can be set up with sprinklers in the backyard, with a giant slip-n-slide to play on (you can make one out of huge sheets of plastic). The second house can be an organized water balloon war, with all the balloons prepared ahead of time. The third house can be a "Water Volleyball" game (regular volleyball played under a "rainfall" created by several sprinklers around the net). The last stop can be a house with a swimming pool, for some relaxed swimming.

You can add any number of attractions along the way, if you live near a beach or near one of those "giant water slides," etc. The extra dimension that this brings to traditional water events is variety. Kids love it! (Contributed by Marge Clark, Cocoa, Florida)

RAIN DANCE

So often our most carefully made plans for an outdoor event are laid to rest by rain or foul weather. So why not, for the fun of it, put a date on your calendar that will be cancelled in the event of sunshine! Call it a "Rain Dance" or a "Rain Out" and plan activities to do in the rain (volleyball, frisbee, water balloon wars, etc.). Afterwards move indoors and have a Bible study on Genesis 7 and 8 (Noah and the flood), listen to appropriate music (Raindrops Keep Falling On My Head, Singing in the Rain, Rainy Day People, Kentucky Rain, etc.), and have a feast on—what else?—watermellon! (Contributed by Rod Klinzing, Columbus, Ohio)

RAINBOW SCAVENGER HUNT

Go to your local paint store and pick up a few paint color charts. Divide into teams, and give each team one of the charts. The object is to go out and find items that match the colors on the chart. Any item will do, but the color has to match *exactly*. Judges can disqualify any item that is questionable. Set a time limit, and the team with the most items matched wins. Extra points can be given for items that have *only* the matched color on it, the *most* of that particular color, and so on. Paint and art stores are off limits. Nothing can be purchased. (Contributed by Dan Brandell, Livonia, Michigan)

SACK LUNCH SHARING

Next time you have an event in which all the kids bring a sack lunch, try this for a change of pace. Lay a blanket out on the ground, and have all the kids dump the contents of their sack lunch onto the blanket. Then have the group gather around the blanket, hold it up by the edges and raise it high as you offer thanks. Then, lower it and allow the kids to "pick and choose" anything they want from the items that are there for lunch.

Tell the kids to keep in mind that everyone needs to eat, so don't be greedy, but share. The result will be a good experiment in cooperation and community. You might want to follow it with a discussion of the group dynamic that took place. (Contributed by Arlene Thaete, Sherburn, Minnesota)

SEARCH AND SCROUNGE SMORGASBORD

Here's a creative and fun way to have your next banquet. Tell the group that the meal will be an "S and S Smorgasbord" (don't tell them what the "S and S" stands for). Each person should pay a certain amount for the meal (like $2.50 per person, or some reasonable amount).

After the kids arrive, they can be told what is going on. You divide the group into five teams and divide the money up among them equally. Each team draws (out of a hat) one course of a five course meal—the appetizer, salad, main dish, dessert, or beverage. The teams are then instructed to go out and beg, barter, scrounge, search, or buy the necessary ingredients to prepare and deliver their assigned course within a given time limit (like one or two hours). They may not spend any more money than they are given.

When the groups return to begin their feast, awards can be given for the most creative, the tastiest, the most unusual, the largest quantity, the best use of the money, and so on. You will genuinely be surprised at what a great meal the kids will come up with. (Contributed by Greg Chantler, Tacoma, Washington)

SMALL WORLD PARTY

Here's a special event that is not only fun, but will help increase world awareness among members of your group. Advertise it as a "Small World Party" and give all the activities an international flavor. Here are some examples:

1. *Name Tag Mixer:* When each person arrives, they make a name tag representing their family's nationality. Emphasize creativity. Allow 15-20 minutes to make the tags. You might want to award prizes to the most creative.
2. *Signature Mixer:* Give everyone a list similar to the one below.

The object is to get a signature for each item.

1. Someone who was born out of the U.S.
2. Someone who has a parent who was born out of the U.S.
3. Someone who has foreign money with them
4. Someone who has been to Europe
5. Someone who can speak a foreign language
6. Someone who carries on their original nationality in their home (customs)
7. Someone who has lived in Canada
8. Someone who knows what "Feliz Navidad" means
9. Someone who knows what Shalom means
10. Someone who can cook a food dish from another country
11. Someone who likes Chinese food
12. Someone who can make a "pinata"
13. Someone who likes Greek food
14. Someone who knows where the coin "Lire" comes from

3. *Costume Fashion Show:* Have everyone come in some kind of international costume and have judges pick the most elaborate, the most creative, the funniest, etc.

4. *Folk Games:* Go to your local library and you will find books full of games from other countries. Perhaps you can find a few people who are familiar with popular folk games from other countries who would be willing to lead them. Play as many as you have time for.

5. *Snacks:* Keep these along the theme, too. Swedish meatballs, tortilla chips and guacamole, tiny pizzas, cheeses from other countries, etc.

6. *Closing Devotion:* Celebrate each person's heritage and uniqueness, emphasizing how all are made one through the Christian faith.

(Contributed by Nancy Wise, St. Petersburg, Florida)

SPY VS. SPY

This is a fun special event that requires cooperation between youth groups from two different churches. It also requires a little advance preparation.

First, you must take a photo of your entire youth group, or get individual photos of each person in the group. These photos are then exchanged with the other group. They should be sent to the other youth group a week or so before the event takes place.

Then, on a given day or evening, the two youth groups go to a busy place, like a shopping mall or an airport. They should meet at predetermined places, but one group should not know where the other one is. Then at a set time, the two groups spread out and try to locate each other, working individually or in pairs. The kids try to pick members of the other youth group out of the crowd by remembering them from the photos. Whenever someone thinks they have spotted someone from the other group, they run up to that person and say, "You're under arrest!" (or some other phrase that has been agreed upon ahead of time). Whoever says this key phrase to the other first gets points for his side. If a person is "arrested" three times, they must go to "jail" (some predetermined place) and wait out the rest of the game there. The game can last 30 minutes to an hour.

If you provide names with the photos, a person can get extra points by saying the spotted person's name—"You're under arrest, Jennifer!" Have a party afterward with refreshments. It's a good way to get to know another youth group.

SUNDAY SCHOOL TAILGATE PARTY

"Tail Gate Parties" have become very popular at sports events in the past few years. People show up hours before the game in their motor homes, cars, campers, trucks, etc. and cook hamburgers, visit with other tailgaters, toss a football around, and so on. So why not try a tail gate party for your church?

Just have everyone come an hour or two early to Sunday School and cook breakfast over a hibachi or camp stove. Serve coffee and orange juice, sausage and eggs, pancakes, and whatever else sounds good. People can bring lawn chairs, frisbees, guitars, and just relax and have a good time before it's time for Sunday School.

One church has made this an annual event, and advertises their tail gate party a few weeks in advance. Lots of people come who normally don't show up for Sunday School. It has become a favorite special event of the church. (Contributed by Dan Craig, San Diego, California)

SUNDAY STUDY HALL

At periodic times throughout the school year (mid-term testing, semester finals), young people feel the rigors of academic pressure more acutely. On the Sundays just prior to these stress weeks, your young people may feel the need to decide whether they are going to youth fellowship or stay home and hit the books. One way to minister to your group during these times is to set up a study hall at the church. Young people can come for their regular activities (recreation, choir, supper) and then, instead of a program, extend the time 1-1/2 to 2 hours and designate it for study. Provide light refreshments and have places available where those who have common classes can review and study together as well as rooms where others can study by themselves. A lot can be accomplished in two hours of uninterrupted study as, in a small way, you minister to your group's educational needs. (Contributed by Vernon Edington, Manchester, Tennessee)

TIN HORN RODEO

Here's an idea that was successfully used by a youth group in Texas. It may not be quite as practical for a youth group in New Jersey, but with a little creativity. . .why not? After all, a "Tin-Horn Rodeo" is a rodeo for city-slickers. It calls for the use of one or more horses (real ones) and some real live goats and pigs, which really aren't that hard to come up with. You will also need to find a good location that has a "rodeo" feel to it, like a fenced-in corral. If you can't come up with any of the above, think of some substitutes that might work. It might even make the whole thing crazier!

This event can be enhanced by emphasizing the "cowboy" theme. Have everyone wear boots and western attire, have some country music on hand, serve a western barbecue, stage mock gunfights, etc. The rodeo can be the main event, with competition for great prizes—like new belt-buckles, cowboy hats, trophies, or whatever. Rodeo events can include the following:

1. *Boot Scramble:* Same thing as the old "Shoe Scramble." Everyone piles their boots into one big pile and then goes back to the starting line. At go, everyone runs to the pile, finds their boots, puts them on and returns to the original line. Have teams sit down to show when their entire team has crossed the line. First team to sit down wins the event.

2. *Barrel Race:* Here's where you need the horse. Two riders are needed, one to ride and one to lead the horse. The rider must ride bareback. The object is to ride a cloverleaf pattern around three oil drums just like they do in the rodeo. The only difference is that at each barrel the person leading the horse stops and hands a water balloon to the rider. Fastest time wins. A two-second penalty is given if a balloon is dropped or busted.

166

3. *Goat Tie:* Stake a goat out in the middle of the arena on a 20 foot rope. The event is run like a calf roping event in the rodeo. Use two kids—one to catch the goat and hold it while the other one ties three of its legs. This is a good event to team older kids with younger ones. The event is timed. Shortest time wins the event.

4. *Rescue:* Each team will need four members for this event. Begin at the starting line. One member rides a horse bareback and a second member leads the horse. At "go" they run to the first barrel, where a third member is waiting. The rider jumps off the horse, the person who led the horse gets on, and the third person now becomes the horse leader. Person #3 leads the horse to the next barrel where the fourth team member is waiting. Again, the rider jumps off, the old leader gets on, and person #4 leads the horse to the finish line. The event is timed. Shortest time wins.

5. *Milking Contest:* Stake a goat out in the middle and tie a surgical glove filled with water around its middle. Place a small stool next to it for the team member to sit on, and a small cup or pail underneath the goat. At "go" the contestant must milk the glove to fill the cup (be sure the fingers of the gloves have pin holes in them). Time the event and the shortest time wins.

6. *Cow Chip Toss:* Take a 20 lb. bag of flour and mark off an area of the arena in semi-circles, much like that when the discus is thrown. Semi-circles should be marked at 10 foot distances. Mark enough area to toss a chip (usually 60 feet or so). Mark a throw line. Have several members of a team line up and toss a chip. A measuring tape of at least 10 feet or more should be on hand to measure the distance. Most of the chips are good for at least two tosses. Farthest toss wins, or you can combine the totals of all the team members. Greatest total wins.

7. *Greased Pig Chase:* Grease a pig with vaseline and let it loose at one end of the arena. It's best to divide the kids up into age groups and let each group have an individual "chase." The object is to catch the pig and bring it back across the finish line. The team members who get it back across the line win.

(Contributed by Elene Harger, Lubbock, Texas)

TYPICAL-SUNDAY-IN-CHURCH PHOTO

This is a great chance for everyone to be a ham. First have the group make a list of things people do in church when they are bored. Your list might include yawning, drawing pictures, touching up one's makeup, or making paper airplanes. Next, think up ways to act out each idea. EXAGGERATING is the key to a hilarious picture. Props and costumes might include choir robes, an offering plate, bubble gum, and a large crayon. You'll need volunteers to dress as young children and old folks (find old hats and funky glasses). The following week everyone brings costumes and props for their star roles. Have someone photograph the group sitting in the pews of your church. Everyone poses, hold it, cheese! Develop 4 x 5 pictures for everyone and an 8 x 10 picture for the church bulletin board. Really ham it up and you will get plenty of laughs. This could be followed up by a discussion on how church can be made more meaningful, or how we can prevent "boredom." (Contributed by Wayne Deibel, Torrance, California)

WATER DAY

This is an excellent event for a hot, summer day. You'll need a lawn, some hoses, a water tub, water balloons, some volleyball gear, and a few other odds and ends. Kids come in swimsuits or shorts, and the games below are played. There are other water games, by the way, in past volumes of *IDEAS*. Check your *IDEAS Index*.

1. *Waterlogged Volleyball:* This one is described in detail in *IDEAS Number 21*. Have sprinklers set up on the net and around the area so that water will be raining down everywhere on the playing area. Then follow regular volleyball rules.

2. *Cup Splash Relay:* For this one, you will need a large tub filled with water. Each group has one large plastic cup. With the sprinklers running and the volleyball net lowered, the participants have to run from one end of the volleyball court to the other. They must slide under the net, get up, run to the tub, fill their cup with water, run back, slide back under the net, run to the group and splash the water in the next person's face. Each person follows the same pattern. If the group is small, go through the event twice.

3. *Water Balloon Race:* With the tub filled with water, put a whole bunch of water balloons in it. Just like the last race, each person must run, slide under the net, run to the tub, get a water balloon, run back, slide under the net, and run to the starting line. This time instead of hitting the next person with the balloon, they must break the water balloon over their own head. Then the rest of the group, one at a time, go through the same process. In both the water balloon race and the cup splash relay, if a person drops their cup of water or pops their balloon, they must go back and get another.

4. *Three-Legged Cup Pour Relay:* Just as a regular track relay is run with several statuins to receive the baton, so is the relay set up in the same way. Only this relay is a three-legged race and the baton is a cup of water. Two people pair up at each station with their legs tied together. The first group is given a cup filled with water, the other stations have an empty cup. Group 1 runs to Group 2 and empties their cup of water into Group 2's cup of water. Group 2 runs to Group 3 and repeats the process and so on. The winner is the group that has the most water left in their cup.

For prizes, give the winners *Perrier* water, second place—Club Soda, and last place—dishwater. Serve Watermelon for refreshments. The kids will love it. (Contributed by Francis Fontana, Houston, Texas)

WINTER PICNIC

If you live in an area where winters are cold and miserable, try having a "Winter Picnic." Decorate a hall or gym so that it looks like an outdoor park in the summertime. Bring in tree branches and put rocks around them to make them stand up. Set up some picnic tables, some "no litter" signs, trash cans, and so on to add to the atmosphere. Play a few outdoor games, cook up some hamburgers or serve typical picnic food, and encourage everyone to wear summer clothes. Use your own creativity and this can be a very refreshing change of pace for your group. (Contributed by Corey Amaro, Belmont, California)

WORLD'S GREATEST FRENCH FRY

Here's an excellent activity that lets your kids become critics or reviewers of the things they consume. The object is to find the very best french-fry in the city. The kids go from one fast food joint to another trying out their french fries. For example, they would go to the McDonalds, Jack in the Box, etc., order up some french fries, and then divide it up between the group. Each member rates the fries on qualities such as taste, appearance, amount per serving, price, saltiness, etc. To really add a professional touch, have each member eat a cracker before they taste to "wash the palate." The group's ratings and any additional comments can be shared in the church's bulletin.

Other foods can be tasted, such as the best hamburger, or the tastiest vanilla ice cream, etc. You could compile a "Christian Consumer's Guide" or something like that. And by notifying the restaurants in advance, you might even get some free food to sample. (Contributed by Milton Hom, Monterey Park, California)

Chapter Five

Youth Group Leadership

BIG BROTHERS AND SISTERS

This idea is designed to involve your more mature young people in ministry and to make it easier for the younger kids to feel accepted and appreciated. Select several of your high school seniors or college students to become "big brothers" or "big sisters" to the incoming freshmen in the group. They can meet with them, make sure they are doing okay, call them up, and help disciple them during the first year that they are part of the group. The main thing is that they try to sincerely be the person's friend. Something like this helps build community and also gives kids a chance to participate in peer ministry. (Contributed by Denny Finnegan, Redondo Beach, California)

COLLEGE CATALOG CORNER

To help your senior highers make decisions about "life after high school," contact private and public colleges and vocational technical institutions with a request for their current catalog, admissions and financial aid information. There is no charge for this service and most schools are eager to reply as well as to pay the return postage.

Then set up a table or corner bookshelf in the senior high room or church library and use a sign-out system to keep track of the catalogs. You might want to post a sign of guidance that reads "Expect God to Guide, Not Decide!" You'll be surprised how many college and career young people and adults find and use the corner too! This is a great way to inform people about possibilities for their continuing education. (Contributed by Matt and Janelle Kuntscher, Lakeville, Minnesota)

DUD POST CARDS

Chances are you have (or have access to) lots of old snapshots that didn't turn out. The setting on your camera wasn't quite right, or you cut somebody's head off, or there wasn't enough light or something. Well, these old photos make excellent post cards—especially the "jumbo" size ones. All you need to do is put a stamp on them, write a note (making reference to the wonderful photo, of course, address them and drop them in the mail. These are very unique one-of-a-kind picture post cards. Kids love to get them. (Contributed by David Amsler, Quincy, Illinois)

EVENT RESPONSE SHEET

Building a consistent youth ministry is a constant yearly challenge. One help for steady improvement is the use of an "Event Response Sheet." The key to effectiveness of such an evaluation tool is using it after each event, recording your data for future planning helps, and using the results when you consider whether to repeat an event or try to develop a new one. The response sheet must be general enough to cover youth events from a service project to a fellowship banquet to a retreat. This is a good way to involve more people in the youth ministry as you continually provide for feedback to your program.

EVENT RESPONSE SHEET

1. Evaluation for project, activity, or study _____

2. Date _____

3. Grade in school and sex of youth _____ M or F

Scoring Key:
90-100 Strongly agree or Yes!
80-90   Mildly agree
70-80   Disagree
60-70   Strongly disagree or No!

Score

I. *"Build-up"*—Were you aware of the event? How well were you informed? Did you have adequate time to prepare to participate in the event? _____

II. *Objectives*—Did you understand what was trying to be accomplished? Was it clear to you what was going on? _____

III. *Value*—Was the event valuable? Was it worth participating in? Was it something you thought was important that youth should consider? _____

IV. *Interest*—Did it meet a need or interest that you have? Did it benefit you in your Christian growth? Was it helpful to Christian living? _____

V. *Leadership*—Did the leaders seem prepared? Did they present the material thoroughly? Did you feel they tried to do a good job? _____

VI. *Repeatability*— Would you recommend repeating this event again? Do you think an annual event of this type would be good? _____

OUTSTANDING FACTORS:

AREAS TO IMPROVE UPON:

(Contributed by Jim Bourne, Douglas, Georgia)

INCLUSIVE ELECTIONS

For many groups, youth group officers are important in the running of the meetings and the planning of the events. Sometimes, however, favorite friends or the most popular people are always the youth group officers. To prevent this from happening, and to give everyone an equal opportunity to serve, you might try one or more of the following ideas:

1. Put all the offices on slips of paper and allow members to draw from a paper bag.
2. Allow members to write down (or the Youth Leader appoint) the officers from this list.
3. Let members write down secretly who they think would be best in each office. Youth Leaders sort out and appoint the new officers.
4. As members arrive have them take a seat in a chair. Beforehand, tape the name of each office on the bottom of the chair. After everyone is seated let them find out who the next slate of officers are.
5. Change officers every three months or so and allow no one to hold an office more than once.
6. After a time when everyone has had an opportunity to serve in a different capacity have an all-out election. By this time the members have seen how different ones perform and can vote more wisely.

(Contributed by Bee Jones, Poway, California)

STORING POSTERS

What a waste to spend time and energy on that poster only to throw it away after one use, or cram it behind a filing cabinet never to retrieve it again. One way to prevent that from happening is to use clothes pant hangers, the kind with the two spring clasps. You can hang several posters on one hanger. Hang them with blank sides together so you can easily check front and back to see the two posters. Then you can hang them in an unused closet or use a door hanger and keep them right where you can find them. (Contributed by Jim Bourne, Douglas, Georgia)

THE US QUIZ

Give your group a "quiz" consisting of 25 questions like those below. The questions may vary from silly to serious. The person with the most correct answers wins a snapshot of the entire group. This is a good way to publicize your group to newcomers, and to remind the regulars of what the group is all about.

1. Name the event when we stayed overnight in a barn.
2. Who is our pastor?
3. Name two people in our group who are related.
4. What's the name of our church newsletter?
5. What were the refreshments last week?
6. Name two service projects that our group did last year.

(Contributed by Corey Amaro, Belmont, California)

WELCOME!

Here's a good way to welcome a new staff member at the church, a new youth sponsor or a new young person in the group. Have all the kids write a letter to the new person introducing themselves, and enclose a "free coupon" that can be redeemed for something. For example. the coupon might say "I will deliver a pie on your request," or "If you want two free guitar lessons, call me," or "I'll buy lunch for you any Saturday," and so on. Then, all the letters and coupons are presented to the newcomer. It really makes them feel wanted and accepted. (Contributed by Corey Amaro, Belmont, California)

WELCOME! II

Another way to help a new person to fit in (especially those who have moved in from out of town) is to give your group the following questionnaire. After the kids have answered all the questions, the survey results can be given to the new person(s). Another way to do this would be to just have a discussion using the same questions, with the new person in attendance.

1. Where can you get the best and cheapest hamburgers in town?
2. Where is the best place to just sit and talk?
3. What's the best radio station?
4. Where is the least expensive movie theater?
5. Where do you go if you want to run into your friends?
6. What should a person be sure and not miss if they can only spend one day in our town?
7. What's the best thing about our youth group?
8. What's the best event that our youth group does every year?

Of course, you can change or add questions as you see fit. (Contributed by Peter Wilkinson, San Anselmo, California)

YOUTH DIRECTOR'S MYSTERY NIGHT

No single event in youth ministry is as important as some close, personal contact with youth and there is no better way to get that personal contact than by adding yourself to a little mystery and time. Kids love to stay overnight at friends homes... why not at the youth director's house? Invite 4 to 6 of them to spend a "mystery night" at your house. Have them bring sleeping bags and sleep in your living room. Take them out to the 99¢ movie in town, out for a pizza, and let them fall asleep watching your TV and talking to their friends. The results are fantastic and a bond can form not only between youth and adult but also between youth who had previously not known each other well or between "in" youth and "out" youth who mingle this way. This event sounds so simple and yet its benefits are so great. (Contributed by John M. Carlson, Mahtomed, Minnesota)

YOUTH GROUP HOTLINE

Here's a good way to keep your group informed about upcoming events and also to give them a way to leave messages for you. Invest in one of those electronic phone answering devices and have the phone company set you up with a private number for it. The message on it should be changed every day, with news of upcoming events, a "thought for the day," jokes, or whatever. Most of these devices allow time for the caller to leave a message, so you can invite kids to do that if they want. You will find that both the young people and their parents will use such a hotline a lot. The charge for the extra line is usually small enough to make it easily affordable. (Contributed by Steve Swanson, Burnsville, Minnesota)

Chapter Six

Fund Raisers

ALLEY SALE

For this unique variation of the "garage sale," you will need to find an alley that has four to eight garages on it that you can "borrow." They should all be located on the same alley. Then, each garage becomes a different "shop" named according to the merchandise sold in each one. One shop can sell household items, another can sell sports equipment, others can sell antiques, or books, or clothing or baked goods, etc. Each shop should be given a clever name (like the shops in a shopping mall) and signs should be posted at each end of the alley calling attention to this "unique shopping experience."

Preparation for this event is obviously crucial to its success. You will need to enlist many people to donate items for sale. Merchandise will have to be collected, sorted, and priced. Advertising will need to be done (newspaper ads, public service announcements on the radio, etc.). Workers will be needed on the day of the sale to do the actual selling, parking cars, directing traffic, etc. The atmosphere should be as festive as possible. You might even get some musicians to play at one end of the alley and some jugglers or clowns to perform at the other end. Use your own creativity to design an event that will attract the most people possible.

If you can't find an alley of this type, use a normal street, using front lawns or garages off the street. You'll find that this event works so well that you may want to make it an annual event. (Contributed by Elizabeth J. Sandell, St. Paul, Minnesota)

BULLISH ON THE YOUTH GROUP

Here's an unusual way to finance your next service project. Print up stock certificates and sell them to members of the church or community as an "investment." Each share can sell for $1.00 with no limit on how many shares a person can buy. Some may want to only buy one share, but others may want to buy a hundred shares. The stock gives them "ownership" in the project and entitles them to attend a "stockholders meeting" so that they can be informed as to how their investment is doing. A "stockholders report" can also be printed. Both the meeting and the report can include photos, testimonies by the kids who participated, a financial statement, and so on. It's an idea that will work. (Contributed by Nancy Freyer, Portland, Oregon)

CALENDAR PAY-OFF

Here's an idea that encourages your kids to be givers. Print up a calendar that has a space for each day of the month. In each space, enter an instruction that will determine how much money they must give that day. The instruction should be humorous, and should vary the amount given from one day to the next. When the month is up, the kids bring in the money they owe. At that time you can give awards for who had to pay the most money, the least, the most expensive day of the month, etc.

A variation of this would be to print the instruction for each day on separate sheets of paper, fold them and staple them, so that they are concealed until the end of each day. The instruction can then be a "fine" for certain things done or not done. For example, it might say "Pay 5¢ for each class you were late to today," or "Pay 25¢ if you forgot to brush your teeth," etc.

Allow a space on the calendar where kids can write in how much they owe each day. They can just total it up at the end of the month. You might add one "extra" space for them to give any amount they choose. This approach adds a little fun and variety to giving.

Sunday	Monday	Tuesday	Wednesday	Thursday	Friday	Saturday
		1 1¢ For each pair of shoes and sneakers you own.	2 3¢ If you disobeyed your parents today.	3 5¢ If you forgot to use a deodorant today.	4 4¢ If you have BLUE eyes.	5 10¢ If you did not clean and straighten up your room.
6 15¢ If you did not attend CHURCH today.	7 5¢ If you washed your hair today.	8 1¢ For each time you talked on the telephone today.	9 5¢ If you get up before seven a.m.	10 3¢ If you wore any type of Jeans today.	11 1¢ For each soda you drank today.	12 2¢ For each hour of sleep you had last night.
13 1¢ For each mile you live away from your church.	14 2¢ If you have a hole in your sock.	15 5¢ If you did not do your homework.	16 2¢ If you have your license to drive a car.	17 4¢ If you have BROWN eyes.	18 1¢ For each letter in your last name.	19 10¢ If you shaved anything today!
20 5¢ If you wore blue today.	21 5¢ For each test you had today.	22 1¢ For each class you had today.	23 50¢ If you were not at Teen Choir tonight.	24 10¢ If you did not eat breakfast **at home** this morning.	25 3¢ For each time you failed to make your bed this week.	26 20¢ If you did not donate any money yesterday.
27 10¢ If you have a pair of Nike's.	28 3¢ For each pair of gloves you own.	29 3¢ If you didn't read your Bible today.	30 10¢ Because it is almost the last day to pay.	31 15¢ If you wore the color red today.		

(Contributed by Dallas Elder, Portland, Oregon)

CRAFTS BOUTIQUE

Crafts and handmade items for the home are very popular nowadays. There are no doubt many people in your church or community who are very talented at making things that will sell in a "boutique" or gift shop. So, why not set up a Crafts Boutique to help finance your next mission project? Pick a good location, advertise it well, and invite everyone to make something in the "arts and crafts" motif and to allow these items to be sold on a consignment basis. You can buy the items from them at a wholesale price, with the profit going to support your project. Some people may be willing to just donate their crafts items altogether.

One church did this in a big way, and on a weekend sold over $20,000 worth of goods. A fixed percentage of the income went to a mission project, and the rest went to the people who had made and sold the items. Needless to say, it was very successful.

GOLF TOURNAMENT

Some youth programs have had good success with sponsoring golf tournaments in the community. This works best if you are in a large church with a lot of golfers in it, or if you have a way of attracting golfers from all over the area. You will need to reserve a local golf course, and work out a "deal" on green fees, if possible. Someone with some golf tournament experience will need to organize the tournament itself, establishing the rules, the tee-off times, and so forth. You can line up some nice prizes (donated) for the lowest score, highest score, closest to the pin on the 18th hole, etc. You might want to enlist some "celebrity" type players to host each foursome. The entry fee can be high enough to make it a good fund raiser, but low enough to attract lots of players. You might want to wrap up the tournament with a banquet where the awards can be presented, the mission project can be explained, and so on.

GRANOLA PARTY

Here's a fund raiser that most people can really sink their teeth into. Get the youth group together for a "Granola Party," in which the kids make their own special brand of granola that can be sold later. Find a good recipe—preferably one that includes lots of "good stuff" like nuts, banana chips, carob chips, coconut, grains, honey, and the like. Have the kids prepare the granola in large quantities, then bag it, put it in decorated coffee cans, and sell it door to door or to friends and relatives. A variation of this would be to make and sell jam, preserves, dried fruit, or other "natural" foods.

HIRE A SUPERKID

This is basically a kind of "employment service" for your youth group. Most unemployed young people have lots of time on their hands after school and on weekends. You and your church can help them to find good part-time jobs which give them meaningful work and which raise money both for them and for the youth group.

To make it happen, print up an attractive flyer that includes information on all of the "odd jobs" that the kids can do: mow yards, wash cars, babysit, clean house, paint, fix cars, etc. After printing up the flyers, distribute them all over the neighborhood and wait for the calls to start coming in. Chances are your response will be very good.

Assign the jobs that come in to the kids according to their abilities and their preferences and give them the responsibility of completing it and doing a good job. If the customer is satisfied, chances are good that they will become a "regular customer." When the jobs start thinning out a little bit, just send out more flyers or get some other free publicity.

A good resource for this is a brochure entitled *"How To Get Plenty of Profitable Part-Time Jobs for your Teenagers"* by Pat Higgins, 1549 Hampton, Grosse Pointe Woods, Michigan, 48236.

Employers can either pay the young people or pay the youth group. You might want to work out a system where a percentage of the money goes towards the youth group project, and the rest is kept by the young person to be used any way he or she wants. (Contributed by John Collins, Houston, Texas)

LE GRANDE CHATEAU

This fund raiser is great fun for everyone. The idea is to open "for one night only" your own fine French restaurant—an elegant dining experience that includes "classy" entertainment. The whole thing, however, is done slightly tongue-in-cheek. The catch is the small print at the bottom of the menu which reads: "Management reserves the right to make substitutions without patron consent." So, regardless of what people order, they all get the same thing.

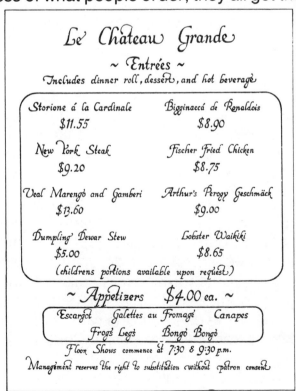

The menu should be elaborate and include extravagant dishes at high prices. It should look like a regular menu (with the exception of the catch line at the bottom, of course). The publicity should include a snooty "reservations only" system so the right amount of food can be prepared. You can also have a "dress code" (ties for the gentlemen, please). Decorations should be as elegant as possible, with cut flowers, candles, linen on the tables, and classical music playing in the background.

The waiters should be dressed to the hilt, with the Maitre'd in tux if possible. The food should be nice but simple. Juice, tossed salad, baked chicken, baked potato, vegetable, roll, dessert. The program after the meal can be anything you want. Be sure to allow a few minutes to explain your project and how the proceeds of the evening will be used.

At the close, the waiters can present the "cheque" to each customer. It can instruct people to make their donations in any amount and to either pay their waiter or pay on their way out. Usually a special event like this gets very good results. It's worth all the work involved. (Contributed by Len Kageler, Seattle, Washington)

MACHO BAKE SALE

The "Bake Sale" has always been successful as a fund raiser, but here it is with a new twist. Get all the men in the church to bake cakes, cookies, and pies, and have a "Macho Bake Sale". You might even want to make it a contest between the men—no women may help them. It will be a lot of fun, generate a lot of enthusiasm, and work great as a fund raiser. (Contributed by Rick Bell, Tucson, Arizona)

PAPER BOOSTER CLUB

In most areas it is possible to pick up some money by recycling used newspapers. It takes a lot of paper to make it very profitable, but if organized properly, it can be a good way to raise dollars for your ongoing projects.

Enlist members of the congregation and neighbors to become members of the "Paper Boosters Club". When they join (you can give them an official membership certificate) they promise to save all their newspapers especially for your group. Then, once a month set up a paper collection route for kids to go around and pick up all the paper. If you get enough people involved, you can earn a lot of money in this way. The same can be done with aluminum cans and other items that can be recycled for cash. (Contributed by Dallas Elder, Portland, Oregon)

SAMPLE FAIR

This idea takes a few months to get ready for, but it is very effective as a fund raiser, and it is different enough to really attract a lot of attention. The first step is to write a form letter (like the one below) to various companies that provide products, foods, or services. This can be sent to nationally known companies or to local companies. You might want to contact some of these personally with a phone call or visit. In the letter, you ask them to give you a large quantity of free samples for your "Sample Fair."

```
Dear Sirs:

    Would you like us to promote your product?
    Our senior high youth group has decided to raise money
to purchase a _____ for our church. We are calling
our project a "Sample Fair". In order for us to be a
success, we are asking you to help...and in return we
will be helping you to promote your product.
    Here is our request: Do you have a sample or "pass-out"
item for promotion? This will not be sold. Tickets in
advance and at the door will be sold. Each person will be
entitled to one of each sample. To complete the evening,
the youth will present a "Home Talent Show".
    We're certain the samples will create interest and
excitement and we will have a good turn-out.
    If you are interested and care to help us with your
"Sample", we would be very pleased. We are setting our
goal to sell 300 tickets. This event will take place
on _____ in our church fellowship room.
    Thank you very much.
                                        Sincerely,
```

If a letter like this is sent to enough companies, you can get hundreds of different free samples for your Sample Fair. Tickets to the Sample Fair can be sold for whatever price you feel is reasonable, and your kids can pass out the samples at the Fair, giving one each to a customer. Some companies may provide plastic bags for people to collect things in, or they may send a representative to help explain the product. At any rate, the overhead is low, and the benefits are high. You can also provide a refreshment booth, or sell baked goods, etc. to add to the festivities. It can be a fun evening that raises a lot of money for a worthwhile cause. (Contributed by Esther Maule, Princeville, Illinois)

Chapter Seven

Holidays

CHRISTMAS MELODRAMA

Here's a Christmas version of the "Spontaneous Melodrama" *(IDEAS Numbers One through Four)*. It's a great skit that requires no rehearsal at all. The characters are selected from the audience, given the props, and the narrator simply reads the script while the characters spontaneously do what the script indicates. Choose people who will really get into it and have some fun with their parts.

CAST: Penelope Pureheart
Dirty Dan
Elmer Schmidlap
Faithful Dog Shep
Christmas Tree
Narrator

Props Needed: Chair
Tree decorations
Clean toilet brush

STORY:

Our action takes place in the deep, snow-covered woods. Poor Penelope Pureheart is out with her faithful dog Shep, trying to find a Christmas tree for their poor, dreary hut. Penelope finds a pretty little tree . . . but . . ., no . . ., Shep's already found it.

After searching some more, she finds the perfect one! She chops it down, yells, "Timber!" and down it falls. She drags it back to her house with the help of her faithful dog Shep.

Now we see the poor, dreary hut. It looks so poor and dreary, except for the beautiful Christmas tree in the corner. She doesn't have any presents to go under it, but it is pretty anyway.

Suddenly, we hear a knock at the door. In bursts Dirty Dan. He demands that Poor Penelope Pureheart pay him the $29.65 plus tax for the tree. She pleads with him to let her have it. Doesn't he know it is more blessed to give than to receive?! "Bah, Humbug!! I'll give you six hours or I'll take it back!" he says as he leaves.

Poor Penelope Pureheart doesn't know what to do. She has no money. She sits down on the chair and starts crying. Her faithful dog Shep comes over to comfort her. She pats him on the head. She scratches him under the chin. She rubs his ears. He loves it!

To comfort her, he licks her hand, then licks her arm all the way to the elbow. She loves it! It makes her feel so much better.

"What will we do?" she asks. "I wish Santa Claus would help us."

All of a sudden, there is a knock on the door. She knows it is Dirty Dan coming to get the money or her tree.

"Come in," she says sadly. But—instead of Dirty Dan—it is Elmer Schmidlap, former Fuller Brush Salesman and now Santa Claus' Vice President in charge of Public Relations. With him, he has his magic toilet brush, with which he performs various and sundry deeds of prestidigitation and other magical acts.

"What's wrong Poor Penelope?" asks Elmer. She tells him and then breaks down crying. This goes on and on. Then her faithful dog Shep starts howling. This goes on and on.

At that moment, in bursts Dirty Dan. He demands the money or the tree.

Elmer says, "Can't you be nice, you dirty thing?"

Dan pushes Elmer and he falls into the beautiful Christmas tree.

"Now look what you've done," says Dirty Dan, "You've ruined the Christmas tree."

Elmer says, "We've had enough of your dirtyness, Dirty Dan. From now on you'll bring joy to the hearts of people." Then Elmer touches Dirty Dan with his Magic Toilet Brush and Dirty Dan turns into the most beautiful Christmas Tree there ever was!

Elmer and Penelope and Penelope's faithful dog Shep go out for a Christmas walk, celebrating with all of Santa's assistants. Dirty Dan just stands in the hut looking beautiful.

And thus our story ends.

Moral: If you get to the root of it all, all dirty, evil people, are really saps.

(Contributed by Tom Lowry, Augusta, Georgia)

CHRISTMAS SITTER SERVICE

As a service project at Christmas, members of your youth group can staff the church's nursery each evening the entire first week of December. Parents of children up to age 10 can then drop off their kids between 6:00 and 10:00 p.m. while they go Christmas shopping. This can be done for free, or donations can be accepted for a worthy project. Most adults really appreciate this kind of service. It is important, by the way, to have some adult supervision present each night. (Contributed by R. Albert Mohler, Jr., Louisville, Kentucky)

CHRISTMAS TREE PICK UP SERVICE

Here's a simple fund raiser for your youth group this Christmas. Spend one or two days after Christmas (before school starts up again) going around with pickup trucks picking up used Christmas trees, oversized gift boxes, etc. Advertise it in advance both in the church and all over the neighborhood. Get it announced in the local newspaper, radio, etc. Get the trucks donated and the only expense will be gas and the fee to dump the trees at your local dump. Charge a flat fee for the service or you can accept donations. This is an especially good idea because many refuse disposal companies will not pick up Christmas trees, or they charge extra for it. (Contributed by R. Albert Mohler, Jr., Louisville, Kentucky)

FAMOUS SWEETHEARTS GAME

This game is great for Valentine parties. It is played just like the old "Newly Wed Game" on T.V. with the exception that participants take on the role of famous sweethearts such as Samson and Delilah, Popeye and Olive Oyl, etc. Have everyone draw a name tag with a famous person's name printed on it out of a hat. (Part of the fun of picking at random is a guy may have to take on the role of Delilah, and a girl that of Samson.) Everyone then finds their mate.

One at a time, the female characters leave the room, while their corresponding mate answers questions, trying to guess and match what their famous sweetheart will say. (Have someone record the answers.) The female characters are brought back in and asked the same questions. Couples are awarded points if they match each others' answers. Then the male characters are taken out and questions are asked of the female characters for round two. Couples with the most points after two rounds wins.

A good way to begin the game would be to award a certain amount of points to the couple that finds their partner the quickest, one point less for the couple to find each other second, two points less for the third couple and so on.

Sample Sweethearts:

Samson and Delilah	Lucy and Ricky Ricardo
Popeye and Olive Oyl	Blondie and Dagwood
Mork and Mindy	George and Martha Washington
Romeo and Juliet	Superman and Lois Lane
Adam and Eve	Kermit the Frog and Miss Piggy

Sample Questions:

A. What would you say your sweetheart is most famous for?
B. Where would you say you and your sweetheart live?
C. What color hair would you say your sweetheart has?

(Contributed by Scott Pogue, Ft. Worth, Texas)

HALLOWEEN DINNER

This is a variation of the "Mystery Dinner" in which people order items from a menu without knowing exactly what it is that they are ordering. All the food items as well as the eating utensils have disguised names. A person orders food in three courses, four items per course, from the menu below. A waitress (dressed as a witch) can fill the orders and bring the food to the table. The person must consume each course (all of it) before the next course can be ordered and received. It's a lot of fun and full of surprises. Here's the menu:

> "Witches Brew" (punch)
> "Lapover" (napkin)
> "Jack's Ripper" (knife)
> "Devil's Right Arm" (fork)
> "Grave Diggers Delight" (spoon)
> "Autumn Nectar" (milk)
> "Pig in a Poke" (hot dog)
> "Tombstone" (bun)
> "Irish Eyes" (fried potatoes)
> "Bones" (beans)
> "Slimy Shivers" (jello)
> "Frosted Pumpkin" (pie)

(Contributed by Malcolm McQueen, Camas, Washington)

GHOST STORY

Obviously this one is for Halloween, but it could be used anytime. Divide your group into several smaller units as specified below. As someone with a deep clear voice reads the story, the young people provide the sound effects as their key word is spoken. It helps to have someone else give hand motions and silent directions. For added fun, rehearse it with the group, then tape record and listen to it together. Here's the story with the key words in bold type:

It was a dark cold night. The moon was full and bright, its light shining through deep grey, menacing clouds. The light cast strange shadows through the woods and across narrow, grassy fields. **Night sounds** echoed through the darkness. (Pause)

Wind whispered through the pines, singing its song so softly. Suddenly, the **wind** increased in intensity, shaking the leaves and branches back and forth, back and forth. A great clap of **thunder** broke through the night as a jagged lightning bolt lighted up the sky. It began to **rain.** (Pause) The rain beat down on the dried leaves and began to fall harder and harder. Soon the ground became slippery and wet as dry, packed earth soaked up the fallen rain, turning it into damp, gooey mud. In the distance the **howling** of dogs could be heard through the **wind** and the **rain.** The sound of **footsteps** could be heard moving slowly through the thick mud. All at once another **thunder** clap broke through the night and a piercing **scream** rose above the trees. As the **rain** began to soften and the **wind** died down, a low **moaning** could be heard through the forest. Suddenly, all became silent. (Pause) And nothing could be heard, (pause) except for the **wind.**

The Sound Effects:

1. *Footsteps:* three or four kids say slowly, "Shlop … Shlop … Shlop"
2. *Wind:* kids make a soft, whistling sound
3. *Howling:* three or four kids howl like hounds
4. *Scream:* group of girls scream like crazy
5. *Thunder:* the entire group claps hands once. Begin on the right side of the room and flow to the left across the crowd
6. *Moan:* group of boys give a long, low moan
7. *Rain:* the entire group begins by snapping their fingers as fast as they can, followed by rubbing their palms together rapidly, then patting their thighs, and finally clapping their hands rapidly. Soften the rain by following the above procedure in reverse.
8. *Night Sounds:* the adult staff can do this one. Everyone picks a vegetable (carrot, pickle, broccoli, lettuce, peas, rutabaga, etc.) and repeats its name over and over softly. It sounds like the noises you might hear deep in the woods. (Contributed by Ben Sharpton, Gainesville, Florida)

HE'S GOING TO WHAT?

The following dialogue, written by Stephen Bly, makes a great short Christmas play for two people. Use your own creativity to come up with props, costumes, or whatever. Be sure your actors memorize their lines and rehearse. The story is also effective simply as a reading or as a discussion starter during the advent season. Use it however you wish.

"He's going down Himself."

"What?"

"I said, He's going down!"

"Who told you?"

"This morning during devotions He called Michael and Gabriel up and began to tell them, in front of us all, about The Plan."

"Why do I always miss the good parts?"

"Where were you?"

"Bythnia. I had to help little Lydia across that icy bridge again. But, do go on. What is The Plan?"

"It has to do with the prophets' predictions."

"So! The Day of the Lord is finally here. I guess I wasted my time helping Lydia. If He's bringing it all to a close now she'll be up here with us soon anyway."

"It's not that simple. He's planning to straighten out the situation down there."

"Well, why doesn't He send Moses? Or Elijah? Or Gabriel?"

"He will—each at their appointed time. But, they can only take a message. I did hear that Gabriel is arranging the entrance preparations."

"Oh, wow! I can see it now . . . all those humans wandering about in their busyness when all of a sudden the sun, stars and sky roll back. Then, out of the deepness of eternity He steps foot on their planet. I wish I could be there to see their faces. How about old Augustus? He'll fall right off his pedestal."

"It's not going to be that way. He doesn't even plan to show up at Rome."

"No Rome? So! He's going to Jerusalem. Imagine, the high priest will look up and suddenly there He is. Won't that wrinkle his robe!"

"I doubt that will happen."

"Oh? Don't tell me He won't see the high priest."

"Yes, He will see the high priest and all his council, but I doubt if they will recognize Him."

"Not recognize the Lord of Glory? Does He plan to disguise Himself?"

"In a way . . ."

"Why doesn't He want them to know who He is?"

"The way I understand it, He wants them to recognize Him by His life and His works, not by His appearance."

"I'm assuming He'll go as a

man, a Jewish man no doubt."

"I hear He's planning His entry as a baby."

"A what?"

"A baby, a humanette."

"Incredible! But, but, isn't He taking a big chance? The security will be fantastic. Why, we'll have to form a couple myriads of bodyguards 24 hours a day."

"He's going to be on His own."

"And turn Him loose with that pack of 'crazies'?"

"Do you honestly think there's any way they can harm Him against His will?"

"Of course, you're right, He'll be taking His power with Him. Can't you see the little tyke lying there in His mother's arms one minute, then jumping up the next to give a Roman soldier a karate chop?"

"I've heard His power will only be used to help others. He doesn't think it necessary to show all His credentials. And He already has the mother picked out."

"I hope it's not Lydia's mother."

"Who?"

"Lydia, the little girl from Bythnia. Imagine letting your four-year-old walk across a slick bridge like that. Anyway, I suppose He's picked out a priest's family or a family of the Pharisees."

"No, she's a poor, young unknown by the name of Mary. And . . . now keep this quiet, I wouldn't want every angel in the galaxy to hear this . . . He's going to be born in a stall, a cattle stable, right in the stench of earthly hay and stubble."

"But, that's criminal! It can't be! I won't allow it! I protest!"

"To whom?"

"I just don't understand the purpose in all this."

"You know as well as I do how He loves them. Now, listen, here's where we fit in. He does want us to line up a few witnesses to record the event for future generations."

"Sure, I've got it. How about 1000 men from each of the 12 tribes of Israel?"

"I said just a few."

"How about 100 each . . .?"

"No. He wants only a few."

"Well, how about a couple scribes, a lawyer, a politician and a news reporter, of course."

"That definitely won't do. Besides, He has them picked out already. Here's the list . . ."

"Let's see . . . three astrologers from Arbela. Where's that?"

"Over on the east side of the Tigris."

"But, they're foreigners, outsiders."

"Don't forget the others too."

"Oh, yes, there's Jason, Demas, and Hakiah. Who are they?"

"Shepherds, I believe."

"Just common, ordinary hillside shepherds?"

"It's His style, you know. Look at Abraham. What was he? And David? And what was Moses doing out there when the bush caught on fire?"

"I see what you mean."

"One thing does bother me, though. Who down there will believe the shepherds?"

"Lydia would."

"Yes, I love those humanettes. They believe whatever we tell them."

"They do until Satan gets a hold of them. By the way, what will he be doing all this time? He won't like this one bit."

"I figure he'll try to incite the humans to hateful and brutal actions."

"You don't suppose they'll keep falling for his old lines, do

187

you?"

"They're like putty in his hands most of the time. But, I do hear that our Lord will pull off some pretty big miracles . . . and then, there's the Final Presentation."

"What's that?"

"I don't know for sure. It's top secret."

"I see. Well, now, let me review. All we have to do is go down, talk to the shepherds and come back here and watch Him do the rest. Right?"

"Right. There's the preliminary signal. It's just about time for us to go down."

"Wow! What a day. I thought I wouldn't have anything to do until the bridge freezes over again."

"Remember, only a few shepherds. And please don't scare them."

"I promise, I promise."

"There's the signal. Let's go."

"Do you think we could stop by Bythnia on the way back? It's about time for Lydia to say her prayers. I just love the way she prays."

"Oh, I guess so. Now, hurry."

"I'm right behind you. But, I was wondering . . . what if it doesn't work out the way we think? What if there's a lot of resistance to His Plan? Down there as a vulnerable human, why, He could get Himself killed!"

"Don't be ridiculous! . . ."

And in the same region there were some shepherds staying out in the fields, and keeping watch over their flock by night. And an angel of the Lord suddenly stood before them, and the glory of the Lord shone around them; and they were terribly frightened. And the angel said to them, 'Do not be afraid; for behold, I bring you good news of a great joy which shall be for all the people; for today in the city of David there has been born for you a Savior, who is Christ the Lord. And this will be a sign for you; you will find a baby wrapped in cloths, and lying in a manger.' And suddenly there appeared with the angel a multitude of the heavenly host praising God, and saying, 'Glory to God in the highest, and on earth peace among men with whom He is pleased.'

(Luke 2:8-14, NASB)

(Contributed by Stephen A. Bly, Winchester, Idaho)

JIGSAW JACK-O-LANTERNS

Here's a great Halloween game for small teams (no more than two or three on a team). Give each team a pumpkin and a sharp knife. Then give each team only one minute to cut up the pumpkin in any way that they want. The pumpkin can be cut into no more than ten pieces.

Then have the teams rotate to a different pumpkin. Have a supply of round wooden toothpicks available. Give each team two minutes to put the "jigsaw puzzle" pumpkin back together, using the toothpicks to hold the pieces in place. The first team to finish is the winner. Pumpkins must be able to stand alone to be considered. (Contributed by Dan Scholten, Rhinelander, Wisconsin)

RUDOLPH GOES TO THE HOSPITAL

Here's a good way to bring a little Christmas cheer to folks in the hospital during the holidays. Have your youth group go caroling or just visiting at your local hospital and allow the kids to wish each patient a Merry Christmas personally by presenting them with a little "Rudolph" that they make ahead of time.

Rudolph is simple, inexpensive and fun to make, and people really enjoy receiving them as gifts. To make one, you'll need three wooden clothespins (not the spring type), some red and green felt, a red marker, cotton ball, little wiggly eyes, scissors and glue. Cut the ears out of green felt in this pattern:

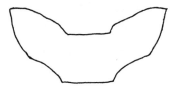

A rectangular piece of red felt is used for the body. Glue two clothespins together at the flat sides for the body, then flip the third clothespin up for the head and antlers. Glue the ears between the body and head. Color the nose, add the tail (cotton) and the eyes, and you have a "Rudolph." You may also glue a loop of fishing line between the head and body to make Rudolph a tree ornament.

You can also write a message like "Get well soon and have a Merry Christmas" on a small piece of paper or card with the name of the church and place it between the antlers. It's a great way to allow your kids to do something nice for others at Christmas. (Contributed by David Oakes, Albuquerque, New Mexico)

MARY'S STORY

The following play is based on the Christmas story, and is excellent for use during the holiday season. But it is perhaps even more effective when presented at a time other than Christmas, to heighten the "element of surprise" at the ending. The names of the characters are not given during the play itself. The setting is modern times. Each of the scenes can be set up any way you choose, and the dialogue has been written in such a way as to allow you the freedom to change or add to it as you see fit. The play was originally written by Beverly Snedden and the youth group of Calvary Baptist Church in Kansas City, Missouri.

Characters Needed:

Mary	Neighbors
Joseph	Elizabeth
Mother	The Doctor
Dad	The Psychiatrist
Mary's Friends (I and II)	The Rabbi
Carpenters (I and II)	Joe's Parents
Teachers (I and II)	

Scene One (Girls sitting around a table discussing the upcoming dance.)

Girl I: What are you going to wear?

Mary: I don't know if I'm going.

Girl II: Everybody's going. It'll be a good dance.

Mary: I can't even dance. Anyway, I wouldn't know how to ask a guy for a date.

Girl I: This is your chance to get around.

Girl II: What about that guy your parents like? Do they still want you to marry him when you get out of school?

Girl I: I hear he's got his own business and a sharp car.

Girl II: The guy I'm going with has a new Corvette.

Scene Two (Mary kneeling beside her bed.)

Mary: (This can be ad-libbed somewhat.) Why me? What am I going to tell Mom and Dad? . . . What will my friends think? . . . What is he going to do? . . . They're never going to believe me . . .

Scene Three (The living room with Mary's parents sitting on the couch.)

Mom: Well, I asked her what was wrong, but I wasn't able to get much out of her. She claims there's a lot of pressure from her teacher giving her a big assignment.

Dad: Well, that doesn't sound like our little girl. She doesn't usually let something like that bother her so much. I've heard a lot about the drug problem at her school. I'm sure our daughter has been raised well enough not to do anything like that, but that doesn't mean the pressure isn't hurting her. Maybe I could talk to her.

Mom: Well, I guess it couldn't hurt but be careful not to hurt her more. She's been awfully touchy lately.

Scene Four (Two girls talking on the phone.)

Girl I: I'm worried about her. She's been acting strange lately. Crying about silly things.

Girl II: Yeah, I've noticed.

190

Girl I:	Have you noticed she's gained weight?
Girl II:	Yeah, maybe it's from all that broccoli and other health food she's been eating.
Girl I:	She won't go out with us—not even to the dance we all went to. She says she's too tired.
Girl II:	She's had the flu a lot lately. Maybe I'll call her and see how she's feeling.

Scene Five (The teacher's lounge at school.)

Teacher I:	She's been acting differently lately.
Teacher II:	Her grades sure have dropped and she's been missing my class a lot.
Teacher I:	She seems lonely. She isn't around her old crowd anymore.
Teacher II:	She's also been putting on weight and wearing those loose tops.
Teacher I:	She's in my first hour English class and she's asked to see the nurse a lot. Do you think she's in trouble? She's so sweet.

Scene Six (Two neighbors talking over the back fence.)

Neighbor I:	I just *know* she is! And with those wonderful parents, too . . . they've tried so hard to bring her up right.
Neighbor II:	I bet I know who the father is . . . that older boy her father knows. He's the only one I've seen at the house.
Neighbor I:	You never know, do you? She just didn't seem the type . . . so well behaved and respectful.
Neighbor II:	She goes to Synagogue every week. What is the world coming to?

Scene Seven (Two carpenters sawing boards.)

Carpenter I:	Poor guy . . . that's too bad.
Carpenter II:	He's got to be crazy to marry her.
Carpenter I:	I'd hate to be in his place.
Carpenter II:	Be quiet, he's coming.

Scene Eight (The living room. Mom and Dad are talking to Mary and Joseph when three men enter.)

Mom:	Where did I go wrong? (Door bell rings. Father gets up to answer it and escorts in three men.)
Father:	Gentlemen, we have discovered our daughter is pregnant and we don't know what to do. We need your expert opinions about what we should do. We don't want her life and future ruined.
Doctor:	As a physician, the only option I can see for a girl her age is to terminate the pregnancy. If you choose abortion, we'll have to act quickly. Then no one else will have to know.
Psychiatrist:	From the viewpoint of a psychiatrist, her emotional stability would probably stand an abortion better than adoption. If you choose for her to give birth to the child, she might want to keep it and I believe that would be a grave mistake.
Rabbi:	They must get married. I know they're young, but with prayer

the marriage can work.

Father:	*(To Joseph)* You got her into this—what do you have to say?
Mary:	I'm going to have my baby and keep him. With the Lord's help, I can handle it.
Joseph:	I had considered breaking it off, but I've prayed about the situation and have decided it's God's will that we should be married. I'll do my best to be a good father to the baby.

Scene Nine (The living room with Mary and Elizabeth)

Mary:	He wonders whether or not our marriage will work. I want it to work.
Elizabeth:	He's a quiet person who loves his work. I'm sure he's worried about the gossip you've told me about.
Mary:	Yes, I feel it's affecting our relationship. He's so practical that he can't believe how I got pregnant. No one believes him when he says he isn't the father.
Elizabeth:	I understand what you are going through, but we know it will be worth it. When the baby is born everything will be okay, you'll see.
Mary:	You're only my cousin, but you're more like a sister to me.

Scene Ten (Mary and Joseph)

Mary:	I'm really frightened about you leaving on this trip. The doctor says that the baby could come anytime now.
Joseph:	Yeah, I know but I have to go! The only solution is having you go with me.
Mary:	Well, I'd rather be with you when the time comes. You know, I am really excited about the baby. God has given me peace that we have done the right thing.
Joseph:	I really feel that way, now. We have a big job ahead of us. We first of all must be sure that we are completely dedicated to God so we can guide our little son.

Scene Eleven	*(Mary and Joseph with the new baby. The Doctor, the Psychiatrist, and the Rabbi enter, bringing gifts for the baby. They kneel and worship Him.)*
Doctor:	*(To Mary and Joseph)* Forgive us, for our prejudice and judgments. We are here to give you and your son our love.
Psychiatrist:	Through prayer we were able to understand your situation.
Rabbi:	Mary, what will you name Him?
Mary:	He has been named . . . Jesus.

(Contributed by Larry Bradford, Hugoton, Kansas)

SANTA'S HELPERS

This is an easy game requiring little advance preparation and only paper and pencil. Announce to your group: "There has been a computer breakdown at the North Pole. Santa has lost everybody's Christmas list. He called wanting your help."

Next, pass out paper and pencils. On a signal, each is to seat another on their lap and ask them what they want for Christmas. Their names and requests are written down for Santa's computers. This continues as each one scrambles to get another person to sit on their lap and make their request. The one with the longest list at the end of five minutes is declared the winner.

To make the game more difficult, do not allow a person to make the same request twice. Encourage them to ask for crazy things, too. Another variation is to require name, address, and phone numbers on the gift lists. This is a sneaky way to build your mailing list. (Contributed by Dave Schultz, Garland, Texas)

TWAS THE NIGHT BEFORE CHRISTMAS

Here's a good crowd breaker for your next Christmas activity. Go around the room with each person taking a turn. On their turn, they must recite the next consecutive couplet of the poem "Twas the Night Before Christmas." For example:

Person 1: "Twas the Night Before Christmas,
And all through the house. . ."

Person 2: "Not a creature was stirring,
Not even a mouse."

If they are correct, then go on to the next person. If they're wrong, they must stand and lead everyone in one verse of a Christmas carol. Then the missed line is read and you go on to the next person. Go around the group as many times as it takes to complete the poem, but carol verses may not be repeated. Carols may be repeated as long as a different verse is used. (Contributed by Scott Davis, Lubbock, Texas)

VALENTINE CAROLS

You've probably gone Christmas caroling, but have you gone *Valentine's Day caroling?* Next Valentine's Day, have your group learn the songs below (or any love songs that you know) and go serenade the people you love—parents, seniors, workers in the church, neighbors, etc. They will love it! If possible, dress everyone up in red and white—and maybe have one member of the group dress up like "cupid." You can also present a box of candy, cookies, or a Valentine's Day card to the people you sing for. You might also sing one or two gospel songs that share the love of Christ as well.

(to the tune of: Deck the Halls)

Deck the halls with hearts of gladness
Fa, la, la, la, la, la, la, la, la.
Tis the day we don't want sadness
Fa, la, la, la, la, la, la, la, la.
Don we now a big wide smile
Fa, la, la, la, la, la, la, la, la.
Sing we love in every mile
Fa, la, la, la, la, la, la, la, la.

(to the tune of: Mistletoe and Holly)

Here we are, it's dandy
It's time for Valentines and candy
Big red presents
Val-en-tine cards
Saying we love you so.

Here we are and caring
It's time for loving
And for sharing
Kissing sweethearts
Big bright red cards
Spreading love wherever we go
(men) Happy Valentines . . .
    (women) Happy Valentines . . .
                . . . to you

(to the tune of: Jingle Bells)

Big red hearts
Flowered carts
Coming through the post
Valentines from someone who
You know will mean the most
(repeat)
Dashing through the snow
In a 4-door or a coupe
We have come to you
To knock you for a loop
Our songs we bring today
To take away your blue
Oh, what fun it is to sing
A Valentine to you

(to the tune of: Oh, Christmas Tree)

Oh, Valentine
Oh, Valentine
We bring you love from Jesus
Oh, Valentine
Oh, Valentine
We bring you love from Jesus
His Love is true in summertime
But also in the wintertime
Oh, Valentine
Oh, Valentine
We bring you love from Jesus

(to the tune of: Jolly Old St. Nicholas)

Jolly old St. Valentine
How'd you ever know
That we'd need a special day
To day, "We love you so!"
Valentine's is here today
So we thought of you
We'll whisper how we love you so
That's just what we will do . . .

(Whisper) "We love you!"

(to the tune of: We Wish You a Merry Christmas)

We wish you a happy Val'tines
We wish you a happy Val'tines
We wish you a happy Val'tines
And a happy heart day.
Good tidings to you
We'll love you always
Good tidings on Val'tines
And a happy heart day.

(Contributed by Donn Williams, Minot, North Dakota)